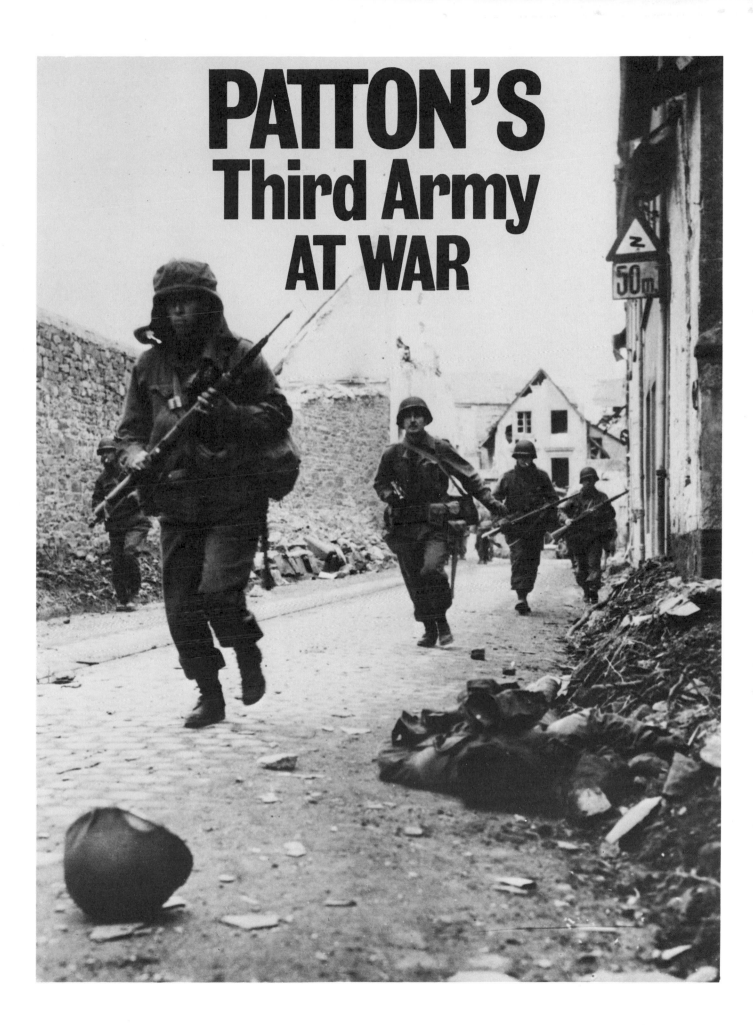

PATTON'S
Third Army
AT WAR

Previous page: GIs of Third Army's 87th Infantry Division (The Acorn Div) pass a dead comrade in the streets of Koblenz./*US Army*

Below: An 8-inch gun pounding the German defences of Brest, second largest naval port in France. Although 3rd Army's brilliant sweep through Brittany took the enemy completely by surprise, the garrison of Brest fought tenaciously and held out till mid-September./*US Army*

PATTON'S
Third Army
AT WAR

George Forty

ARMS AND
ARMOUR

Bibliography

Books

Allen, Colonel Robert S.: *Lucky Forward* (The Vanguard Press Inc)

Ayer, Fred: *Before the Colours Fade* (Cassell and Co Ltd)

Army Times, editors of: *Warrior* (Army Times Publishing Co)

Blumenson, Martin: *The Patton Papers* two volumes, (Houghton Mifflin Co)

Chamberlain Peter, and Ellis, Chris: *British and American Tanks of World War II* (Arms and Armour Press)

Chamberlain Peter, and Gander, Terry: *World War Two Fact Files* (Macdonald and Janes)

Dyer, Lt-Col George: *XII Corps, Spearhead of Patton's Third Army* (Herbert S. Benjamin Associate, Inc)

Eisenhower, Dwight D. *Crusade in Europe* (William Heinemann Ltd)

Ellis, William Donohue and Cunningham, Col Thomas T.: *Clarke of St Vith* (Dillon/Liederbach)

Farago, Ladislas: *Patton: Ordeal and Triumph* (Arthur Baker Ltd)

Harkins, Gen Paul D., with the editors of the Army Times Pub Co: *When the Third Cracked Europe* (Army Times Pub Co/Stackpole Books)

Hart, B. H. Liddell: *History of the Second World War* (Cassell & Co Ltd)

Hofmann, George F.: *The Super Sixth* (6th Armd Div Assoc)

Patton, George S.: *War as I knew it* (Houghton Mifflin Co)

Toland, John: *The Last Hundred Days* (Arthur Barker Ltd) and *Battle, the story of the Bulge* (Frederick Muller Ltd)

Wallace, Col Brenton G.: *Patton and his Third Army* (Stackpole Books)

Wise, Terence: *American Military Camouflage and Markings* 1939-1945 (Almark Publications)

76th Div Association: *We Ripened Fast, the unofficial history of the 76th Infantry Division* (privately published)

Periodicals

Armor, the Magazine of Mobile Warfare, Editor in Chief: Lt-Col Burton S. Boudinot

After the Battle, Editor: Winston G. Ramsey

Army in Europe Magazine, Editor: Capt Emil L. Havach

Highlights from Yank the Army weekly, published by Universal Publishing and Distributing Corporation

Articles

The Nancy Bridgehead by Brig Hal C. Pattison

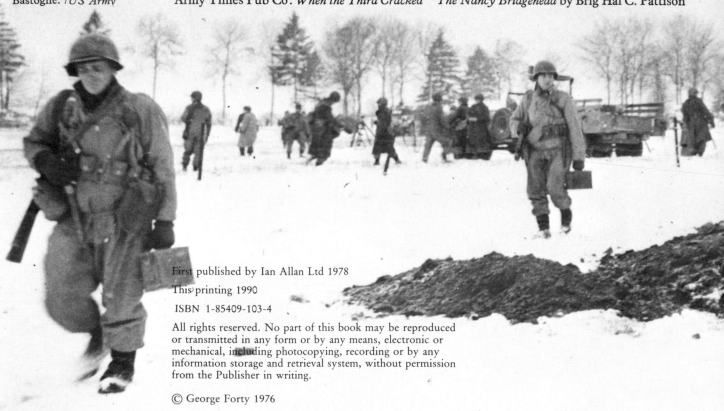

Below: Armoured infantry of Third Army, supported by tanks, move up to attack the Germans surrounding Bastogne. /*US Army*

First published by Ian Allan Ltd 1978

This printing 1990

ISBN 1-85409-103-4

© George Forty 1976

This edition published by Arms and Armour Press, Villiers House, 41/47 Strand, London WC2N 5JE

Printed and bound in Great Britain by the Bath Press, Avon

Contents

To the men of the United States Third Army and their great commander General George S. Patton, Jr, who went further faster than any other army has done in the history of war.

'*No words the saga full to tell,*
No voice the vict'ry song to sing,
No pen the epic to inscribe,
No chisel, brush . . .

The giant deeds achieved
In answer to the nation's need,
Mirrored, stand but part revealed –
Like sun, its form, the hue of it
Which man may aptly duplicate
But for its heat goes to the sun,
Sole vivid master.

Thus unfolds the tale,
Reflections feeble, thin
Attenuated images
Remotely kin to gallant sons,
Living and dead, whose valiant strides
Outstrip all power to describe;
Model's meager replica,
Faint, unfully sung,
In wonder framed,
With pride retold'*

*Quoted from *We ripened fast!* The unofficial history of the 76th Infantry Division and published here by kind permission of the Board of Directors of the 76th Infantry Officers' Association.

Foreword
General Bruce C. Clarke
United States Army, Ret.

It is most difficult to do justice in introducing a book about Patton's Third Army. Patton was a unique commander, and a unique person, and had a unique influence over the officers and men under him and, I am sure, over his enemies in battle, as well.

General George S. Patton, Jr changed the United States Army's concept of the role of the tanks in World War I, from an accompanying and supporting weapon of foot infantry, to that of the principal component of a balanced, combined arms division made up of tanks, armoured cavalry, armoured infantry, armoured field artillery, and armoured engineers, supported by tactical air and by adequate logistics units. This transition took twenty years in our army. But after World War II, it became necessary to provide our Army school system with this new concept for use in its teachings. Lt Colonel Creighton W. Abrams, a great tank battalion commander was with me in the 4th Armored Division, and again with me on the faculty of the US Army Armor School. With Colonel Abram's great help, I wrote the new concept based upon the great successes of armoured divisions in Patton's Third Army. It was published in service journals in 1948 and repeated in 1967 under the title of: *The Principles of the Employment of Armor.*

A copy of this latter publication came to the attention of General Dwight D. Eisenhower, our Supreme SHAEF Commander in Europe in World War II. He wrote me this letter:

D D E
Gettysburg
Pennsylvania 17323
15 September 1967

Dear Bruce,
Regarding the attached brochure on tank tactics, it may amuse you to know that in 1920 and 1921 George Patton and I publicly and earnestly expounded similar ideas in the service journals of that day. Such a doctrine was so revolutionary, as compared to the World War I practice, that we were threatened with court martial. Our championship of the basic principles, which you now so rightly support, was anathema to the high military officials of that day.
With all the best,

Sincerely, D.D.E.

General Bruce C. Clarke,
USA. Ret.

Thus, many of the tactics, operations and exploits of Patton's Third Army in France, Belgium and Germany did not astound the Supreme Commander Eisenhower. In fact, I feel he gloried in them.

Bruce C. Clarke

Above: General Bruce C. Clarke, United States Army, Retired./*Charles Laikin*

Left: 'God Bless America!' A triumphant GI of 83rd Infantry Division plants the Stars and Stripes in the muzzle of a knocked out German anti-aircraft gun on top of the Citadel, St Malo, where the last Nazi resistance in the town ended on 17 August 1944./*IWM*

Below: The secret of Third Army's success was good teamwork at all levels. Here machine gunners of the 10th Infantry, 4th Armored Division, cover a tank crossing snow covered fields in the Bastogne corridor, 3 January 1945./*US Army*

Introduction

Far right, top: General George S. Patton, Jr, was born in San Gabriel, California, on 11 November 1885. He was appointed to the United States Military Academy in 1904, and commissioned a second lieutenant of cavalry on 11 June 1909. He served as a member of General Pershing's staff both in Mexico and in World War I. He left the staff to join the new Tank Corps where he rose to the rank of colonel and served until the Corps was abolished in 1920.

His cavalry assignments included Hawaii, Fort Riley, and Washington DC. In 1940 he transferred to the 2nd Armored Division at Fort Benning. He was assigned as CG of the 2nd Armored Division on 19 April 1941. On 8 November 1942, when American forces landed in North Africa, Patton was in command of the units landing on the west coast. In February 1943, he became CG of the Western Task Force, and subsequently assumed command of all American forces in the Tunisian combat area. He became CG, Seventh Army, during the invasion of Sicily, in July 1943, serving until March 1944, when he was assigned to the ETO and chosen to command the Third Army. In October 1945 he assumed command of the Fifteenth Army in American occupied Germany, and on 21 December 1945, died in Germany as a result of an automobile accident. His decorations included the Distinguished Service Cross with Oak Leaf Cluster, Distinguished Service Medal with Oak Leaf Cluster, Silver Star, Legion of Merit, Bronze Star, Purple Heart and numerous other US and foreign decorations, including Knight of the British Empire, Companion of the Bath and the Croix de Guerre from both France and Luxembourg. /US Army

Far right, bottom: It was men like this tank driver, Sergeant Hobart Drew, who were the backbone of Third Army. He drove 'Blockbuster 3d', the command tank of B Company, 37th Tank Battalion, 4th Armored Division./US Army

Right: 'Patton's Ghosts'. Men of the 4th Armored Division read about their exploits in the Stars and Stripes, 14 November 1944./US Army

My first subject in Ian Allan's 'At War' series was a study of that famous British 7th Armoured Division – 'The Desert Rats'; my second featured a German Corps, namely Erwin Rommel's peerless Afrika Korps; so perhaps it is appropriate that my third subject should be the next largest formation, namely a complete Army, and that the Army chosen should be American. What better choice in the circumstances, therefore, than the late General George S. Patton's magnificent United States Third Army? The only major problem which I have had to face is exactly the same one that beset me with my other books, and that is trying to get a quart into a pint pot. I found it quite impossible to do full justice to the British Seventh Armoured Division in one volume, so it is equally impossible for me again to attempt to do so with the great United States Third Army. This book can only give a brief indication of what it was like to serve in *Lucky* – the codename which was chosen for Third Army by Patton himself – during their triumphal progress across Europe. So this book is in no way a detailed history of that progress, but rather a pictorial evocation of 'Georgie's Boys' at war. 'Triumphal' is perhaps a good way of describing their progress, because in the nine months and eight days of campaigning, Third Army completed a record of offensive operations that can only be measured by using such superlatives. Their actions in France, Belgium, Luxembourg, Germany, Czechoslovakia and Austria gave a new dimension to the term 'fluid warfare'. They only needed one general order – to seek out the enemy, trap and destroy him. This they did, driving on in fair weather and foul, across good going and bad. Their story is one of team work, of armour, infantry and aircraft, working together with a perfection that even amazed the Germans, who had always considered themselves as the masters of the Blitzkreig. It is also the story of a triumph of administration as thousands of trucks carried forward the supplies so vital to keep an Army of that size moving and fighting. It is the story of American ingenuity, of meeting every challenge with new battle winning ideas. But above all it is the story of American soldiers, those in the front line, those behind who kept them fighting and those above who did the planning and issued the orders. Reduced to cold figures, the feats which they achieved in 281 days of campaigning make incredible reading. In that time Third Army liberated or captured 81,522 square miles of territory, containing an estimated 12,000 cities, towns and communities, which included 27 cities of more than 50,000 people. They killed 144,500 enemy, wounded 386,200 and captured a staggering 1,280,688. In contrast with the total enemy casualty figure of 1,811,388, Third Army suffered 160,692 casualties, including 27,104 killed. But enough of mere statistics, suffice it to say that Third Army went further and faster than any other Army has *ever* done in the whole history of war. Much of their greatness, their driving force, their will to win, they owed to one man, their commander – General George Smith Patton, Junior – and I have in consequence, devoted a section of the book to him alone.

As usual I have many people to thank for their invaluable help in providing me with material and photographs for this book. Most

of their names appear with their stories and pictures, however, I would like to single out three for special mention. Firstly, Colonel James H. Leach, ex-member of the great 4th Armored Division, now living and working in Arlington, Virginia. I was fortunate enough to be put in contact with him by a mutual friend and it is largely through his efforts that I was able to contact such a comprehensive selection of ex-members of the Third Army. One of them made a point which it is perhaps relevant for me to make here, and that concerns the codename. Although Patton was a great believer in luck I would hate anyone reading this book to go away with the idea that Third Army's achievements were based on good luck alone. Of course luck played its part, but the main reasons for their success were well trained, brave and devoted soldiers, sound planning and excellent weapons and material. Secondly, I must thank Mrs Ruth Ellen Patton Totten for her contribution, as it gives such a marvellous glimpse of her late father which I could not possibly have obtained elsewhere. Thirdly, I must thank General Bruce C. Clarke for doing me the great honour of writing the foreword. His name and prowess are renowned all over the world. 'Clarke of St Vith' has directly commanded more troops than any other United States officer. His heroic defence of St Vith is now legendary, and of course he did command Combat Command A of 4th Armored Division in Third Army at the beginning of their victorious sweep through France in 1944.

My thanks go as usual to the Ministry of Defence Library and to the Imperial War Museum, London, for their invaluable help; also to the US Army Audio Visual Agency for obtaining for me many of the battle photographs; to LTC Burton S. Boudinot, the editor of *Armor* for allowing me to quote freely from his excellent magazine; to Philip M. Cavanaugh, Curator of the Patton Museum, Fort Knox, for lending me much basic material and photographs; to Colonel John Hind of the British Defence Staff, Washington, Colonel Bunny Warren, British LO at Fort Knox and Major Mike Weaver, American LO at Bovington Camp, all of whom have given me so much help and assistance that it is impossible for me to begin to list here their many kindnesses; to all the Divisional Associations who have helped me, in particular the 4th and 6th Armored and 76th and 80th Infantry Divisions, who have all allowed me to quote from their histories. My ever patient and hard working typist has again done a grand job, whilst my long suffering family has allowed me to make their life unbearable. I hope the result is worth all their efforts.

Bradford, West Yorkshire,   *George Forty*
December 1977

The Shoulder Patch and the Codename

The Shoulder Patch

The Third United States Army first came into existence on 15 November 1918, at Ligny-en-Barrois, France, four days after the Armistice had ended World War I. Two days later it moved into Germany with its headquarters at Koblenz. It remained there until deactivated to 'American Forces Germany' about six months later on 2 July 1919. Thirteen years later the Third Army was reactivated and became one of four armies created within the geographical limits of the United States. From 1932 until leaving for Europe in 1944, the headquarters alternated between Fort Sam Houston, Texas, and Atlanta, Georgia. From 1941 until the end of 1943 it was basically a training army, by far the largest in the country. It comprised hundreds of units from full corps to small detachments, occupying many camps, posts, manoeuvre areas and other installations, stretching from Mississippi to Arizona, and from Arkansas to the Mexican border. The average monthly troop strength was over 750,000 men. Among other formations which Third Army trained were the three best negro divisions of the war, the 92nd and 93rd Infantry Divisions at Fort Huachuca, Arizona and the 2nd Cavalry Division at Fort Clark, Texas. From 1941 to 1943 Third Army was commanded by Lieutenant-General Courtney H. Hodges and even when the advance elements arrived in UK in January 1944, they were still under his command, Third Army having been transferred to combat army status on 31 December 1943. General Patton took over in England, indeed, the advance party were the first to hear the news shortly after they had disembarked from the *Ile de France*. The shoulder patch derives from World War I, being a white 'A' on a blue background, circled by a red 'O', standing for 'Army of Occupation'. When Third Army was reactivated the shoulder patch was also revived and worn again by all members of Headquarters Third Army and Third Army troops. The line and air units had their own shoulder patches and I have included elsewhere in this book drawings of those worn by all the corps and divisions that served with Third Army between 1 August 1944 and 9 May 1945.

The Codename

General Patton was a great believer in luck. He said it was 'the instantaneous realisation of a problem by the inner mind before the outer mind could get into gear'*. *Lucky* was therefore his own personal choice as the codename for Third Army. He felt that it would epitomise the victorious career and ebullient character of his newest and largest command and certainly time has proved him to be correct on both scores. His Battle Command Post was known as *Lucky Forward*. Other such codenames used were, for example, *Liberty* (Supreme Headquarters Allied Expeditionary Force), *Eagle* (Twelfth Army Group) and *Master* (First Army).

*Quoted from a talk given by his daughter, Mrs Ruth Ellen Patton Totten, to the Topsfield Historical Society, 30 December 1974.

Below: An excellent close up of the Third Army shoulder patch worn by the Commander himself./*IWM*

The Organisation of an Army

The total number of soldiers in any of the American armies of World War II varied considerably from month to month, depending upon how many corps and divisions were assigned under command at any one time. During the 281 days (from 1 August 1944 to 8 May 1945) whilst 3rd Army was in continuous combat, no fewer than six corps and 42 divisions were at one time or another under its command, including the 2nd French Armoured Division. Third Army strength varied from about 200,000 to a staggering 540,000, when V Corps was assigned to it in early May 1945, and a total of 18 divisions were under command at the same time. General Patton, in his book *War as I knew it*, laid down the following priorities for an army: 'First, it must fight. Second it must eat. Third it must be capable of rapid movement. And last but not least, it must be equipped with all essentials necessary to the accomplishment of its mission. In reality, an army provides most of the necessities of life found in a community of equal size . . .'. He goes on to explain that under the army headquarters there are the corps headquarters, each HQ having specialist troops to provide for its own 'house-keeping, protection and administration'. Within each corps are the infantry and armoured divisions who do the fighting, plus the many and varied supporting troops who help them to accomplish their missions. He explains that: 'The supporting troops are made up of fighting units; such as cavalry, artillery, engineers, anti-aircraft artillery, tank destroyer and chemical warfare units. There are military police units to enforce law and order and medical units to take care of the sick and wounded and to supervise the general health of the command. The quartermaster handles the general supplies, such as gas, food, clothing and so forth. The transportation corps hauls these supplies. Signal units provide all types of communication and the engineers have many types of units which enable them to do anything from fighting the enemy and fires to building railroad bridges over rivers. Civil affairs detachments handle the civilian population in liberated or captured towns and special service units provide entertainment for all the troops. Several miscellaneous detachments, such as secret intelligence units, finance units, prisoner of war interpreters and the like, finish off the list. Most units are complete with transportation and cooking detachments. If not, they are assigned or attached to other units which have facilities to provide for them'.

Tactical Air Command

In addition to the ground forces which were assigned to an army, a tactical air command was also assigned for air support and reconnaissance. Squadrons of the tactical air force were daily allocated for duty with each corps. In the case of Third Army, XIX Tactical Air Command worked very closely with their ground forces, quickly establishing a very strong relationship which lasted throughout all the many hard fought campaigns to eventual victory. XIX Tactical Air Command flew 7,326 missions and 74,447 sorties during the campaigns, dropping 17,500 tons of bombs, over 3,000 napalm tanks and over 4,500 rockets. Targets destroyed or damaged included 3,833 tanks and armoured cars, 38,541 motor vehicles and 4,337 locomotives!

Composition of HQ Third Army

At the top of the headquarters was the commanding general (CG) who, like any other commander, was ultimately responsible for everything that went on in his command. Directly under him was the chief of staff (COS), the CG's chief assistant and the co-ordinator of the staff. He in turn, had a deputy chief of staff to assist him. Beneath this 'top brass' the Army headquarters comprised two basic groups, one consisting of the five general staff sections, the other of the 18 special staff sections, viz:

a *General Staff:* G1 – Personnel; G2 – Intelligence; G3 – Operations; G4 – Supply; G5 – Civil Affairs or Military Government (including Displaced Persons).

b *Special Staff:* Adjutant general, artillery, anti-aircraft artillery, chaplain, chemical warfare, engineer, finance, HQ commandant, inspector general, judge advocate, medical, ordnance, provost marshal, public relations, quartermaster, signal, special services and tank destroyers.

Army troops were those units not in corps but directly under HQ Third Army command. They consisted mostly of MP battalions, car companies, intelligence, engineer, ordnance, quartermaster, signal and other specialist units. The staff was there to assist the commander in the exercise of command. It collected information, made plans, arranged details and made recommendations. A well organised staff had to work together at all levels, keeping each other fully informed all

All quotations from *War as I knew it* reprinted by kind permission of Houghton Mifflin Co.

All quotations from *Lucky Forward* reprinted by kind permission of The Vanguard Press Inc.

All quotations from *The Patton Papers* reprinted by kind permission of Houghton Mifflin Co and Blanche C. Gregory Inc.

the time. Colonel Brenton G. Wallace, who was Patton's Assistant Chief of Staff (G3 Liaison) says in his book *Patton and his Third Army* that the qualifications of a good staff officer are: 'Ability, tact, the confidence of the commander, courageous frankness and loyalty'. It was clear that General Patton inspired the best qualities in his staff and Colonel Wallace goes on to say: 'The "Old Man" hated show and sham. He was interested in one thing only – efficiency; and his spirit permeated the whole organisation. You had a feeling that Third Army was going in only one direction – forward'.

Basic Organisations

As I have explained the numbers and composition of the corps assigned to 3rd Army varied according to the task they were carrying out at a particular time, so it would be inappropriate to give organisational details above divisional level. The two charts that follow, therefore, deal only with the outline organisations of the two basic divisions, viz: armoured and infantry, circa 1944.

The Armoured Division

In 1943 the armoured division underwent a thorough reorganisation as well as being reduced in manpower by over 3,600 men. The light tank strength was halved (from 158 to 77) and the armoured infantry element increased. Service elements were trimmed, so as to increase their mobility and unnecessary command echelons, such as the tank regimental level, were eliminated. The new streamlined division had five commands under divisional control, namely: Combat Command A (CCA), Combat Command B (CCB) Reserve Command (Res Cmd), Artillery Command, (Divarty), and Trains Command (Tns Cmd). Each command headquarters consisted of a headquarters, plus an HQ company or detachment. It was designed to control whatever subordinate units were assigned to it for a particular mission. CCA and CCB, the strike forces, were set up to control a number of combat units (battalions or companies) and/or support units. The major units in the division were three tank battalions, each comprising an HQ and HQ company, three medium tank companies, one light tank company and a service company. Total manpower of a tank battalion was 729. Each medium or light tank company contained 17 tanks, three platoons of 5 tanks and 2 tanks in Company HQ. Towards the end of the war, an extra M4, mounting a 105mm howitzer, was added to each Coy HQ, increasing the medium tank strength per armoured division to 195. Balancing the three tank battalions were three armoured infantry battalions each composed of an HQ and HQ company, a service company and three rifle companies. Total battalion manpower was 1,001. The tank and infantry battalions were supported by three armoured field artillery battalions, each equipped with 18 105mm self propelled howitzers (M7). Auxiliary units such as the divisional reconnaissance squadron, attached medical personnel and unit chaplains, brought the armoured division strength to 10,937. In addition, other battalions, such as tank destroyers or anti-aircraft artillery, were normally attached. By way of example, the order of battle of the 6th Armored Division included 603d Tank Destroyer Battalion and 777th Anti-Aircraft

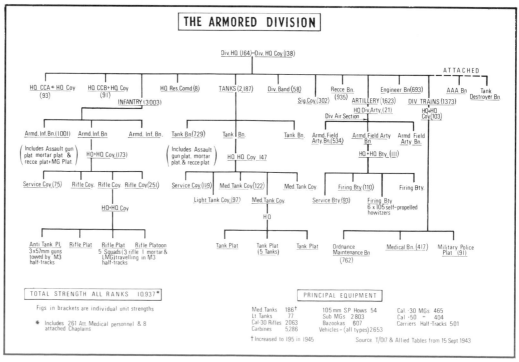

Artillery Battalion, throughout the campaigns in North West Europe.

The Infantry Division

The 1943 reorganisation also covered the infantry division, when the overall divisional manpower was reduced by 1,200, but no major structural changes were made to its 'triangular' organisation. There were no permanent combat command headquarters as with the armoured division. When combined arms teams were formed for independent missions, one of the three infantry regimental headquarters was used to command them and the groups were called 'Combat Teams' (eg 385th CT). Within the infantry regiments the smallest sub unit was the rifle squad of 12 men, armed with 10 M1 (Garand) rifles, one Browning automatic rifle (BAR) and one M1903 Springfield rifle. Three squads made up a rifle platoon and three rifle platoons and one weapons platoon were grouped together to form a rifle company. The weapons platoon had two .30cal light machine guns (LMG), three 60mm mortars, three anti-tank rocket launchers (Bazookas), and one .50cal heavy machine gun (HMG) primarily for anti-aircraft defence. The total strength of a rifle company was 193 all ranks. The infantry battalion consisted of three such rifle companies, plus a heavy weapons company of six 81mm mortars, eight .30cal HMGs, seven bazookas and three .50cal HMGs. Headquarters company of the battalion held an anti-tank platoon of three 37mm anti-tank guns (later replaced by 57mm guns). Total strength of an infantry battalion was 871. An infantry regiment consisted of three battalions, together with the following regimental units

HQ and HQ Company; a cannon company of six short barrelled, towed 105mm howitzers; an anti-tank company of 12 37mm or 57mm anti-tank guns and a mine-laying platoon. Finally there was the service company, with the task of transporting supplies for the line battalions. There were three infantry regiments in the 'triangular' infantry division, making a total of 9,354 infantrymen. The field artillery of the division had at its head an HQ and HQ battery, division artillery; there were three light artillery battalions, and one medium artillery battalion. The former each comprised an headquarters battery, a service battery and three firing batteries of four 105mm towed howitzers, making 36 guns in the division artillery. The medium battalion had a similar organisation with three firing batteries each of four 155mm towed howitzers. Total artillery manpower was 2,160; auxiliary units in the division included a reconnaissance troop, an engineer battalion, medical battalion, quartermaster company, ordnance company, signal company and a military police platoon. Together with attached personnel, such as medical sections and the chaplains with units, the total all ranks strength of the division was 14,253 men. For specific operations infantry divisions might be reinforced with a mechanised cavalry squadron, by one or more field artillery battalions of any appropriate calibre, by a chemical battalion manning 4.2 inch mortars, by tank, tank destroyer or anti-aircraft artillery units. These attachments became the 'norm' when combat developed on a large scale in 1944. The result was the infantry divisional commander usually commanded well over 15,000 men.

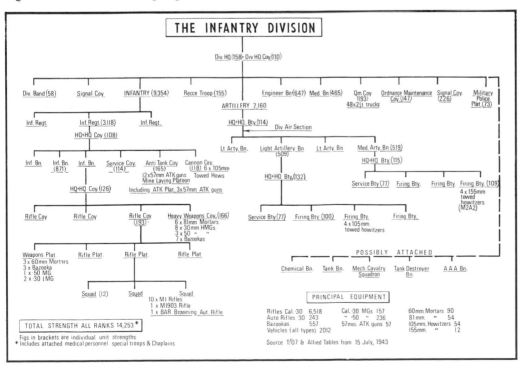

15

Below: Standing in a jeep, General Patton reviews some of his newly arrived troops 'somewhere in England'. /Associated Press

The Yanks are coming!

Goodbye America

In company with thousands of other doughboys, WACs and nurses, the GIs of Third Army had first to make the dangerous, uncomfortable crossing of the Atlantic Ocean. Many travelled on the *Queen Mary* (SS490 as she was known in wartime) or on her sister ship the *Queen Elizabeth*. The impressions gained at the beginning of these voyages were indelibly stamped on the minds of all those who experienced them. The lights, the bustle, the magnificent panorama of New York City, as the harbour boat swung down the East River, around the Battery and up the Hudson. The band playing on the pier as troops transferred to their ocean going home; the Red Cross 'Doughnut' girls handing out mugs of steaming coffee, and finally the long climb, with full equipment, up the steep gangplank. Here is how such an embarkation was described by one GI:

'Now, visualize the long queue of khaki-clad men which is filing slowly across the narrow gangway into the maw of the waiting monster. This is not a mere figure of speech, for the *Queen Mary* and the *Queen Elizabeth* and other great liners used for troop carrying are known affectionately in the navies of both America and Britain as the "monsters" . . . At the dark entrance stands a white-helmeted MP. "Keep goin', soldier" he will say, and those three words will ring in your ears like the refrain of a litany throughout the trip, varied on occasion by the sharp command, "Put out that cigarette!" In your hand is a blue card and, once inside, you will find yourself in a long alleyway with a staircase at the

18

far end. It smells hot and stuffy, but you bump your way down it until you reach the stairway and then climb up or down. Here and there you will catch a glimpse of a steward in a white coat or a British seaman in dark blue trousers and a polo-necked pullover. They are members of a crew of 800 Britishers in whose hands you will be until the ship is safely in the Clyde. At last you reach your standee bed. One of eighteen, it is situated in an oblong box, in peacetime a stateroom on D deck which held at most four. Next to it is a bathroom with more cots in it. You won't trouble much about baths during the voyage. Presently a loud impersonal voice coming from the public address systems tells you the evening meal is beginning and you shuffle off to the main dining room with its decorations of polished wood and steel where once first-class passengers ate. Thence, after eating you will if you are wise, find out the whereabouts of the PX canteen, note the hours of opening and realize that if you want Coca-Cola, that is where you go for it . . .'*

The *Queen Mary* and *Queen Elizabeth* both made the voyage unescorted, ploughing effortlessly through the waves at an average speed of 28½ knots. They were loaded to the gunwhales on every crossing. Experience had shown that hammocks were unsuitable for land-lubbers, so 'standee' bunks were installed, anything up to eight tiers high! They could be folded flat when not in use and were put up practically everywhere, so that nearly 8,000 could sleep at a time. However, even this was not enough, and a two shift system had to be instituted, two men being allocated to every bunk. In this way up to 15,000 troops were carried on each voyage, roughly the equivalent of an entire infantry division. Two of the major headaches whilst on board were feeding and safety. Imagine, for example, cooking three *tons* of sausages at a time! Safety was of course paramount, boat and raft drill being practised daily and everyone was made to carry a lifebelt at all times. Anyone seen without one immediately had to surrender their shoes. These were impounded on the spot by the military police and returned only when the culprit presented himself with his lifebelt at the shoe store. 'The finest incident I saw on any of my trips,' reported one distinguished official who crossed the Atlantic many times during the war, 'was the sight of an American admiral stopped by a GI sentry and ordered to remove his shoes because he had no lifebelt. I can see the great man now, padding obediently away in his socks over the wet decks and returning meekly with the belt.'*

*Both quotes from *XII Corps – Spearhead of Patton's Third Army* by Lt-Col George Dyer.

I have included in this section photographs which show GIs embarking for the European Theatre of Operations (ETO) but I cannot swear that they actually feature members of Third Army. However, they are I believe typical of the thousands and thousands who made the crossing. Typical also is this account of the journey sent to me by Frank J. Paskvan of Lorain, Ohio, who served with the Engineers in Third Army:
'After receiving my basic training I was transferred to the 995th Engineer Treadway Bridge Company. I had no previous training in building a bridge but was told my training would be finished when we were shipped overseas. My outfit left Camp Barkley, Texas in January 1944 and moved to Camp Kilmer, New Jersey, an embarkation centre for the European theatre of war. Receiving more shots and a little training in gas warfare, all of us were given a night off to visit New York City. I went with a buddy of mine, who called his wife and told her that he would soon be leaving for overseas duty. I didn't call my wife, but his wife called her and told her what was happening. The next day we were paraded

Below: A well equipped GI looking for his 'Stateroom'. Although not Joe Di Maggio (he was in the Air Force) this doughboy is apparently determined to play baseball as well as fight!
/*US Office of War Information*

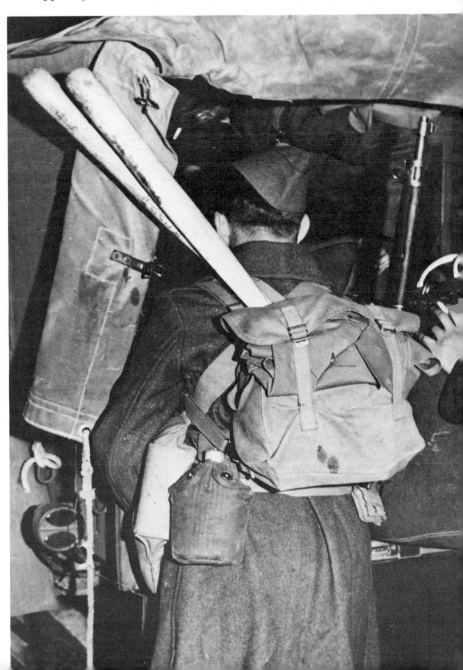

Right: A bit crowded, but these soldiers don't seem to mind. 'Standee' bunks, sometimes eight tiers high, were used instead of hammocks on most of the larger troopships. /*US Office of War Information*

Below: Home made entertainment. A couple of guitar playing doughboys entertain their comrades in a crowded mess hall on board the *Queen Mary* during one of her many wartime voyages across the Atlantic./*Stewart Bale Ltd*

and told to get rid of all civilian clothing and material not issued by the United States Army and to place it on a pile in one of the empty barrack rooms. When my turn came to pass through the barrack room the pile was almost up to the ceiling, we never did find out what happened to all those extra towels, soap, socks, shorts etc. When we had ridded ourselves of all this fine material they said the reason was that we were only allowed so many pounds to a man on the ship. Another thing they told us was that when we boarded the ship there would be two men to each stateroom and that we had to stay in the staterooms until orders were given for us to be allowed to move about. On 28 January 1944, we embarked for England on a ship called the *Andes*. As we boarded through an opening in the side of the ship a band played the *Star Spangled Banner* and all of us slowly went up the gangplank and inside the ship. Down, down, down we went, until I thought we would come out at the bottom. By this time my pack was so heavy that I'd lost all interest and only wanted to sleep in my stateroom. Someone asked the Captain when we

would be allowed to go to our staterooms. He said, "Staterooms, this is your stateroom" and he left in a hurry! To make something out of nothing, one of the sailors gave us some hammocks and I hung one up, almost fell out a couple of times, but found out if I held my breath I didn't fall out and was soon asleep. Morning was breaking when I noticed the lamp above me swaying slowly. I told my buddy that the ship was moving. He looked at me then at the lamp and said "Naw, no way is this ship moving". I told him to listen and you could hear the motors of the ship. When he heard them he immediately got sea sick, so did several others. It took us ten days to cross the Atlantic and my buddy was sick for the whole ten days, I thought he was going to die. We all managed to survive, however, and landed in Liverpool, England, boarded a bus and the driver scared hell out of me by driving on the wrong side of the street. Anyhow he got us to our destination, the railway station, and we were soon on our way to Southern England, to a small town called Ross-on-the-Wye where we were billeted in Nissen huts and given a bucket of coal!'

Below: RMS *Queen Mary* (or SS 490 as she was known in wartime) leaving America with a full complement of passengers. As can be seen it was 'standing room only' on deck when 15,000 passengers all try to catch a last glimpse of their native shore!/*Stewart Bale Ltd*

Left: Well wrapped up against the English weather, General Patton talks to some of his troops during a training exercise. His 'off the cuff' talks were aimed at instilling confidence and a determination to fight./*IWM*

Right: Patton talking to men of the 10th Infantry Regiment after they had completed an assault demonstration near Kilkeel, County Down, Northern Ireland, 30 March 1944./*US Army*

Below right: Map 1a HQ Third Army: location in England 21 March–28 June 1944.

Below: An American jeep driver gets expert help from some young garage attendants in a small village 'somewhere in England', one works the pump, another holds back the seat, a third holds the hose, whilst a fourth cleans the windscreen. /*IWM*

HQ Third Army Arrives in England

Third Army HQ was located at Fort Sam Houston, Texas, when, on 1 January 1944, it was alerted for overseas movement to ETO. An advance party of 13 officers and 26 enlisted men left on 12 January and travelled over on the *Queen Mary*, reaching the Firth of Clyde on the 29th. Colonel Robert S. Allen in his book *Lucky Forward* describes their arrival: 'When their ship docked at Glasgow, they were assembled in a mess hall. They assumed this was to hear a welcoming speech, as was the practice. Even when Patton entered, aglitter with gleaming brass and boots, they still suspected nothing. They thought he would do the spieling. He did. But not what they expected. "I am your new commander", he said, "I'm glad to see you. I hope it's mutual. There's a lot of work to be done and there's little time to do it. There's a special train waiting on the docks to take you to the CP (Command Post). We will leave in an hour". That was it. On the train, the Advance Echelon was ordered not to say or write anything about the new Commanding General'.

Their destination was in fact Peover Camp, about three miles from Knutsford, Cheshire, (see Sketch Map 1a) which, together with Toft Camp about two miles distant, was to be used by the headquarters personnel. Patton's personal residence and HQ were in Peover

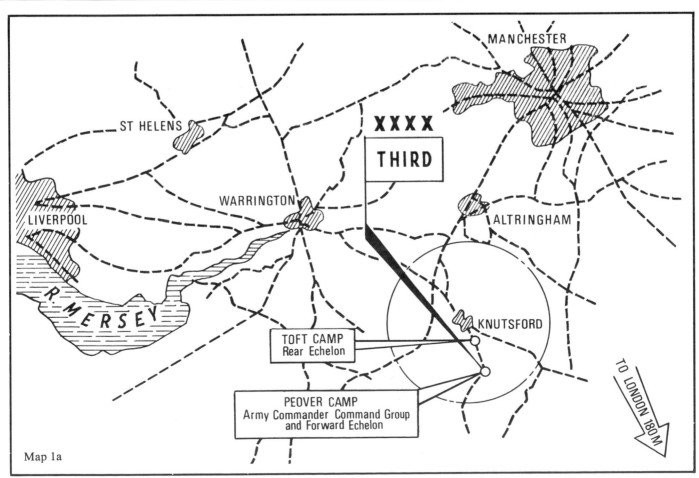

Map 1a

Hall, an 11th century manor house. Here, in two high ceilinged chambers, under constant armed guard, all Third Army's invasion planning was done. Patton also held all his war councils and briefings for corps and divisional commanders at Peover. He described his new surroundings in letters to his wife Beatrice, firstly as 'a huge house last repaired in 1627 or thereabouts' and secondly as 'quite impressive and the most inconvenient that I have so far occupied, as all the leaded windows leak and the fires don't heat and the water is scarce. However, part of it was built in 1528 and the new stable is inscribed "To my beloved son from his mother in 1658" . . . half Tudor and half Georgian and they don't blend well. . . .'*

The main body arrived at Knutsford on 23 March. They too were addressed by the Army Commander, here is how Colonel Allen described the meeting:

'The day after they were billeted all officers and enlisted men were assembled on the large terrace in front of Peover. It was a raw, gloomy, early spring day. Patton stood on the wide stone steps facing the Staff. On his left was his Chief of Staff, Brigadier General "Hap" Gay, and on the right, Willie, Patton's pugnacious-looking, white English bull terrier. On the portal over Patton's head was a weather-beaten stone shield bearing the date 1536. But there was nothing medieval about him. He was attired in a superbly tailored, form fitting, brass buttoned battle jacket, studded,

*The Patton Papers (Vol 2) by Martin Blumenson.

with four rows of campaign ribbons and decorations, pink whipcord riding breeches, and gleaming high-topped cavalry boots and spurs. Around his waist was a hand-tooled wide leather belt with a large, embossed, shiny brass buckle. In his hand was a long riding crop; on his shoulders, shirt collar, and helmet, fifteen large stars. Characteristically, Patton didn't talk long. Also characteristically, what he said was pungent and to the point. "I have been given command of Third Army", he said, "for reasons which will become clear later on. You made an outstanding record as an able and hard-working staff under my predecessor. I have no doubt you will do the same for me. We now have two staffs merging into one, each with its own procedures. By working harmoniously and intelligently together, a third Staff will be developed with a third procedure, which should be better than either of the other two. I am here because of the confidence of two men: the President of the United States and the Theatre Commander. They have confidence in me and also because they know I mean business when I fight. I don't fight for fun and I won't tolerate anyone on my Staff who does. You are here to fight. This is an active Theatre of War. Ahead of you lies battle. That means just one thing. You can't afford to be a goddamned fool, because in battle fools mean dead men. It is inevitable for men to be killed and wounded in battle. But there is no reason why such losses should be increased because of the incompetence and carelessness of some stupid son-of-a-bitch. I don't tolerate such men on my Staff. There are three reasons why we are fighting this war. The first is because we are determined to preserve our traditional liberties. Some crazy German bastards decided they were supermen and that it was their holy mission to rule the world. They've been pushing people around all over the world, looting, killing and abusing millions of innocent men, women and children. They were getting set to do the same thing to us. We had to fight to prevent being subjugated. The second reason we are fighting is to defeat and wipe out the Nazis who started all this goddamned son-of-bitchery. They didn't think we could or would fight, and they weren't the only ones who thought that, either. There are certain people back home who had the same idea. Both were wrong. The third reason we are fighting is because men like to fight. They always have and they always will. Some sophists and other crackpots deny that. They don't know what they are talking about. They are either goddamned fools or cowards or both. Men like to fight and if they don't they are not real men. If you don't like to fight, I don't want you around. You'd better get out before I kick you out. But there is one thing to remember. In war, it takes more than the

Below: Willie's Birthday Party. One night at Peover Hall the staff held a birthday party for General Patton's dog Willie with a cake and all the trimmings. Here GSP, Jr, cuts the cake whilst 'Pvt Willie Alexander' looks on approvingly./*US Army*

desire to fight to win. You've got to have more than guts to lick the enemy. You must also have brains. It takes brains and guts to win wars. We licked the Germans in Africa and Sicily because we had brains as well as guts. We're going to lick them in Europe for the same reason. That's all and good luck".'

Preparing for Overlord

The spring and early summer months of 1944 were hectic ones for all, as the detailed preparations and planning were made for the great assault on Hitler's 'Fortress Europe'. As the Army assembled, General Patton made personal inspections of his troops throughout the United Kingdom, visiting all principal units and talking with the officers and non-commissioned officers – quite an undertaking when one considers that by 31 May, the strength of Third Army was 253,500 men. Patton always spoke 'off the cuff', so there were many versions of his famous speech to the troops. However, the message was always the same – the need to fight, to kill the enemy and for everyone to do their duty no matter what their job might be. The enlisted men loved his profanity, such as:

'There's one great thing you men can say when it's all over and you're home once more. You can thank God that twenty years from now, when you're sitting around the fireside with your grandson on your knee and he asks you what you did in the war you won't have to shift him to the other knee, cough and say, "I shovelled shit in Louisiana".'*

Training had to take place and, after the almost limitless space of the training areas they were used to, tank units in particular found that England offered a few problems they had not previously encountered, as Colonel Crosby P. Miller recalls:

'I was commanding a tank company (C Company, 35th Tank Battalion, 4th Armored Division), stationed at Devizes. There were plenty of training areas nearby for platoon tactical exercises, but when it came to company size operations, an interesting problem always developed. Picture two tank platoons abreast and a third on a flank in echelon right – fifteen medium tanks charging across country. Suddenly, all come to a halt, laboriously form column, carefully cross over a narrow churned up strip of green grass, redeploy and go charging on again. Perhaps you have guessed it – a horse gallop. We had orders to cross only at designated points, and we did it – frustrating was the word!'

*The Patton Papers (Vol 2) by Martin Blumenson.

During the planning stage a great deal of co-ordination was necessary with higher headquarters which required the presence of Third Army personnel in London. So a small HQ was established in Bryanston Square under the Deputy Chief of Staff (Tactical), which acted as a liaison cell. Close contact was also maintained with the Western and Southern Base Sections who were responsible for the equipping, marshalling and movement of Third Army troops to the Continent. Third Army Divisions lined up in UK as follows (the dates are when they were first assigned to *Lucky*):

XV Corps
5 Inf ⎫
6 Inf ⎭ (2 Jan)
4 Armd (1 Feb)
35 Inf (26 Apr)

VIII Corps
79 Inf (4 Apr)
83 Inf (4 Apr)

XX Corps
5 Armd ⎫
6 Armd ⎭ (3 Mar)
90 Inf (5 Mar, attached to First Army 27 Mar-30 Jul)
28 Inf (14 Apr)
7 Armd (26 Apr)

XII Corps
2 French Armd (attached 21 Apr)
80 Inf (11 Jun)

Below: Captain (later Major) E. Ray Taylor, one of Patton's ADCs, poses in the garden of Peover Hall in May 1944. Major Taylor writes: 'Although the furnishings were sparse, each room had a fireplace, bed and chair and each of us had a private room with large shower and bath on each floor. I'm afraid we used too much coal for our fireplaces during those cold winter nights. . . . The Knutsford people were most kind to us. On one occasion Gen Patton was invited to a cocktail party and decided to go without aides, just Driver Sgt Mims. The return that night was rather unusual in that the driver and the drivee switched places. Sgt Mims was invited into the hostess's kitchen where he got a snoot full. Gen Patton had to drive Sgt Mims home. Sgt Mims woke up as Pvt Mims the following morning. Most of the days were spent preparing for the invasion. Sunday was usually a quiet day. We all attended the little church in the grounds. Recreation consisted of a baseball game in the afternoons, weather permitting, or a walk. We would all get together for a cocktail or two before dinner. Gen Patton enjoyed scotch and soda. All meals were prepared there in the Peover's kitchen and were usually very good.'
/E. R. Taylor

Right: The Knutsford incident. General Patton speaking at the opening of the Knutsford 'Welcome Club', 25 April 1944. Mrs Constantine Smith is on his immediate right, then Miss Foster-Jeffries. On Patton's left is Mr Johnson, Knutsford Council Chairman.
/*The Hon Mrs Constantine Smith, OBE*

Below right: The actor George C. Scott, who gave a memorable performance as General Patton, waits for the set to be prepared outside the Knutsford Town Hall.
/*Editor*, The Knutsford Guardian

Below: The flag of the United States of America which hangs in Over Peover church. It was presented by the Commanding General and Staff of the American Third Army who worshipped there in 1944.
/*J. P. Haworth*

The Knutsford Incident

In their usual forthright, friendly way the GIs of 3rd Army soon made themselves popular with the local population. General Patton was much in demand at all manner of functions and greatly enjoyed himself. Typical of the events he attended was the seemingly innocent opening of a Welcome Club for American officers in Knutsford, at which he was asked to make an impromptu speech. I have researched, what came to be known as 'The Knutsford Incident' very carefully indeed and am satisfied that Patton was deliberately misquoted by the American press, either maliciously or for sensation seeking reasons. The Hon Mrs Constantine-Smith, OBE, who was then head of the Knutsford WVS, and instrumental in arranging the opening of the Club, has told me categorically that General Patton very definitely did include the Russians in his remarks about who would rule the world after the war viz:

'. . . I feel that such Clubs as this are a very real value, because I believe with Mr Bernard Shaw, I think it was he, that the British and Americans are two people separated by a common language, and since it is the evident destiny of the British and the Americans, and, of course the Russians, to rule the world, the better we know each other, the better job we will do. . . .'*

His words were correctly reported by the British press and it was only when the story was reprinted in America that the phrase 'and of course the Russians' was deliberately omitted. The resulting storm reached such unbelievable proportions that it was not until Henry L. Stimson, the United States Secretary of State for War himself, intervened on Patton's behalf, that some element of sanity was restored. But as Winston G. Ramsey explains in his excellent *After the Battle* coverage of this and other incidents of Patton's life: 'Despite the exoneration we are told the whole incident left General Patton with a deep seated bitterness that was never to leave him, innocent as he was of any wrong doing'.

The Patton Papers (Vol 2) by Martin Blumenson.

Below: Preparations being made to the film set in front of the Old Town Hall, Knutsford, (now a furniture store) during the filming there of *Patton* by 20th Century-Fox. /*Editor*, The Knutsford Guardian

On the Roll

With movement to the continent imminent the headquarters moved by road on 29 June, to Breamore, near Salisbury (see Sketch Map 1b). An advance detachment had already left for France on 23 June, together with VIII Corps, in order to maintain close liaison with US First Army and to establish a new headquarters site for 3rd Army. They chose an apple orchard near Nehou on the Cotentin Peninsula.

'Late in the afternoon of 3 July, we got word that there would be a staff meeting of Section Chiefs of the Headquarters at 1730 hours. It was an unusual time for a staff meeting. We assembled quietly. There was little of the usual talk as we waited for General Patton. Exactly at the appointed time of 1730, General Patton strode quickly but quietly in and took his place before us. For just a moment his glance roved over the ranks of his staff, the men who would be carrying out and putting into effect his battle orders. Then he spoke: "Gentlemen, the moment for which we have all been working and training so long has at last arrived. Tomorrow we go to war! I congratulate you. And I prophesy that your names and the name of the Third Army will go down in history – or they will go down in the records of the Graves Registration Bureau. Thank you. Good night!''. The Third Army was on the roll!' *

The Move to France

The UK planning phase came to a close about 5 July, when the Forward Echelon sailed from Southampton, crossing the Channel in about 14 hours. They travelled in Liberty ships and Landing Ships Tank (LST). The transports anchored offshore and loads were transferred to small craft and amphibious trucks for unloading on Utah Beach, vehicles driving ashore through the shallow water. The LSTs were beached at high tide, left dry when the tide ebbed, and debarkation was then carried out across dry land. All vehicles moved inland about eight miles to a transit area for dewaterproofing and then drove in convoy a distance of some 28 miles to the headquarters

Patton and his Third Army by Col Brenton G. Wallace.

Left: Ready for 'Jump-Off'. A tough looking bunch of tank crewmen after completing their training at Devizes, Wilts, May 1944. They are members of 1st Platoon, B Company, 37 Tank Battalion, 4th Armored Division (1-Lt Leach, the platoon leader, is sitting on the tank gun, right arm on knee). /Col James H. Leach

Below: Map 1b HQ Third Army: location in England 29 June-5 July 1944.

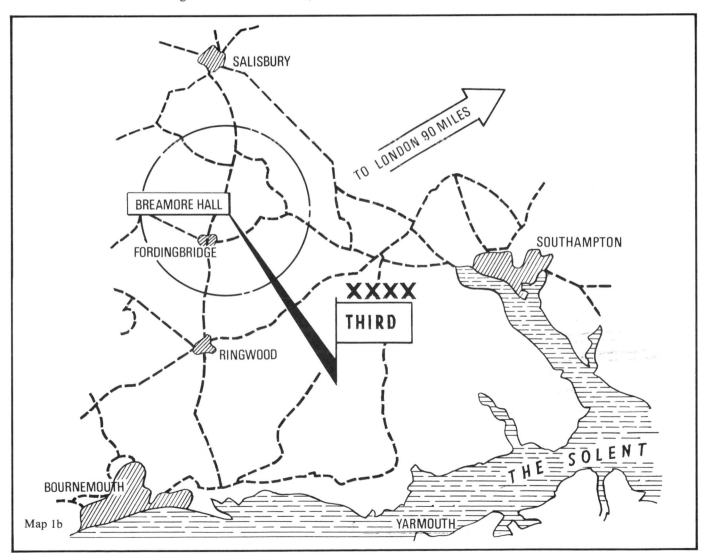

Map 1b

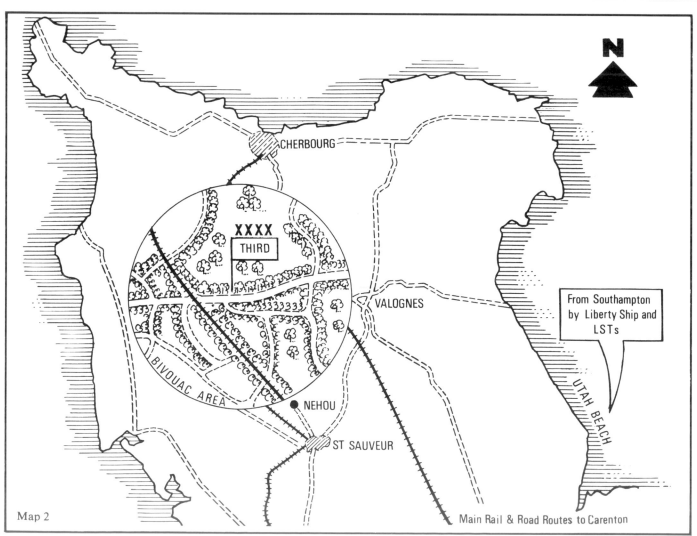

Map 2

XXXX
THIRD

CHERBOURG

VALOGNES

From Southampton
by Liberty Ship and
LSTs

UTAH BEACH

BIVOUAC AREA

NEHOU

ST SAUVEUR

Main Rail & Road Routes to Carenton

Left: The invasion begins. American troops embarking onto landing craft at a British port./*Associated Press*

Below left: Map 2 HQ Third Army: location during pre-operational phase 7 July–1 August 1944.

Right: Landing craft loaded with GIs get ready to sail for Normandy. Note the small barrage balloons attached to each landing craft for anti-aircraft protection. /*Associated Press*

Below: A stretcher bearer gives a nonchalant wave as his landing craft gets ready to leave a British port bound for Normandy./*Associated Press*

bivouac area at Nehou (see Sketch Map 2). Here is how Colonel Brenton G. Wallace described the crossing in his book *Patton and his Third Army*:

'Late in the afternoon of 4 July the headquarters started to motor down to the port of Southampton in the embarkation area, to board the ships for the passage across the Channel. As we neared the port, our column moved slower and slower, and finally came to a halt in the centre of the city. Despite the light, we finally realised that it was almost midnight, and decided that we would probably be stuck there for the rest of the night. So we tried to make the best of it. We all had our own motor equipment, of course, for we had been made independently mobile for the campaign. I personally had my own jeep and trailer and my sergeant driver. All of my equipment, including my CP tent, bedding roll and other personal belongings, as well as those belonging to my driver, were in the trailer, covered with a tarpaulin. Earlier in the evening we had become pretty hungry so opened some K rations and ate them for the first time. They were supposed to be full of vitamins, but to us they tasted terrible. Later on in France we changed our minds and thought they were excellent. Some time after midnight, we located an army kitchen and got some hot coffee. Some of us tried to sleep on the benches in a park, opposite which we were stopped, but I never realised how hard park benches really were. It got pretty cool toward morning and I finally crawled in under the tarpaulin on top of the baggage in the trailer

31

and got a little sleep. The following morning we drove our vehicles aboard an LST (Landing Ship Tank), which is larger than an LCT (Landing Craft Tank). Both have fronts which drop down as the vessel hits the beach, and the vehicles aboard run off the ship to the beach over the ramp. The LST has two decks, the upper one reached by a large elevator which carries vehicles from deck to deck. The LST was equipped with triple-tier bunks and blankets for the enlisted men and junior officers. The senior officers had bunks in staterooms. The meals going across the Channel were hot, and were really excellent. The whole trip was surprisingly comfortable. It took practically all day for our ships to be loaded and our convoy formed and we did not sail till the night of 5 July. When we came on deck the next morning, it was a beautiful clear day and the Channel was quite a sight. In front of us and behind us, as far as the eye could see, were LSTs, Liberty and Victory ships in double column plowing across the Channel. Each ship carried a silver barrage balloon, extending on a cable from its stern. It was really a bridge of ships. On either side of the double column, destroyers flitted here and there and off in the distance could occasionally be seen the low outline of a cruiser or a battleship. As we neared the French coast we began to hear the rumble of guns, demolition charges along the coast, with once in a while the explosion of a mine. As we approached Utah Beach we saw a great deal of wreckage, smashed craft and vehicles, and many underwater obstacles, although many of these things had been removed. Our LST beached shortly after noon of 6 July and we drove ashore over the ramp formed by our dropped bow. The beach traffic was fairly well organized although dozens of ships were lined up on both sides of us discharging their loads onto the sand. We drove over a sort of highway marked by the vehicles along the beach and then up a ramp built through an opening in the sea wall onto the land above. Beach strongpoints and enemy gun emplacements which had been captured or smashed, were of course visible everywhere. We began to see minefields placed by the Heinies, marked with a skull and crossbones and the words *Achtung-Minen*. They told us the white signs marked dummy minefields and the yellow ones the real thing. As we went inland we saw the barbed wire entanglements and the French grey stone houses which had been wrecked by the naval and artillery shells and also small fields of crosses where the dead had been buried. When we came to Ste. Mere Eglise and other towns we found that many civilians still lived there and they welcomed us warmly with smiles and hand waving and an occasional *Vive l'Amerique!* As we got farther inland they even offered us calvados to drink

and threw apples to us. One of the amusing things, however, was to see the little children, six or seven years old, try to give us Churchill's famous victory sign made with the first two fingers of the hand. These little youngsters, having been taught the Nazi salute by the Heinies, and of course knowing no better, would first give us a stiff Nazi salute and then immediately open two fingers making the V sign at the same time'.

Frank Paskvan left for France on 21 July also landing at Utah Beach. The planes were bombing Cherbourg at the time and in the distance he could see a pall of heavy black smoke:

'Our landing was not perfect, the ship hit a sand bar and we were stuck out in the water about two hundred feet from shore and yet the orders were that as soon as the ramp was lowered the first truck was to leave the ship immediately. Our truck was in the middle of the LCT so I walked over to watch the first truck leaving the ship, but something was wrong, I didn't see any ramp. The captain of the ship also sensing something was wrong immediately picked up a measuring device and found that the water was eleven feet deep! So we waited for the tide to go out and the first truck and first bridge outfit then landed in France'.

Colonel Crosby Miller left England with his tank company on 29 June crammed into the tank deck of an LST with a light tank company:

'The trip across was uneventful until the last few minutes. Just before the LST hit the beach, all our tank engines were started for warm up. Unfortunately at the same time, the ventilating system was shut off, and in a matter of minutes the tank deck was filled with exhaust fumes so thick that we could barely see two tanks away. The main concern was how long we would be cooped up with the exhaust fumes and the effect of carbon monoxide on the tankers. Fortunately, we grounded very shortly, the doors opened, the ramp dropped and we were out in the fresh air. A few of the tankers had splitting headaches for a while, but there were no lasting ill effects. Later, all I could think of was what a ridiculous way we might have entered the war – asphyxiated in the hold of an LST!'

To illustrate this section I have included some typical photos of US troops embarking for France. Except where stated I cannot confirm that these pictures actually show Third Army troops, but they are representative of embarkation conditions.

Patton Arrives

General Patton and his Chief of Staff flew to France to join the headquarters, leaving England at 1025 hours on 6 July. They flew in a flight of three C-47s, each carrying a jeep and were escorted by four P-47s. Flying down the eastern side of the Cotentin Peninsula, they landed at an airstrip near Omaha Beach. 'News of his arrival in France spread like wildfire and army and navy personnel rushed to see him . . . When his jeep was ready, he got in, remained standing and gave a short impromptu speech: "I'm proud to be here

to fight beside you. I am going personally to shoot that paper-hanging goddamned son-of-a-bitch just like I would a snake". The troops cheered.'* Leaving the airstrip they drove to General Bradley's headquarters south of Isigny, where Patton spent his first night in the middle of 'the most infernal artillery preparation I have ever heard'** – the HQ being very close to a number of gun positions of divisional units of First Army. Next day they drove on to Nehou, crossing the bridge in Carentan which was supposed to be under enemy fire and had to be crossed at high speed. 'When I went over, I saw four of our soldiers sitting on it fishing. However, every visiting fireman whom I subsequently met told me of the dangers he had encountered crossing the bridge.'** Arriving at his Nehou apple orchard Patton spent a frustrating period of waiting, obsessed with the belief that the war would be over before he could get into it. During the remainder of July, thousands of his Third Army troops arrived. Their movements were still heavily cloaked in secrecy, but they were eager and ready to fight. The Staff spent the time making liaison visits to units already involved with the enemy, but on strict orders that the Third Army patch was not to be seen.

* *The Patton Papers* (Vol 2) by Martin Blumenson.

** Both quotes from *War as I knew it* by George S. Patton, Jr.

Below: Patton in France. The Commander of Third Army conferring with Maj-Gen Lindsey McD. Silvester at his Divisional HQ in the field, 26 August 1944./US Army

Breakout!

Breakout from the Bocage

Having established strong bridgeheads to the east of the Orne River around Caen, the British 21st Army Group issued a general directive for an offensive to break out of the Cotentin Peninsula, gain control of Brittany and swing wide to the east. The British and Canadian Armies on the left flank were to attack continually to the south and east, to screen the location of the main effort, which was to be undertaken by the First US Army in a pivoting move on its left flank and a swing south on its right flank, which would secure the whole of the Cotentin Peninsula. On reaching the base of the peninsula, it was to turn VIII Corps west into Brittany towards Rennes and St Malo. Third US Army was instructed to follow the advance of VIII Corps on the extreme right flank and to take command of the operation when ordered. The First Army's operation was known as Cobra.

Its aim was to effect a penetration of the enemy defences west of St Lo, with VIII Corps, and to exploit this penetration with a strong armoured and motorised thrust deep into the enemy's rear at Coutances. It was assumed that the enemy would be forced to make a gradual withdrawal and that VIII Corps would continue to exert direct pressure during this withdrawal. H-hour was fixed at 1300 hours on 24 July, but had to be postponed for 24 hours because of bad flying weather. Heavy artillery barrages and saturation bombing preceded the attack. Here is now it was described in the history of 704th Tank Destroyer Battalion:

'25 July 1944, an unforgettable day for the men of 4th Armored Division – the start of the Normandy breakthrough. Fortresses, Liberators, Marauders, Mustangs and Thunderbolts filled the sky – a sky full of the black balls of bursting ack ack. But they flew steadily

Below: Breakout! A medium tank of 37th Tank Bn, 4th Armd Div, on the road to Coutances, turns out of Periers and begins it journey to the front lines, 29 July 1944. Note the 'B-11' on the Sherman's right rear. This denotes that it is from 2nd Platoon of B Company./*US Army*

on and spilled tons of bombs that shook the ground on which we stood three miles away from the target area. Three thousand planes were involved and when the last one had finished its work the 4th Armored Division plunged through the dazed enemy, cutting down and overrunning anything that presented opposition'.

They rolled on to Coutances and concentrated to refuel. Snipers and small isolated groups of enemy caused minor delays, but they were quickly wiped out. 'In Avranches several well camouflaged German tanks opened fire and knocked out five halftracks. Lt Addison of the 2nd Platoon, A Company, 704th Tank Destroyer Battalion roared past the column with two guns to flush the Jerries out. Sgt Joe Shedvey, tank commander, spotted the enemy tanks first. T/S Bleemel Beck, driver, whipped the tank around into a firing position. Pfc Manuel Alviso shoved home a 76mm APC, the breech block snapped shut, Cpl Clinton Threet laid the crosshairs on the centre of the swastika and the first round fired at an enemy tank by an M18 of the battalion tore to its mark. Before the Hell Cat had stopped rocking, another round was in the chamber and Threet was traversing the tube with swift coolness to another tank partly hidden behind a hedgerow. The Jerry, already laid, fired and missed which cost him

his life for the second round from Shedvey's gun left the Kraut tank burning. Two other tanks in the vicinity saw the action and, panic stricken, tried to escape and exposed their positions. Four more rounds were expended and two more enemy tanks were stopped in their tracks, a holocaust of flame. The battle was won and confidence in men and machines was secure. Lt Addison, instantly killed in this battle, was the first officer of the battalion killed in action'.

Third Army Operational

On 28 July General Bradley issued verbal orders to General Patton to assume operational command of all troops then in the VIII Corps Zone and to supervise the lightning-like follow up which had hit the enemy. The 4th and 6th Armored Divisions were quickly thrown into the battle, followed closely by 8th and 79th Infantry Divisions. At 1230 hours on 1 August 1944, a warm clear day with good visibility, the Third US Army became officially operational, but under a veil of official secrecy, although the enemy had already suggested their presence in France. In addition to VIII Corps, commanded by Maj-Gen Troy H. Middleton, Third Army took operational control of XII Corps (Maj-Gen Gilbert R. Cook), XV Corps (Maj-Gen Wade E. Haislip) and XX Corps (Maj-Gen Walton H. Walker). (See Sketch Map 3 for layout of

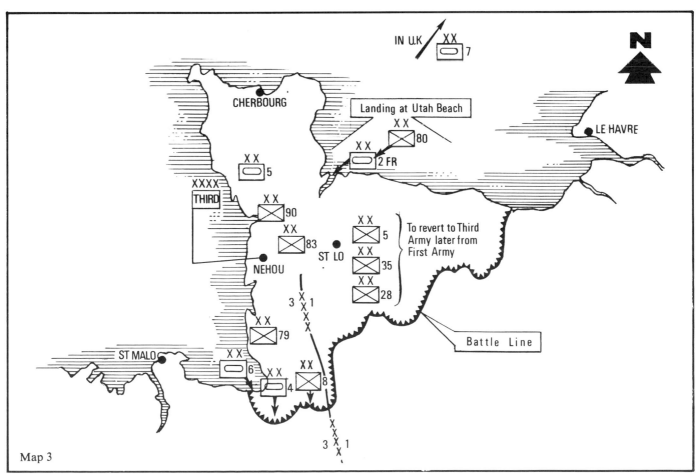

IN U.K XX 7

N

CHERBOURG

Landing at Utah Beach

LE HAVRE

XX 80

XX 2 FR

XX 5

XXXX
THIRD

XX 90

XX 83

ST LO

XX 5

To revert to Third
Army later from
First Army

XX 35

XX 28

NEHOU

3 X 1
X
X
X

Battle Line

XX 79

ST MALO

XX 6

XX 4

XX 8

X
X
X
3 X 1
X

Map 3

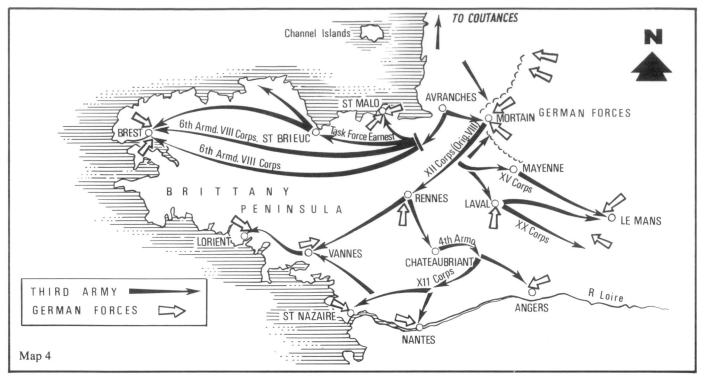

Map 4

Third Army on 1 August 1944, and Sketch Map 4 for details of the initial thrust lines 1-10 August.)

The Breakout

I have chosen three short battle stories by men of Third Army who took part in the breakout. The first concerns C Company 35th Tank Battalion of 4th Armored Division. Colonel Crosby P. Miller recalls:

'After the breakout, we were heading into Brittany towards Rennes. Just outside of Rennes, at a small place called La Charbonniere, the column ran into heavy anti-tank and small arms fire. B Company was called forward to clear out the resistance. Within a very short time, my company was called forward. Nearing the area, I could see several tanks burning and others out of action. I was told there was an anti-tank gun off to the right of the road and to knock it out. Seeing what had happened to B Company, I sent one platoon on down the left side of the road to move beyond and swing back in on the other side of the gun position. I took a second platoon off to the right of the road, formed a line and started sweeping slowly toward the suspected position. Suddenly, a round hit one of my tanks, penetrating the front slope, passing through the transmission, up into the turret and knocking out the main gun. Everyone finally got out safely but with a little delay because the tank commander had to climb back on the tank to tell the gunner to get out – he was still trying to fire his gun. Just as both men hit the ground, another round hit the tank and set it afire. At this point, none of my tank commanders had

spotted the enemy position. From the damage already inflicted, that gunner was clearly extremely accurate. Consequently I ordered all tanks to stand fast. I moved my own tank slowly forward along a sunken road, trying to spot the position. Suddenly, what sounded like a freight train roared by under my tank, and I realized I was square in the enemy gunner's sights. I immediately began backing up, became enveloped in smoke and thought we had been hit. But as we backed farther and into cover, I saw that the smoke was from an old mattress lying on the road and set afire by the enemy round. By this time, it was obvious that every approach was covered by anti-tank gun fire. I stayed put and asked for artillery and mortars to blanket the area and infantry to mop it up. We did get mortar fire into the area and two P-47s also bombed it. By this time it was dark. I asked for infantry to outpost my tanks, was told none were available, so each tank crew set up its own security. One German was killed during the night by a tanker, and when dawn came, an infantry force came through and found the position to have been abandoned during the night. I was told later that the position was primarily anti-aircraft guns. There was a ring of six 88mm guns in concrete emplacements, but each gun could fire at ground targets based on pictures painted on the emplacement walls which showed the exact range to a given point in front of the gun where a US vehicle might appear. This was C Company's first direct exposure to combat, and it came through it quite well. As for me, I was thoroughly scared from start to finish!'

Frank Paskvan was also with 4th Armored, as an assistant truck driver and hoist operator with an engineer bridge building detachment, working with the spearhead of the 25th Cavalry, a platoon of tanks, the 51st Infantry and some other divisional units.

'As we broke out the enemy was in a daze from the bombing until we got close to Avranches, then they started to take pot shots at us from all directions until our truck looked like a sieve. Suddenly we hit a road block and the enemy must have had direct communications to the 88mm guns because they threw everything in on us but the kitchen sink. Finally a major asked me which way the shells were coming from but I was so scared I pointed one way and my buddy Fred Devries, driver of our truck, pointed the other. He then radioed in for some P-47s. They were in the air about five minutes later and dropped some bombs and that was that. Beside the road block the Germans had planted mines, a half track started around the road block when a mine went off, it even blew the spark plugs out of the engine. So this was what war was all about. After the mines were cleared we started for Avranches. My buddy and I were pulled out of the column and told to go to the advance guard. When we reached Avranches I looked down into the valley and saw the Salune river bridge and it was intact. The enemy was giving up by the hundreds and I looked alongside of the road and saw the bushes moving and gave a yell ''Come out of there''. About 20 or 30 of the enemy jumped up. They scared hell out of me, but by this time I thought we had got them by the ass. There was a jeep in front of us and he started up the other side

Above: French civilians crowd into a narrow street in Angers to welcome XX Corps troops as they enter the town, while two young Frenchmen hold a welcoming banner./*IWM*

Top left: Map 4 Breakout! 1-10 August 1944.

Bottom left: French civilians applaud enthusiastically during the ceremony, on 4 August 1944, celebrating their liberation in the Place de la Mairie, Rennes, after the city had been freed by VIII Corps troops. /*IWM*

Left: Kamerad! A 14-year old sniper lifts his arms in surrender after being captured by US troops in the Coutances area./*IWM*

Below: Prisoners to the rear. Armoured forces push forward to the south and east after the capture of Avranches. Some of 20,000 German prisoners taken in the battle for Avranches (captured by US First Army 30 July 1944) are seen here on their way to POW cages./*IWM*

Above: American tanks push on through Avranches, as they follow up the retreating German forces./*US Army*

of the valley and we went down and across the bridge. Just as we started across a bus came busting over the hill full of Germans, the tank that was sitting along the river with four others let go and the bus started to burn and the enemy came out of the windows, doors or any opening, tearing off their insignias and clothes. I jumped out of the truck and picked up some shoulder patches etc – don't know what made me do it. As the jeep got to the top of the hill he suddenly turned around and came back full speed and yelled "Get the hell off the road, the whole German Army is on the other side!" Our platoon leader told us to go about two fields away with a platoon of 24th Engineers who were with us all the time for protection. My lieutenant told our platoon and also the 24th, to dig in, dig deep and camouflage all the equipment. There was a lot of firing going on and then it got quiet, Fred and I crawled into our foxhole and I started to pray. About midnight the Germans started back toward the bridge, we had only left five tanks there so they could only do so much. The enemy went right by us but the men we had left along the road really got clobbered, the screams of the wounded and dying I can still hear to this day. About five in the morning it got quiet again. The Lieutenant asked me to check if everybody was OK and as I crawled from hole to hole everybody said OK. We then started to get up and look around and when we looked to the left there were Germans, to the front there were Germans, and to the right was the river and then a hill and on top of the hill a hospital or rest home with a wall all around it. We could see the Germans peering down at us from the openings and top of the wall. The Lieutenant from the 24th Engineer Platoon told his men to put on their bayonets as we would have hand to hand combat, but the Germans never fired. Our Lieutenant got a radio message that a bridge was needed at once on the See river,

this was about a mile or two down the road. Guess who he picked – Fred and I, and a squad of the 24th, to go and build a Treadway Steel Bridge across the bridge that was blown. As we got to the road the Germans were looking down into our faces. On the road we stopped to assemble the squad on to an empty truck. I jumped out of the truck and stood behind a tree so did the others, can't hit anything you can't see was my thinking. Finally the Lieutenant of the 24th came up the road with his jeep and we slowly took off and still the Germans did not fire. As we drove along the road we found a small cart loaded with whiskey, white calvados, beer and a box which was full of money. The booze was more important as we needed some Dutch courage. As we got to the bridge we turned the truck around and ran the hoist to get the treadway steel bridge parts off. When all four sections were assembled I started to lift it and the whole front of the truck went into the air, the front wheels were about 2 feet off the road. The Lieutenant of the 24th made everyone grab a stone and crawl on the hood to hold the front end down and it worked. As I started to lift, my buddy started to back the truck and we placed the bridge into position, by this time the Germans saw what we were up to and opened up on us. The ground really shook, I never heard so much noise in my life, but by an act of God no one got hit bad. Later I felt as if I had stepped in some water, and found I had a 2½-inch gash across my knee, the blood ran down my leg into my shoe. Funny how you can be hit and not feel it. Anyhow the 24th Engineers went out looking for the Germans and came back with 30 prisoners including one pissed-off SS trooper. He wouldn't even walk with the other men so to aggravate him one of the 24th took his watch and broke it, then took his bayonet and started to prod him from behind, this made him walk faster. With all the prisoners in front

Above: Frank J. Paskvan pictured here with his buddy Fred Derries (minus hat) standing beside their truck 'Helen', named after Fred's sister./*Frank J. Paskvan*

of us we came back to the original place that we had started out from in the morning. The dead and wounded were all laying out alongside a big barn and the German and American medics were trying to save the lives of the ones who were still breathing. I remember thinking just a couple of hours ago all were alive, and the enemy could have given up and all this bloodshed could have been avoided. Our truck was empty so the Lieutenant told us to take the prisoners to the rear, whilst we were taking them back we passed our company coming to the front. I was sitting on the hood of the truck guarding them and there must have been a couple of hundred in this bunch. The look on the faces of our company is still instilled in my mind. They were amazed that we had so many prisoners. We only took them so far and then the military police took over. As we assembled a sniper started to fire out of a tree about 500 feet away. My carbine would never reach him if I tried to fire back, so I crawled over to a ditch that I had passed the previous evening and took a rifle from a dead soldier. As I did so I thought that he looked so young and in my mind it could have been me and I was thinking what will his mother do when she gets the telegram "Killed in Action"? Killed in Action, it was a slaughter, he never had a chance. When I got his rifle I started to aim when a jeep came down the road and I yelled for him to get down. He was a photographer and he said, "Shoot when I tell you to" but I couldn't wait and I fired as soon as he hit the road. The enemy sniper who had pinned us down came tumbling out of the tree. Somewhere there is a picture of me shooting the sniper out of a tree. We were then able to move out and we went over the same route that we took that morning and crossed over our own bridge. This was the breakout and Fred and I had a big hand in doing it with the squad of the 24th Engineers. Remember

the box we had thrown on the truck? It was a German payroll. I thought it was fake money and later was throwing it to the French civilians who were picking it up Must have been a million dollars'

The third anecdote is about a member of the Quartermaster Corps It was written by Sgt Saul Levitt and appeared in *Highlights from Yank* which was published in 1955 and is reproduced here with the kind permission of the Universal Publishing and Distributing Corporation of New York:

'From the record itself, you realize immediately that Major Charles W. Ketterman of Pasadena, California, of the QM was a frustrated infantryman. He had been in the infantry in the last war and at Soissons had won the Croix de Guerre for knocking out a brace of German machine guns. But early in this war the Army had shoved him into a QM outfit, thereby blighting any combat plans he might have worked out for himself. As for Pvt Ernest Jenkins, who drives the major, it is not very clear what his outlook on combat was. He is a very close-mouthed negro of 21, from New York City. He is a QM soldier armed with an '03 Springfield rifle. He had never said he wanted to kill Germans, and he'd never said that he didn't. Under the routine conditions of his job, the only way the major could ever get close to combat was to have his jeep get around to the scene of action as often as possible, which he did. He always went with Jenkins at the wheel, and they picked up things like hand grenades which they held onto. After the breakthrough at St Lo the major's QM battalion, following hard on the track of armour through France, was hard to hold together in one piece. It was the time of splendid confusion in France. The major played tag with his battalion. Now he had it, now it was gone. It was in one of the periods, when his battalion was gone and he was looking for it, that the major and the private found themselves driving down from Brou towards Chateaudun on a day in August. As the jeep went south it was very quiet, the kind of quietness that is disturbing to a soldier. The major was aware of the quietness, but that didn't stop him from going on. Maybe he was looking for something. They had both been without sleep for 24 hours. Along the road out of Chateaudun and coming toward them was a jeep rolling along at a pretty fair clip. The two vehicles stopped. "Where are you going, major?" asked one of the soldiers in the other jeep. "Through Chateaudun and south" said the major. "I don't think you're going through Chateaudun, major", said the soldier, "because we're shelling hell out of that town, and what's more the Germans are in Chateaudun". The major considered that for a minute. If we were shelling it was probably to catch the movement of the Germans eastward. Hell, he could probably slip around to the east of the town and capture some Germans. Maybe, however, he and Jenkins ought to have a little support. Between them they had only the '03 rifle and a .45 pistol. Maybe the boys in the jeep, which mounted a .30 calibre machine gun, would like to help capture some Germans. The major told them about his plan, and they were distinctly disinterested. In the end, however, they turned toward Chateaudun. As they came over a rise of ground that showed Chateaudun below them, shells broke around them whistling from the other side of the Loire River and splattering the road. It was clearly enemy shelling. This burst had been aimed at them. It meant that German guns covered the road with direct observation. The men in the jeeps got under cover of a stone wall at the side of the road. The men out of the other jeep stayed for a while and then thought of something they ought to be doing right away. They left. The major and the private were now alone in a garden behind a wall on the outskirts of the town. An old Frenchman showed himself. The major was thinking fast. He had discarded the out-flanking move to

the east of town. What was more important was the German big gun on the other side of the river that covered this road. Americans coming this way would receive pointblank fire. But if he could get close enough to the German gun to note its position accurately and report it back to our artillery . . . "Jenkins" said the major, "Yessir", "I got a plan", "Yessir". The major gave Jenkins the plan. "So we'll go down to the river and look for that gun. How do you feel about that?" "It's all right with me", said Jenkins. The old Frenchman showed them a way down to the river through which they couldn't be seen. They made it to another parapet on the edge of the river, and from behind the wall the major spotted the gun. It was a big gun all right and camouflaged. They could see the Germans moving around the gun. It was a hundred yards across the river to the gun. They waited until dusk fell. And then it happened by itself. Our artillery was falling on the town, which made it fairly safe in a way, but not if the Germans saw the flash from the barrel. Jenkins had never fired the thing before except for the ordinary amount of target practice in basic training back in the States. The German stood up there clearly, and Jenkins let go and the German went

Below: Prisoners taken in the bocage 'battle of the hedgerows' are quizzed before being sent to the rear.
/US Army

down. That was all. "Good boy" said the major. "Jenkins", "Yessir", "Gimme that gun". Jenkins handed it over. From behind the other end of that wall the major fired. Around the gun now there was a flurry of motion and the sound of voices. One man looked directly toward the wall. He looked at it steadily but that was all. It was now dark, but they had looked at the gun site for a long time. For three hours the '03 went back and forth between the major and the private. They were still there at midnight, a clear star-filled moonless midnight – 16 August. They knew they had killed and wounded men around that gun. And now the movement began. The unmistakable sounds of motors. Then it was quiet again. "Jenkins", "Yessir", "How about our getting across the river and looking around?" "It's OK with me, sir". In the darkness they tried to cross a bridge into the heart of Chateaudun, and halfway across almost fell into the river. The Germans had blown the centre span. The major and the private went back to the stone wall and slept until dawn, and when they awoke and looked across the river the gun and the men were gone. Some French people came out of the houses. The French said to the two Americans that they didn't know who was in the town

now. Undoubtedly there must be some Americans because they had heard some rifle fire going back over the river toward the German positions. "It was our rifle fire", explained the major. "Well, then", declared the French, "you are the only ones here". The major and the private now crossed to the other side of the river, walking carefully across a thread of bridgeway that still held in the centre. As they reached the other side, crowds caught them up. It was spreading through Chateaudun that here were the liberators, the first Americans to show. And there were still Germans in the town – 15 of them, said the prefect of police, hidden in a dugout on the hospital grounds, and there was one German prisoner in the town jail. The major brought his mind to bear on this military problem and concentrated, and then he consulted with his one-man army in the person of Private Jenkins. "Jenkins", said the major, "I've got an idea", "Yessir", "We've got hand grenades, haven't we, plus the rifle and the .45? I think we could take those Germans. What do you say?" "It's OK with me, sir" said Jenkins. Through an interpreter the major explained to the German prisoner how he was to deliver from the Americans the ultimatum that grenades would be fired into the dugout if the Germans did not surrender. The crowds lay around the border of the hospital grounds surrounding the dugout. The two Americans stood 25 feet in front of the dugout and waited. It was a long wait, a long five-minute wait – and then the Germans came out – without arms. In the dugout lay some of their wounded. Three had been killed last night by rifle fire from some place, they said, and the others in the dugout had been wounded by the same fire. The 15 of them were in the rear guard left behind; the gun and the other men had gone eastward out of town. Chateaudun swelled now with the joy of liberation, giving to the two Americans that kind of welcome which always accompanies the first hours of freedom. And that was long ago, in those ancient days of breakthrough after St Lo, as we charged through France. They shook Chateaudun from them, a little at a time, making their way out of town, the major who had once been an infantryman and couldn't forget it, and the private who had never fired a gun in anger. As the jeep drove out of town it was warm and they felt drowsy. "Jenkins" said the major, "I've got an idea", "Yessir"; "If we keep on going through Chateaudun we should hit that damn CP OK and get some sleep. How about it?" "It's OK with me, sir" said Jenkins, wheeling the jeep southward out of town. Note: A Silver Star was awarded to the major and the private and was pinned on by Lt-Gen George S. Patton, Jr.'

Below: On 20 August 1944 infantrymen of XV Corps stride past the battered sign at the entrance to the ancient French town of Argentan, after finally driving the Germans out of the village which was first reached by armoured columns on 12 August./*US Army*

Patton

Hero or Clown?

It is one of the quirks of our modern Western society that we are inclined to treat a hero badly during his lifetime and only heap praises on his head when he is dead and gone. General Patton was a perfect example. Can anyone honestly imagine Alexander the Great, Hannibal or Napoleon being subjected to the indignities that Patton had to endure for merely slapping an hysterical soldier? And what other great military commander has nearly lost his command before a vital campaign because he was deliberately misquoted by the press of his own country, after speaking 'off the record' at a minor function in a small out of the way town in a foreign country? Of course he was a flamboyant, larger than life character, with a vocabulary of four letter words which delighted most of his audiences and offended a few. He was, like so many great men, a complete mixture of opposites. Loyal and dependable, he could still be unpredictable and capricious. Brutal yet sensitive, gregarious yet always a loner, as easily moved to tears as to anger, the list of opposites is endless. It is inevitable that such a man should have had critics, but despite everything that has been said or written against him, no one can truthfully find anything derogatory to say about his ability to win battles. And surely isn't that what good generalship is really all about in wartime? In this brief look at the character of the commander of Third Army there is only space to highlight some facets of his life, but I hope that in so doing my admiration for his professional ability will not be lost to the reader. He was undoubtedly one of the greatest field commanders ever, a fact which was apparently more obvious to the Axis than to the Allies! Why else would they have swallowed so obediently the complicated deception plan, known as 'Fortitude', designed to convince them that Patton, who had not been used in operations since Sicily because of the slapping incident, was actually the head of an Army Group that was preparing to launch the real invasion across the Channel into the Pas de Calais area? There were many other instances of their respect for his prowess, for example, during the highly successful operations of 4th Armored Division in the Nancy area in September 1944, one of the prisoners taken was an SS colonel, Standarten Führer Theodore Werner. He gave Patton this unsolicited testimonial:

'I would be pleased to know the commander of this division and I am sure that it must be part of General Patton's Third Army. *General Patton is for the American Army what Rommel stands for in the German Army*, and to know the commander of this armoured division would help explain to me how this Army managed to achieve such speed of advance which in many instances caught us completely unprepared'[*]

No mean compliment from a man who commanded a division in Russia, only served with the SS for a short time and was the possessor of the Order of the German Cross in Gold.

Patton the Man

Many people have written books and articles about Patton, some more accurate than others and there are a wealth of anecdotes attributed to him. Whilst I was determined to present as accurate a picture as possible, I also wanted to find a new approach. Therefore, I was delighted when General Patton's daughter, Mrs Ruth Ellen Patton Totten, widow of the late Major-General James W. Totten, kindly agreed to help me. An historian in her own right, Mrs Totten has lectured in many subjects, varying from military heritage to witchcraft. She has allowed me to quote at length from a talk she gave about her father to the Topsfield Historical Society in 1974. It does, I believe, present a fascinating picture of him and of his forebears, whose influence was so great upon his life:

'George Smith Patton, Jr, came from a family of civilians, people who had been lawyers and ministers for generations. The only soldiers in the family had been the men who went to war for a cause, and who went back to civilian life, if they were still alive, when the battles were over and the cause lost or won. But from the age of five, Georgie had always wanted to be a soldier (up until then he wanted to be a fireman). He was the most literate man I have

Right: Cadet Patton at West Point 1909. Cadet Adjutant Patton flashes a triumphant grin during his final year at West Point. He excelled in 'Drill Regulations' and at the end of his second year was top of his class in conduct, being appointed second-ranking corporal at Summer Camp. He maintained his high standing throughout his final year (1908-09) when he was adjutant. Scholastically he graduated 46th out of 103; he was awarded his A for athletics, and played in the West Point football team for the last four of his five years there, breaking both arms, his nose (three times) and dislocating a shoulder. It is also interesting to note that he graduated six years before both Eisenhower and Bradley./*Patton Museum*

[*] *The Nancy Bridgehead* by Lt-Col (now Brig-Gen, Retd) Hal C. Pattison.

ever known and also the most well-read, but he had a terrible time getting through school – The Virginia Military Institute (VMI) and West Point – because his Aunt Nannie Wilson, gentle as the dove and stubborn as the mule, decided out of hand that Georgie, whom she worshipped, was too delicate to go to school, so she kept him home and read aloud to him. For this reason he didn't learn to read or write until he was 12 years old, when his father, driven to the wall, forcibly sent him off to the local grammar school. To make a vignette of Aunt Nannie's force of character, my grandmother, her sister, once told my mother that she never punished Georgie without first turning down Nannie's bed and sending for the doctor.

'My father was born on 11 November 1885, on his grandfather's working ranch in San Gabriel, California. His grandfather, Benjamin Davis Wilson, was a famous pioneer from Wilson County, Tennessee. He went West as a guide in the 1840s, and stayed to make a fortune and to make Californian history. He was always known as Don Benito. He built the big rambling house, where Georgie was born, for his third wife, Margaret Hereford Wilson, my father's grandmother, and while Georgie and his sister Anita were growing up,

the whole family lived there together, as people did in those days. Don Benito was a story-book character, his adventures ranged from being tied to a stake and burned – for a while – by hostile Indians, to being rushed and savaged by a wounded bear, shot by a poisoned Indian arrow and captured by bandits. Don Benito's grandfather had been a hero of the Revolutionary War, and the Continental Congress gave him 2,000 acres of howling wilderness, later to become part of the state of Tennessee, as a reward. Two of Don Benito's aunts had been captured, as girls, by Indians; one was rapidly recovered but the other disappeared and was found years later, a white squaw with several babies. The soldiers tried to take her back to her family, but she ran away in the night and went back to her Indian people. Georgie was brought up on this rich fare. Don Benito Wilson died in 1878, when his two daughters, Nannie and Ruth, were young girls. The girls both fell in love with young George Patton, whose widowed mother had come West after the Civil War to live with her brother, who was a lawyer in Los Angeles. George married Ruth Wilson, and moved into the family home – the ranch was called Lake Vineyard. Years later, when George finally built a home of his own, Nannie moved in with them and lived there till she died. Aunt Nannie was a tremendous influence in George's life. In her way, she was a great educator. She pressed the study of the Bible on him, as a library of

history and religion. He knew a great deal of it by heart, and one of his favourite quotes was, "As a man thinketh, so is he". Aunt Nannie read aloud all of the Iliad, the Odyssey, Pliny, Plutarch's Lives, all the books on Napoleon – my father's super hero next to Achilles – and Xenophon, and the March of the Ten Thousand, all about Alexander the Great, Shakespeare, Ben Jonson, Marlowe, Piers Plowman, Pilgrim's Progress – all the books we all should read and never have time to (except my sister and brother and I *had* to read them and give my father book reports). Georgie inherited the Patton trait of total recall, and all his life he could come up with a quotation for anything and everything. History was his playmate and his mentor and probably the greatest influence in his life. All his games, as a boy, were historic games. He was a hero worshipper. His sister, my Aunt Anita, told us that one time he wanted to play Achilles, dragging the body of Hector around the walls of Troy behind his pony Peachblossom, and the only way she avoided being Hector was by finding a huge dead rat to take her place. He brought himself up in the company of heroes, and he wanted to be among them.

'Another great influence in his life was his grandmother Susan Patton. His grandfather, the gallant Confederate Colonel George Patton, was killed at the Battle of Cedar Creek in Winchester, Virginia, in 1864. The widow came to California, via the Isthmus of Panama, with her four children, her blind father, and her brother, who had been an officer in the Confederate Navy and had skippered the ironside *Little David* in Charleston Harbor. He had been captured by the Yankees and was dying of TB which he had caught in a Yankee prison. This most gallant of heroines later married her husband's first cousin, and best friend, Colonel George Hugh Smith, a hero himself. He never took the oath of allegiance to the USA after the Civil War, but he was such a distinguished lawyer and person that the authorities overlooked it. He was a wonderful stepfather and grandfather to the Pattons, and brought them all up on the heroism of the dead Colonel George Patton; of the dramatic mortal wound of George's brother, Colonel Walter Tazewell Patton, who charged with Pickett at Gettysburg and was hit in the final wave that broke against the Yankee artillery and died in the Union Hospital there, murmuring, "In Christ alone, perfectly resigned, perfectly resigned". And of the youngest Patton son, Willie, who marched to the Battle of Newmarket with the other VMI cadets, to the music of fife and drum playing, "Will you come to the bower I have builded for you, your bed shall be of roses bespangled with dew". Georgie's father, and Georgie himself, and all of us as the years went by, including my own children, would hear these stories, holding in our hands the iron shell fragment that killed the first George Patton, with his blood soaked shirt and blood

Above: Colonel Patton and members of his Staff, Fort Myer, June 1940. Between the wars Patton went back to the horse cavalry, attending the Cavalry School at Fort Riley, Kansas in 1923. After service in Leavenworth, Boston and Hawaii he was promoted Colonel in 1937 (20 years after attaining it temporarily in World War I) and assigned to a cavalry command. Shortly after the Germans had conquered France and the Low Countries in 1940, he was given command of an armoured brigade at Ft Benning, Georgia, by Gen Marshall, who was desperately trying to modernise the Army. A few months later he was commanding 2nd Armored Division, earning the nickname 'Old Blood and Guts' about this time. ('An armoured division', Patton is supposed to have asserted at a staff conference, 'needs blood and brains'. Newspaper reports garbled his phraseology, crediting him with having called for blood and guts.) /*Patton Museum*

stained pass book, brought back to his widow by the negro slave, Peter, who refused his freedom because he had to look after "his family". The first George Patton, that beautiful, dark-eyed colonel only 33 years old when he died, was another hero to be emulated.

'Then there were the other stories – about the first Patton to come to Virginia in the late 1760s. He bragged that he had a price on his head, dead or alive, of 500 British pounds sterling, and that the name Patton was an alias. On his death bed he raved about his grandfather's funeral, when the Lords of the Isles carried the casket and there were games and feasting at the castle for a week, but he would never tell his wife his real name. He said "A Patton I've lived and a Patton I'll die; better a new name in a new country". This romantic rascal married the daughter of General Hugh Mercer, who had come as a Jacobite refugee to this country and met George Washington on a surveying trip in Pennsylvania. He had been a surgeon in the Army of Bonnie Prince Charlie, and ended up on General Washington's staff. Mercer was mortally wounded at the Battle of Princeton, and being a doctor, treated himself with the help of a British surgeon sent by the sympathetic British commandant. He received his mortal wound when his horse was shot out from under him and he was clubbed on the head by a red coat and then stabbed under the arm by his bayonet when he refused to surrender saying, "I would rather die honourably as a rebel than be hung as a traitor" – reference no doubt to having been on the wrong side in Scotland.

'These are the stuff that young Georgie's dreams were made of, and they were instrumental in making the man. He felt, all his life, that he owed a vast debt to his ancestors and to the country they had made for him, and he constantly worried that he would not be worthy of them. He used to tell us of a strange thing that happened to him when he went into the Meuse Argonne offensive in September 1918. He was to take his light tank brigade into combat and was waiting for the command. Their position was being sprayed with German machine gun fire, and the bullets were cutting the grass along the ridge. Occasionally a man would be hit and he said he could tell by the grunt or scream and the way the body fell whether the hit was high or low. He said he was getting more and more scared, his mouth was dry and his hands were sweating, and he felt like turning and running like hell toward the rear. He happened to look up, and there, on a low lying bank of cloud he saw the faces of his ancestors, watching him; he recognized his grandfather, George Patton and his great Uncle Tazewell, and General Mercer, from their pictures, but he said there were scores of others, in different dress, some almost fading into the cloud, but they all had a family look and he said to himself, "Here is where another Patton gets his". The command came to move forward, and he suddenly was not scared at all. That was the day he was wounded critically. "As a man thinketh, so is he".

'As I said, Georgie was great on quotations and in consequence, we are a family of quoters. Almost everything our parents taught us had a tag. When we were old enough, we were each given a motto, my father telling us that the knights of old had their escutcheons blazoned on their shields, and we should have the same, by which to set our standards. To my older sister, Beatrice, they gave, "Be loyal to the royal in thyself". To me they gave, "Of him to whom much hath been given, much shall be required". and to my younger brother George, they gave, "Act well thy part, therein all honour lies". In retrospect, I should like to emblazon my father's shield with a verse he taught us. I have no idea where it comes from:

To set the cause above renown
To love the game beyond the prize
To honor, while you strike him down
The foe that comes with fearless eyes,
To count the life of battle good,
And dear the land that gave you birth,
And dearer still the brotherhood
That binds the brave to all the earth.

'The movie *Patton* was a very interesting experience for us in the family. We fought it tooth and nail for 20 years, of course, but when we saw it we had to admit with the critics, that it is one of the great movies. Of course, it is an anti-war movie, which is interesting, but the most interesting point on

Above: Pistol Packin' Patton. Monty eyes GSP's six-shooters with a slightly quizzical stare during this meeting between Patton, Bradley and Montgomery in France. Patton's ivory handled pistols were one of his trademarks, but they were not, as some people have written, pearl handled. 'Goddammit' said GSP, Jr, when asked 'my guns are ivory handled. Nobody but a pimp from a cheap New Orleans whorehouse would carry one with pearl grips!'/*IWM*

Left: Patton the Orator. GSP, Jr, addresses some newly arrived troops of Third Army, 'somewhere in England' 1 April 1944. His 'off the cuff' speeches were greatly enjoyed by most of his audiences, the main theme being to get to grips with the enemy and kill them./*US Army*

Above: Another splendid view of one of Patton's ivory handled six-shooters as he rides in a T8E1 Reconnaissance vehicle with Averell Harriman, Ambassador to Russia, who visited the Third Army during the Saar campaign, November 1944. Whether he is merely steadying himself on the .50cal Browning machine gun, or just about to use it on some 'Goddam Krauts' is not recorded./*Patton Museum*

Left: Visiting XX Corps. Patton congratulating some of the officers and men of XX Corps on their achievements in France. Major-General Walton H. Walker, CG XX Corps, is standing next to him. /*US Army*

Above: Looking his usual immaculate self, General Patton stands out in this group of American generals gathered at 12th Army Headquarters, Bad Wildungen, Germany, 11 May 1945. His uniform was never quite 'regulation pattern' – note the brass buttons, belt, riding breeches and riding boots, in contrast with the more conservative battledress worn by the rest of the group. (Front row are, left to right: Gen William H. Simpson, CG US Ninth Army; GSP, Jr; Gen Carl A. Spaatz, CG USATAF; Gen Dwight D. Eisenhower, Supreme Allied Commander; Gen Omar N. Bradley, CG 12th Army Group; Gen Courtney H. Hodges, CG US First Army and Lt-Gen Leonard T. Gerow, CG US Fifteenth Army. Standing in rear, are left to right: Brig-Gen Ralph F. Stearley, CG IX Tactical Air Command; Lt-Gen Hoyt S. Vandenburg, CG 9th Air Force; Lt-Gen Walter H. Smith, Chief of Staff SHAEF; Maj-Gen Otto P. Weyland, CG XIX Tactical Air Command and Brig-Gen Richard E. Nugent, CG XXIX Tactical Air Command.)/*US Army*

which 90 per cent of the reviews agree, was that it was – to quote – "a film with a gap in it". One critic says, "The man remains a mystery until the end". Another says, "At the end of almost three hours one is still waiting for something to happen which really opens up the man whom it is all about". A third says, "Star and camera give a sophisticated performance, but they are also equivocal performances, oddly evasive, an inconclusive portrait – we still lack a comprehensive idea of the man. Patton is a movie to see but after it is over you feel quizzical and empty, wishing you had learned more, understood more had more to go on".

'I don't think anybody really knew Georgie, not even my mother. He was such a stratified person, so many pressures from so many traditions and impossible comparisons to the great and beloved dead heroes. He would have very much liked the fact that the movie could not strip him to the soul, for the world to remark. One of his favorite poems, could have been written for him. It is called, "The Soul Speaks".

Here is Honor, the dying knight
And here is Truth, the snuffed out light
And here is Faith, the broken staff,
And there is Knowledge, the throttled laugh,
And here is Fame, the lost surprise,
Virtue, the uncontested prize,
And Sacrifice, the suicide,
And there, the wilted flower, Pride,
Under the crust of things that die
Living, unfathomed, here am I.

'Of course, in the movie, you only saw what he called his "war face". As a young man, and even as an old man, in repose, he was almost painfully beautiful, curly blonde hair, big blue eyes with long dark lashes, a gorgeous aristocratic nose, in other words, "the works". He spent hours practicing his war face in front of mirrors. I can well remember him doing it – and once, I will never forget it, he was reciting this:

In peace, there's nothing so becomes a man
As modest stillness and humility
But when the blast of war blows in our ears
Then imitate the action of the tiger
Stiffen the sinews, summon up the blood
Then lend the eye a terrible aspect
Now set the teeth and stretch the nostril wide
Hold hard the breath and bend up every spirit
To his full height! On, On, you noblest English!

'It was years before I found out – in boarding school – that it was from Act III of Shakespeare's *Henry V*, but my sister and I always shouted, "On, On, you noblest English", to our horses going over jumps in horseshows – it was very inspiring. I was impressed by the movie, and by all it accomplished in three hours, but when hard pressed by friends for real criticism, I must say that they did not emphasise that he was a strategist, they did not give him enough credit for his accurate predictions of what would happen if we let the Russians take Berlin – that *they* were the real enemy, and that we would in the end suffer from their mailed fist. Eisenhower said

Above: Commander of the Legion of Honor. GSP, Jr, pictured here with Lt-Gen William H. Simpson, CG US Ninth Army, Lt-Gen Courtney H. Hodges, CG US First Army, Lt-Gen Omar N. Bradley, CG 12th Army Group and Lt-Gen Leonard T. Gerow, CG US Fifteenth Army, after the presentation of the Commander of the Legion of Honor award, 3 September 1945./*US Army*

Left: Patton the Tactician. GSP, Jr, discusses the battle situation with one of his Corps commanders (Maj-Gen Manton S. Eddy, CG XII Corps) as they view the area near Oppenheim on the Rhine, where 5th Infantry Division made its initial crossing 22 March 1945./*US Army*

of General Patton, "The more he drives his men the more he will save lives and the men in the Third Army know this to be true". Patton's hard nosed toughness and seemingly merciless drive did not make him a beloved figure, but he repeatedly said, when criticized for being too hard on his men, as he had been many years before for being too hard on his children, "Goddamnit, I'm not running for Shah of Persia. There are no practice games in life. It's eat or be eaten, kill or be killed. I want my bunch to get in there first, to be the 'fustest with the mostest'. They won't do it if I ask them kindly. That was the only mistake that Robert E. Lee ever made. He gave suggestions instead of orders and it cost him the war".

'Georgie was the kindest man that ever lived, and he spent a great deal of his life trying not to show it – he thought it was a sign of weakness. Animals, dogs, old ladies and little children adored him. His mother-in-law had his picture on her dressing table – I have it now on mine – and across the back of it is written in her hand, "The bravest are the tenderest; the loving are the daring". When one of his family got hurt, as we frequently did because we spent most of our waking moments on the backs of his horses, he was always there first to cut off the riding boot, grab off his shirt and stuff it under the broken collarbone, or apply one of his huge linen handkerchiefs to whatever was bleeding.

Above: An eye for detail. Patton learns the use of a special valve grinder from Sgt Woodrow W. Smith, during a visit to the 520th Ordnance Maintenance Workshops./*IWM*

Left: Patton the planner. GSP, Jr, confers with his Chief of Staff, Maj-Gen Hugh G. Gaffey and Major M. C. Helfers, Special Intelligence Officer, on the operations of German forces opposing the Third Army in the Seine River area, 26 August 1944. Patton was a meticulous planner but did not let this prevent him taking opportunities when they were presented./*US Army*

'His belief in God was the cornerstone of his existence. He felt that the hand of Fate, the hands of the past reaching forward to influence the present, was the hand of God. He genuinely believed that God was on the side of the right and not on the side of the biggest battalions, and he was always, in his own mind, very close to God. When he prayed, as he did constantly, he prayed directly to God and told us to do the same. He said, "Start at the top and work down". He said to Chaplain O'Neil when he instructed him to write the famous Christmas prayer, "Those who pray do more for the world than those who fight; and if the world goes from bad to worse it is because there are more battles than prayers". "Hands lifted up", said Bossuet, "smash more battalions than hands that strike". Part of the *Star Spangled Banner* could have been written just for him – "Yet conquer we must, for our cause it is just, and this is our motto, in God is our trust". My father was a good church-going, tithing Episcopalian all of his life, but he believed implicitly in reincarnation, and brought all of us up to believe in it. He said it was the only acceptable explanation for injustice and in-equality. He believed that we were put on earth to better our souls and bring them closer to the perfection of God, and he quoted Revelations Chapter III verse 12 "Him that overcometh shall I make a pillar in the temple of my God and he shall go no more forth".

Above: Is somebody getting a rocket? It looks suspiciously as though this young major is receiving a blasting from the 'old man' for unpunctuality – but I could be wrong! /US Army

Left: Conference in the Ardennes. GSP, Jr, talks with grim faced Eisenhower and Bradley in the centre of the battered town of Bastogne, 5 February 1945. Both Eisenhower and Bradley found Patton difficult to control. Neither of them liked taking risks, which did much to hold up Third Army's sweep through France./US Army

Left: The expression on Patton's face clearly reveals his feelings of frustration, having just been told by Gen Eisenhower that Third Army's victorious advance must halt and they must 'assume an aggressive defensive posture'. GSP, Jr's dog Willie standing by its master, was a bull terrier which Patton had bought in England. Willie had originally belonged to an RAF pilot killed on operations. He was 'pure white except for a little lemin [sic] on his tail, which to a cursory glance would seem to indicate that he had not used toilet paper'. Willie (or 'William the Conqueror' to give his full title) was not a very aggressive dog 'even afraid of rabbits', but was a great favourite in the headquarters and a constant companion to GSP, Jr.
/*US Army*

Below: A cheerful Patton greets French General Henri Giraud at XX Corps Headquarters in Thionville 25 November 1944. Giraud was reported as remarking during the visit that Patton was the 'Liberator of France', so clearly GSP, Jr, had much to smile about. Also in the picture are Col William A. Collier, Chief of Staff XX Corps and Maj-Gen Walton H. Walker, CG XX Corps.
/*US Army*

He knew quantities of the Bible by heart, and had memorized the book of Common Prayer, but on his way to Africa he read the Koran to enable himself to understand the religion and the customs of the Moslems. He had read the Bhagavad-Gita – the Bible of the Brahman sect in India – many times. He used to recite it to us, especially, "As a man, casting off worn out bodies, entereth into others that are new. For sure is the death of him that is born, and sure the birth of him that is dead, therefore, over the inevitable thou shalt not grieve". Georgie himself was totally unafraid of death, but he said he was always afraid in battle and anyone who said he was not was either a liar or a moron. My mother asked him why, if he wasn't afraid of death, he was afraid in battle and he told her he was afraid of being maimed and was ashamed of such a fear, and he also said he was a little bit afraid of dying because he knew, by experience, that it could be long, drawn out and painful. His mother, Ruth Wilson Patton, was the first person to die in the family when my sister and I were old enough to realize the sense of loss. My father called us into his room and said, "Your grandmother just went back out of the door she came in. Do new-born babies have complaints? Yet bet they do! They yell like hell because they liked it better where they were, both their bodies and their souls did. Believe me, God is not a hypocrite. He didn't make a great world like

this one, and go to make one on the other side that isn't just as great". The chaplain once asked him if he believed in hell and he said, "You're in hell when you lie or cheat or destroy anything unnecessarily, or when you feel sorry for yourself. That's the only hell there is. That's enough". The chaplain asked him about the devil and he said, "there is light and there is dark; every coin has two sides, every man has a god in him and a devil and it's up to him to see that God keeps the upper hand. It's his personal responsibility".

'Our family was great on what we called "interesting conversation" which took place at the dinner table, which was about the only time of day we all came together in leisure. Our father was great on history, and often illustrated his stories with his memories of lives he had lived and places he had been. He was one of those less-than-rare people who could remember part of their other lives. True or not, as a man thinketh so is he. Georgie connected this "far memory" with luck. He said luck was the instantaneous realization of a problem by the inner mind before the outer mind could get in gear. Intuition was part of it, perhaps hidden memories, but history too, was his mentor. When he and my mother were at the sabre school in Saumur in France in 1912 they toured over all the routes across

Above: Patton with a Russian General. GSP, Jr, and Lt-Gen Nikonov Dimitrievitch Zahwataeff, CG of the 4th Russian Guards Army, salute a guard of honour composed of 65th Inf Div soldiers near Linz, Austria, 12 May 1945. Patton was violently suspicious of the Russians and saw them as a far greater menace than the Germans. 'The whole damned world is going communist' he wrote bitterly to his wife in November 1945, 'The last US troops to leave Europe will be fighting a rearguard action'. /*Patton Museum*

Right: Talking to wounded. Despite the notorious 'slapping incident' Patton was genuinely moved by the sight of wounded soldiers and did everything he could to improve their lot. Here he talks to Private Frank A. Read, 7th Infantry, 3rd Division, suffering from shrapnel wound, with others nearby waiting to be evacuated by air from Sicily, 25 July 1943. /*US Army*

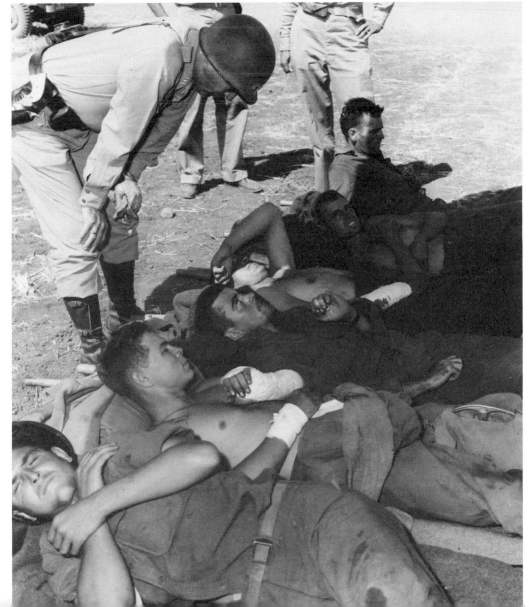

Above: Ladies' Man. Gen Patton talking with some Red Cross hostesses at the opening of the new Red Cross Club in Nancy, France. He was always most gallant towards women and they invariably responded. His feelings were well expressed in a 'toast to the ladies' he gave at a West Point dinner in April 1924, in which he said: 'In the chapel of Leavenworth, on the monument at Riley, on the walls of Cullum Hall, are names, names of officers dead on the field of honour . . . little plaques tell the story and fame, such as it is, and high honour from us who know, is accorded Willie. But where is Mrs Willie's tablet? Such were the women who year after harrowing year made homes for officers in these bleak Western posts; such as the women who today uncomplainingly share the "luxury" of cantonment quarters . . . May we live to make them happy, or, and the Great Day come, so die to make them proud. The Army Women, God bless them.' (Taken from *Before the Colours Fade* by Fred Ayer.) /US Army

that part of France that Caesar had taken in 58 to 49 BC and Attila the Hun re-traced in 451 AD. He said that in those days, before roads, the armies followed the contour of the land and that Caesar and Attila had done his scouting for him. He told mother that he had fought over that land before and would fight over it again, and actually, his knowledge of the terrain is what made him able to make the famous dash across France. Much of his military success has been attributed to his luck – Napoleon never promoted anyone, you know, until he found out if they were lucky. Georgie "knew" what the enemy was going to do, just as he had always known that a certain horse would perform well in a race and another would fall. He knew certain people who went into battle would not return. He knew he would see mother again, but not us, and told us so when we said goodbye to him in July of 1945. He had always prayed to die in battle – he wanted to die as Confederate General Bee had died at the 2nd Manassas, standing in his stirrups and rallying his men with, "There stands Jackson like a stonewall! Rally behind the Virginians". General Bee was another of his heroes. But just the same, he knew he would not die as he wanted to. Just before he died he said to mother, "I guess I wasn't good enough".

'My father has been called lots of names – he has been called a bully, an actor, a prima donna, a son of a bitch. He was not a bully, but he was a great actor and acted not only to entertain us – you should have heard him recite poetry – but he used his acting as an adjunct to leadership. For instance, in battle he always went to the front in an open jeep or plane, so the men could see him, but when he went back to Headquarters he always went in a closed car or plane so the men did not see the General with his back to the enemy.

'People always end up asking me about the soldier slapping incident in Sicily and the answer is simple to those who knew him. He hated to see men killed; he honestly did not believe in battle fatigue – he called it cowardice – and he felt a coward had less of a chance to stay alive, because fear dulls intuition, and cowardice is catching – the ancient Greeks called it panic. He said, "One must fear, but one must conquer fear to continue with the scheme of God". He slapped that soldier, as he had, years before, slapped hysterical daughters, because he thought the man needed to be snapped out of his collapse and restored to some pride. He afterwards wrote mother that he knew no officer should ever lay a hand on an enlisted man and he had been wrong and that he had apologized. That's all there was to it.

'You cannot sum up a human being. Georgie Patton was the result of his life long training, sitting beside his Aunt Nannie in

Left: Patton with his grandchildren June 1945. He loved children, who responded by adoring him. In this group are (l to r) George Patton Waters, aged 4; Michael Walker Totten, aged 3; Beatrice Willoughby Totten, aged 2; John K. Waters, Jr, aged 7./*Patton Museum*

Below: Patton's jeep flag. At the 6 Armd Div Association reunion in Cincinnati in 1955, Major General Robert W. Grow, Divisional Commander throughout the war, presented to the Association a framed cloth flag which had originally flown on the front bumper of Gen Patton's jeep in Europe in 1945. It was personally autographed 'To 6th Armd Div from G. S. Patton, Jr'. Patton had given the four star flag to Brig-Gen George W. Read (Asst Div Comd) in 1945 and over the years he had cherished and safely guarded the treasured memento of Patton's respect for the great 6th Armored./*6 Armd Div Assoc /George F. Hofmann*

Below: In sombre mood. GSP, Jr, photographed in a light liaison aircraft ready to take off from Kirchdorf, Germany, where he attended a review of 103rd Infantry Division just before their departure for the States, 21 August 1945. Patton's grim countenance perhaps mirrors the inner growing bitterness which was building up against the criticisms appearing in the US press for his handling of civil matters, such as the denazification of the Third Army area./*IWM*

front of the fire, at the ranch, hearing of the fearless trek of his grandfather across the plains to California; sitting with his grandmother Patton, holding in his hand the rusty iron fragment that had split the guts of her husband, his grandfather; hearing from his own father how he was taken in front of *his* father's saddle to see the body of the great Confederate hero, Jeb Stuart, lying on the billiard table at the Yellow Tavern, like a statue of a God, his form outlined beneath a damp white sheet, his great bronze beard spilling over his silent breast, and the lines of weeping Confederate soldiers filing by; hearing in his mind the dying words of General Mercer, at Princeton, and of Tazewell Patton at Gettysburg – and behind them, the parade of the mighty heroes, Alexander, and Achilles, Hannibal crossing the Alps, Harold at Hastings, Napoleon, Nathan Hale. All this combined in George S. Patton, Jr, to make him the man he was. He always wanted to be among the heroes. All his life he summoned unto himself a company of heroes, alive and dead, and in his death he lies among heroes to whom he was a hero. As a man thinketh, so is he.'

In the pictures which accompany this section I have tried to capture some of Patton's many moods – in one quiet and reflective, in another impatient and irascible; a 'pistol-packing' showman when he thought it would achieve the desired results, yet always immaculate and well groomed, so that he stands out like a beacon even in a group of senior officers. Above all a general who fought his battles from the front as did Rommel, who took chances but justified the risks by getting the results. As General Omar Bradley wrote of him:

'A leader – military or civilian – must be judged by results. Patton was certainly a successful battle leader. He had a battle sense – a sixth sense if I may call it that – which enabled him to foresee situations that were developing and make dispositions to meet them. . . . Yes, when you add up all the pluses and minuses – all of his good points and his faults – and consider his accomplishments we must conclude that General Patton was a great leader in battle.'*

*Foreword to *Before the Colours Fade* by Fred Ayer.

The Gallop across France

Georgie's Boys

'A recon sergeant from another outfit, knowing he was far out in front of his main body where he had a better chance to see Germans rather than Americans, dropped his jaw when a column of 4th Armored mediums went churning by in single file like it was the Fourth of July at Pine Camp. He cupped his hands and yelled to one of the turrets, "Who are you guys?" – "Georgie's Boys!" came the reply.'*

*Clarke of St Vith by W. D. Ellis and Col T. J. Cunningham Jr.

August Operations

The quote above sets the pace for Third Army's operations in August 1944 as they raced through France. Briefly, they can be divided into five phases (see Sketch Map 5):

1 *The conquest of Brittany.* Third Army swept through the peninsula catching the enemy completely by surprise. By the end of the month St Malo had been captured and Brest, Lorient and St Nazaire contained.

2 *The encirclement of the enemy in the Argentan, Falaise, Mortain area.* The Germans made their first attempt at a counter attack in force in the Mortain area, committing

Below: Map 5 The five phases of August operations, 1944.

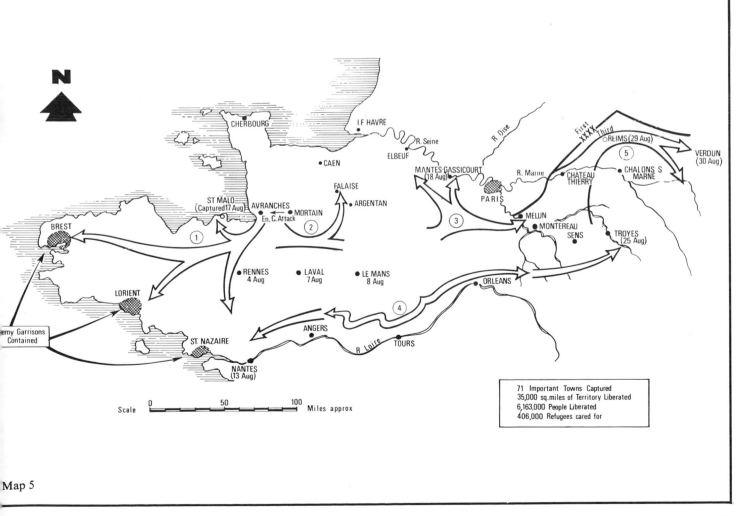

Map 5

armour, infantry and artillery, with air support, in a determined drive towards Avranches and the Channel coast. After three days, when threatened with complete encirclement, they withdrew, having suffered tremendous losses.

3 *The advance to the Seine and the envelopment of the Mantes Gassicourt-Elbeuf area.* In this third phase, which was carried out at the same time as the Argentan encirclement, *Lucky* continued to advance east, swinging NW of Paris to seize a bridgehead across the Seine near Mantes Gassicourt. Simultaneously they drove towards Elbeuf and Rouen, along the west bank of the river. Faced with the threat of another encirclement so soon after the Argentan debacle, the Germans fought desperately to prevent their escape routes across the Seine being cut and began to withdraw forces east of the river. To the south, armoured columns drove towards Paris, the French 2nd Armoured Division fittingly being given the honour to be the eventual liberators of the capital.

4 *The enemy evacuation of South West France.* Remnants of enemy divisions from Normandy, Brittany and the Franco-Spanish border, plus those overrun in the Rennes – St Malo area, were now located in the Loire towns of Nantes, Angers, Saumur, Tours, Blois and Orleans. Together with the regular garrisons of these places, they attempted to defend the towns and constituted a continual threat to Third Army's right flank. By the end of the month, however, they were more concerned with retreating towards the Fatherland, before Third Army cut their escape routes.

5 *The rout of the enemy across the Marne, Aisne and Meuse Rivers.* This was the fifth and final phase. Continual hammering by the 19th Tactical Air Command, coupled with thrusts by Third Army's tanks and infantry, destroyed all enemy hopes of holding the line of the Seine. The line of the Somme-Marne rivers was turned even before it could be occupied, and in the resulting confusion the enemy withdrew on all fronts. The speed of Third Army's advance across the Marne, Aisne and Meuse rivers, forced the enemy into headlong retreat. However, despite shattered communications, disorganisation and enormous losses, the Germans were still able to maintain some semblance of overall control, so at no time was there a complete collapse.

By the end of the month, it was clear that Third Army's advance would have to be slowed down in order to allow the resupply echelons to catch up. However, there was only one more major river barrier before the Siegfried Line and Germany, namely the Moselle, and any delay might well result in a build up there, right in the path of Third Army. At the time HQ Third Army was responsible for operations on two fronts 600 miles apart, and an exposed right flank over 1,000 miles long (covered by less than two divisions!). The 19th Tactical Air Force was always ready to break up any concentrated enemy attack should one develop and a very close relationship was built up between the air and ground troops in much the same way as that existing between tanks and infantry.

Top right: Map 6a The liberation of Paris: advance 23-24 August 1944.

Bottom right: The German commander, Colonel von Aulock, carries his own baggage as he leaves the fortress of St Malo to surrender to 83rd Inf Div, VII Corps. (Note GI, with white flag, leading the surrender party.)/*US Army*

Below: Infantrymen of 83rd Inf Div take aim at a German sniper's position during house to house fighting in St Malo. When the citadel was captured on 17 August 1944 the commander and his staff declared that it was the accuracy of the American artillery which had destroyed all their guns, that brought about their eventual surrender. /*US Army*

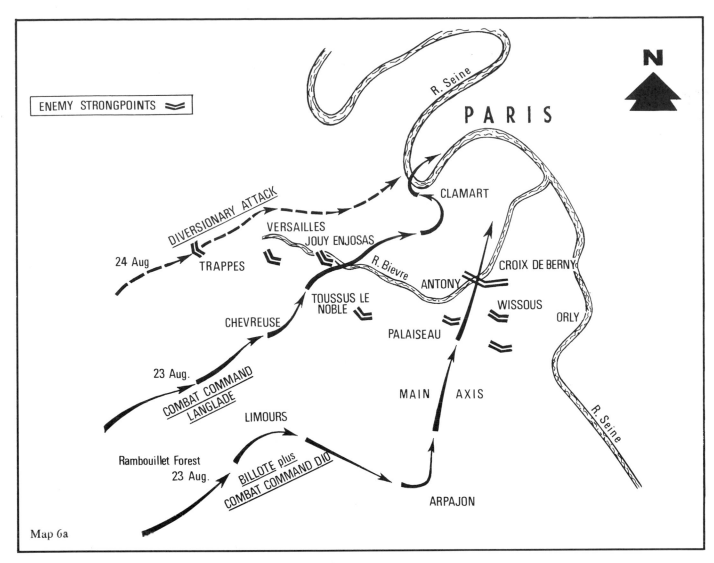

ENEMY STRONGPOINTS

N

PARIS

R. Seine

DIVERSIONARY ATTACK

CLAMART

24 Aug

TRAPPES

VERSAILLES
JOUY ENJOSAS

R. Bievre

CROIX DE BERNY

ANTONY

TOUSSUS LE
NOBLE

WISSOUS

ORLY

CHEVREUSE

PALAISEAU

23 Aug.

COMBAT COMMAND
LANGLADE

MAIN   AXIS

LIMOURS

R. Seine

Rambouillet Forest
23 Aug.

BILLOTE plus
COMBAT COMMAND DIO

ARPAJON

Map 6a

The Liberation of Paris

I felt that the task of telling the story of the liberation of Paris must surely be given to a Frenchman. I have been fortunate enough to obtain this account, written especially for me, by General André Gribius, Grand Officer of the Legion of Honour and holder of the Bronze Star. He has now retired from the French Army and is the Mayor of Villebernier, near Saumur, but in August 1944, as a Chef D'Escadrons (Major), he was the Operations Officer (G3) of the 2nd French Armoured Division under command of General Leclerc. He writes:

'On the improvised grass runway of Fleure airfield, we are waiting anxiously for our General to return. At last he arrives, accompanied by Repiton, who always escorts him on liaison visits to our friends, the British and Americans, because he has a good knowledge of their language and is used to working with them. General Leclerc jumps down and asks me to prepare straight away movement orders for the division to get us to Rambouillet [see Sketch Map 6a] which I know has already been taken by Allied forces. (Colonel de

Above: Closing in on Brest. Troops set up their M5 anti-tank gun on the outskirts of war wrecked Recouvrance, en route to Brest./*IWM*

Guillebon confirmed this on his radio link to a small detachment of tanks and half tracks which he had clandestinely sent, some 48 hours ago, to work closely with the advancing US forces.) Their mission is to occupy Les Invalides should these forces reach Paris first. Thus, Guillebon would be immediately able to become the French military commander of "Liberated Paris". In fact the orders coming from the Allied Army Group give us only the mission to capture the downstream sweeps of the Seine River but not Paris itself. On the other hand, if we meet strong resistance, then the 4th US Division and the 2nd French Armoured Division must work together to capture Paris under the command of a general who is unknown to us – General Gerow, commander of the 5th US Army Corps. But for us these orders are sufficient, they mean "Go and liberate Paris. . . .!"

'It takes some time to write and broadcast the message which, for the moment, covers merely the administrative movement to Rambouillet through Seez, Mortagne, La Loupe and Maintenon. At dawn, the huge armoured snake, which is an armoured division using only one axis, begins its move with the punctuality of a clock, guided by the road traffic units of our friend Peschaud who was in charge of all our movement. Thus, we advance, living in the hope of holding our next parade in the Champs Elysees, even if our present directive gives only Rambouillet as our destination point. However, most of the command know instinctively that the advance will take them to the Place de la Concorde.

'At Rambouillet we again find Guillebon who gives us information about enemy activities. Some enemy strongpoints are dangerously close to Trappes, the enemy strength seems less effective to the east, especially towards Arpajon. That's more than enough for General Leclerc to make his decision. Immediately he briefs me, and, hastily sitting in the main drive leading to the Chateau under century-old trees, I write battle orders, very short ones, just three pages, including the essential sentence written in four words: "*S'emparer de Paris*" (to capture Paris).

'The main axis is through Arpajon and Antony. Another, thirty kilometres to the west begins at Rambouillet but avoids Trappes and Versailles. Of course it is along the first axis that Leclerc hopes for success. He gives it to Billotte followed by Combat Command Dio, whereas Langlade will try to find a way along the second route. When the target has an historical importance it is normal for the mission to be given to one of the first De Gaulle Companions.* Billotte attached to the Division by General de Gaulle for this mission, has been given the axis which has the best opportunity of reaching the Hotel Meurice first, there to receive the surrender of the German commander of Paris.

*The De Gaulle Companions were the first men, women or units who rejoined General de Gaulle in 1940 or 1941. Most of them became members of the Liberation Order (*Ordre de la Liberation*) sometimes posthumously. The only rank in the Liberation Order is *Compagnon*.

'On the 23rd August General de Gaulle visits us at the very moment when the historic order is being signed. He says to General Leclerc: "You are lucky". Indeed, in his mind, events are beyond the military aspect, the political problems of the liberation of Paris are for him the most crucial ones. For these reasons, he orders us to keep him well informed of our advance hour by hour.

'The battle begins at dawn on 24 August 1944. It will be more murderous in the country around Paris than inside the capital itself. Combat Command Langlade, by-passing Rambouillet from the Chevreuse valley jumps off into Toussus le Noble, where, after an initial easy fight against a German column on the upland, must break through a belt of 88mm Flak guns protected on the flanks by 20mm AA machine guns, which bars the way to Paris. Massu attacks, loses two tanks, while Minjonnet by-passes and Mirambeau makes a first gap with his artillery. At Jouy en Josas, having linked up with the neighbouring combat team, Langlade crosses the Bievre river. At Clamart he attacks the last hastily gathered German tank resistance, and makes them withdraw, leaving him a clear route.

'Combat Command Billotte, as foreseen, meets only light resistance on their route. Nevertheless, he is obliged to attack a line of 88mm guns between Palaiseau and Orly. One part of this battle is led by Warabiot at Wissous, while Buis swings to Croix de Berny. Understanding our manoeuvre, the Germans throw all their forces into the battle. Even their military prisoners from Fresnes

Jail, and those ones wearing light khaki linen uniforms, who give Buis the feeling that he is again fighting his old adversaries from the Afrika Korps. At night while Langlade has reached Pont de Sevres, Billotte continues to fight in front of Antony.

'General Leclerc, who has leaguered us in a disused quarry near the main Orleans to Paris road, realises his Division will be unable to give a helping hand to the insurgents in Paris before nightfall. The announcement of our coming has galvanised the FFI [*Forces Françaises de L'Interieur:* French Insurgent Forces], but we know that the Germans still control the situation, and are in a position to destroy large parts of the city, and above all, to massacre our countrymen. He sends Callet, with his Piper-Cub light recce aircraft, to drop a message of encouragement to the FFI in their battle positions at the Prefecture de Police. On his return, mission completed, Callet describes the empty streets. This reinforces our opinion that the Germans still control most of the capital.

'Meanwhile, however, General von Choltitz, the German Commander of Paris, feels that although the game is over, he must still obey Hitler and destroy all bridges and monuments in the capital. Happily this man is far sighted and a long time before made contact with Mr Nordling, the Swedish Consul. Von Choltitz is an officer of the old school who accepts the Führer's orders only with difficulty when they are not motivated by tactical or national interests. But at this moment we don't know that, on 23 August, after a further intervention from Mr Nordling, Von Choltitz

Above: A Hellcat (tank destroyer) fires its 76mm gun at point blank range at a pillbox, to clear a path through a side street in Brest, during the savage fighting which took place there in the summer of 1944. The enemy garrison was contained, but the port (second largest naval port in France) was not completely cleared until 14 September 1944./*IWM*

Above: As Third Army's armoured columns raced through the Brittany peninsula the FFI (*Forces Francaises de L'Interieur* – French Insurgent Forces) began to come out into the open. /6 *Armd Div Assoc*/*George F. Hofmann*

has given the promise "Paris will not be destroyed".

'However, we, in front of the gates, fear the worst. Mr Petit, an emissary from Chaban Delmas, who co-ordinates the resistance action in Paris with London, asks us to hurry our coming. General Leclerc gives him a message to give to General von Choltitz making the German commander personally responsible for any destruction. But Von Choltitz never receives this message, as the emissary and the NCO of the escort squad are killed.

'Leclerc moves quickly to the forward elements of Billotte's force. Understanding the threat to our countrymen, he wants to do something tonight. Despite the fact that the tanks are unable to fight at night (because at that time they are not equipped with infra-red viewing devices) it is necessary to take a risk to obtain a psychological advantage. For this delicate mission, Leclerc must find Dronne, and he finds him. The general knows all his officers and he employs each of them for the right mission at the right time. Dronne, General Leclerc knows, is a leader, an untiring man, who always understands and faithfully carries out the mission of his commander. Leclerc gives orders to Dronne to lead a light detachment (one tank troop, two mechanised infantry platoons and one troop of armoured engineers) and to thread his own way through the maze of small streets to the Hotel de Ville (the Town Hall) [see Sketch Map 6b]. Reaching it before dawn Dronne carries out his important mission perfectly. General Leclerc is also confident that he will be successful, and when he comes back to our

quarry (I could never find it again after the battle), he says that even if we don't receive any message he is confident that Dronne will succeed. Indeed, communications with Paris are jammed with messages and Dronne will only communicate if he meets real opposition. The Eiffel Tower slowly disappears into the darkness while some artillery salvoes rumble around the town which lives its last "occupation night". Even if we are unable to hear the full peal of bells of Notre Dame de Paris, we know that an historical feat has taken place and that tomorrow at dawn, our columns will also hurry to the city centre. Through La Porte de Gentilly, then to La Cité Universitaire and along Rue Saint Jacques, Billotte's combat command speedily reaches La Prefecture de Police where, as foreseen, Dronne has been established since midnight.

'Dio has organised two combat teams. One moves along the boulevards up to the Seine and seizes the bridges. The other moves through Montparnasse and Les Invalides and has a target La Chambre des Deputes. Langlade's force stretches from Pont de Sèvres to L'Etoile, ready to go down to the Place de la Concorde. No reserves. If we meet difficult strong points, we shall try to employ the FFI or by-pass them. The principal aim is to reach the Hotel Meurice where General von Choltitz is located and obtain his surrender as quickly as possible.

'Under the protection of De Boissieu's squadron, the Divisional headquarters moves quickly to the main railway station at Montparnasse. Here we shall be able to use the telephone network and when we arrive the

Left: Link up of Third and Seventh Armies. The crew of a scout car belonging to the 86th Recon Squadron, 6th Armd Div, shaking hands with their opposite numbers from a French unit serving with US 7th Army, 11 September 1944, in Autun, a small town in central France. Seventh Army, under command of Lt-Gen Alexander M. Patch, had landed in southern France on 14 and 15 August 1944 in order to protect the southern flank of the Allied advance from Normandy. */6 Armd Div Assoc/George F. Hofmann*

Below: Map 6b The liberation of Paris: into the city 25 August 1944.

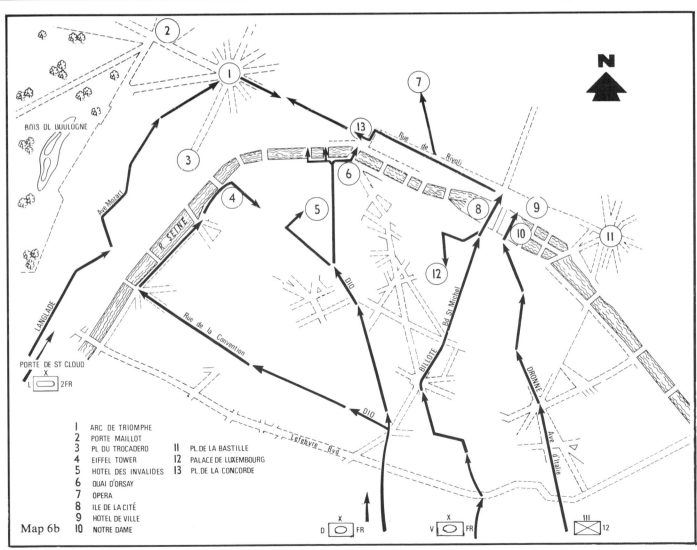

Map 6b

1	ARC DE TRIOMPHE
2	PORTE MAILLOT
3	PL DU TROCADERO
4	EIFFEL TOWER
5	HOTEL DES INVALIDES
6	QUAI D'ORSAY
7	OPERA
8	ILE DE LA CITÉ
9	HOTEL DE VILLE
10	NOTRE DAME
11	PL. DE LA BASTILLE
12	PALACE DE LUXEMBOURG
13	PL. DE LA CONCORDE

BOIS DE BOULOGNE

Ave Mozart

R. SEINE

LANGLADE

PORTE DE ST CLOUD

Rue de la Convention

Lefebvre Bvd

Rue de Rivoli

Bd St Michel

BILLOTE

DRONNE

Ave d'Italie

DIO

Below: Tanks of the 8th Tank Bn, 4th Armd Div, churn through the mud as they cross the National Canal near Bayon, 20 September 1944.
/US Army

personnel of the SNCF (French Railways) give us their offices, mine is in the main departure lounge! We examine the situation, and now after three hours siege the Gross-Paris Commander has capitulated. Encircled by La Horie Combat Team and the Spanish of Putz, General von Choltitz, having received an ultimatum from Billotte, which has been confirmed by La Horie, gives no answer. He wants a fight with honour (a *Baroud d'honneur*: *Baroud* is an Arab word for battle or fight). This attitude is brave. But after a short battle, supported only by seventeen officers of his headquarters, he gives his surrender to the French officers who arrive in his office. Through the crowd, La Horie drives his prisoners of war to La Prefecture de Police where General Leclerc is waiting for them. It is 3 pm when, in the midst of a huge "hubbub" made by the crowd booing, General von Choltitz enters the room where the three liberators of Paris, Leclerc, Chaban Delmas and Rol Tanguy,* have taken their places. He seems exhausted, astonished to still be alive, but also offended at the aggressive attitude of the Parisian crowd against a high ranking German general officer. Indeed, during the journey by half track between the Hotel Meurice and La Prefecture de Police, he had to be protected by a French officer as the crowd grew more and more dangerous.

*Rol Tanguy was, with the rank of colonel, chief of all the French Insurgent Forces (FFI) for Paris and its suburban area. He was also a communist and a member of the Paris political communist committee trying to seize the power in France.

Above: The Army commander prepares to go aloft, inspecting the progress of his forces from the air, 29 August 1944./*US Army*

Above left: Tanks and infantry wait hull down behind a convenient embankment during a German counter-attack near Moncel, France. (Note the white vertical stripe on the sponson of the two central tanks which indicates that they belong to the 1st Platoon.) /*US Army*

Centre left: Flotsam of the Nazi dreams of conquest. His life forfeit to the dream of world conquest by his Führer, this German soldier lies sprawled in the high grass where he fell during the Allied advance across France./*IWM*

Bottom left: A knocked out PzKpfw V Panther in Fenetrange, France. This excellent AFV weighed 44.8 tons, had a crew of five, was armed with a 75mm KwK42 (L/70) gun and two 7.92mm MG 34 machine guns. 79 rounds were carried for the main gun. With a road speed of 34mph and a range of 110 miles the Panther saw service on all fronts. A later model, the Jagdpanther, mounted an 88mm gun./*Col Crosby P. Miller*

Right: 88mm with 'banana peeled' barrel. This 88mm anti-aircraft/anti-tank gun will never fire again and forms a bizarre piece of battlefield flotsam and jetsam./*IWM*

Right: Visit of Gen George S. Marshall, US Army Chief of Staff, to 80 Infantry Division at Dieulouard, France, during the crossing of the Moselle. During the visit a presentation of medals ceremony took place, Silver Stars being the order of the day. Patton with tears streaming down his face as he read the citation for an aid-man who had been heroic under fire, turned to Marshall and said, 'By God, this man doesn't deserve the Silver Star, he should have received the Distinguished Service Cross', and turned to his aide directing him to depart and get one. As the aide hastily took off, Marshall pinned the Silver Star on the soldier and said, 'This will have to suffice until Gen Patton's DSC gets here!'. /80th Inf Div Assoc

76

'After signing the Capitulation Agreement, General Leclerc drives Von Choltitz to the main railway station at Montparnasse through the same crowd. Doubtless General Leclerc did not want to make this humiliating journey through the town and many times he struck out with his walking stick. However, it was necessary as the orders to cease battle could only be passed on by ourselves and our German equivalents, who follow their General in a truck. At 1600 hours General von Choltitz and his HQ reach Montparnasse. General Leclerc gives them to me and explains quickly what has been done. According to my own orders, some teams, consisting of both French and German officers, are organised with the, aim of taking the cease fire orders to all elements of the garrison. In a small office I sit with the ex-German Commander of Paris and an interpreter – Lt Betz. With an exemplary correctness, Betz (the interpreter) explains what we want of the German Commander.

Above: Major-General Jacques Philippe Leclerc, Commanding General 2nd French Armoured Division. The photograph was taken in Casablanca, Morocco, in 1943 during a parade, before the Division moved to England. /*Gen. A. Gribius*

Right: Landing in Normandy not far from Isigny, 1 August 1944. Chef D'Escadrons Gribius can be seen just behind Gen Leclerc's left shoulder./*Gen. A. Gribius*

Below right: French tank aids patriots in street battle. Aided by a tank of the 2nd French Armoured Division, French resistance fighters engage the enemy during the street battles that preceded the German surrender. The tank has just fired at an enemy strongpoint and smoke pours from its gun. (Note the Free French Cross of Lorraine on the rear of the tank.)/*IWM*

The effect of a super heavy railway gun is shown in these three photographs taken by Col Crosby P. Miller. *Centre left:* Bousonville before the round hit. *Far left:* Same house after receiving a direct hit from the railway gun. *Bottom left:* Shell hole made by super heavy shell, with Col Miller standing inside it (he was sleeping just across the street when the barrage started and as he put it 'Whatta' night!'). /*Col Crosby P. Miller*

Von Choltitz then writes in German the following words:

Paris 25 August 1944
Order
All resistance in the strongpoints and their surrounding area must cease immediately.
  Signed: Von Choltitz – General of Infantry

'I translate it straight away and after getting it approved by General Leclerc I type ten copies, which are read by a French-speaking German officer and immediately signed. It is a great pity that I was unable to keep one of these documents to copy but to gain time I have to memorise them and then to type them separately, but at last they are all finished. The copies are then given to the joint officer teams who, protected by a white flag, go off to their different destinations.

'At the Palais du Luxembourg, Colonel Crepin must hold a parley for two hours with a unit, including many SS, before they agree to surrender. From the barracks of the Kriegmarine, Lt Boris will see three hundred men emerging and will have the utmost difficulty in disarming them.

'At Avenue Victor Hugo the most dramatic incident takes place, preceded by Lt Bailou's tank, a column of prisoners of war is suddenly fired on by snipers. The Germans rush towards the tanks and half tracks of the Massu Combat Team which is close by ... and nearby machine-guns begin to fire. Is it a genuine mistake or deliberate provocation? It will never be possible to know, but some tens of German soldiers are killed here, while a young girl dips her handkerchief in the blood

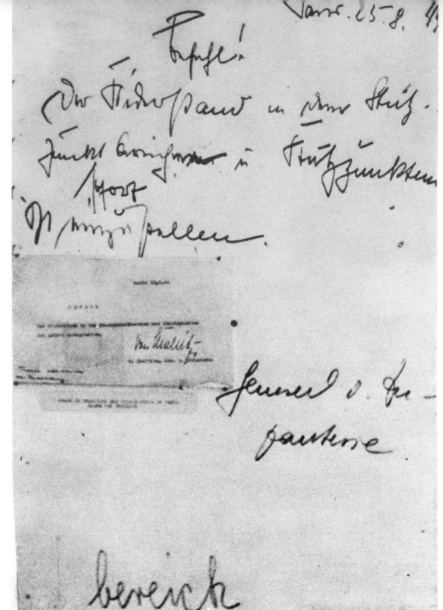

Above: This photograph shows the original surrender order written by Gen von Choltitz himself to all the German forces in Paris. (In the middle are instructions for the officer teams who took the order around the streets to all the German strongpoints.) /*Gen A. Gribius*

Left: General Dietrich von Choltitz, Commander of German Forces in Paris, sits at a desk in the Montparnasse station as he signs the terms of surrender of the 10,000 German troops in Paris, 25 August 1944./*IWM*

which is flowing and cries "this one, I shall never wash it . . ."

'Another bloody event takes place at Palaiseau where Laferriere stays all night long talking with some German officers who say they cannot accept orders from Von Choltitz. Finally, the Commanding Officer assembles his troops, disarms them and walking back, commits suicide by holding a hand grenade to his stomach. In another location the German officer plenipotentiary, is shot, whilst at Vincennes Py is taken prisoner and driven out of Paris and is only liberated by our forces at Metz several days later.

'During the surrender operations, Langlade, who has mopped up the Renault factories, continues his action to La Porte de St Cloud, La Rue Michel Ange, L'Avenue Mozart, La Rue de la Pompe and L'Avenue Victor Hugo, knocking out strongpoint after strongpoint. At last he arrives at La Place de L'Etoile.

'Under the Arc de Triomphe men of the Fire Brigade unfurl an immense flag whilst some snipers on the roof of Hotel Majestic try to prevent them. An 88 shell from a Panther goes straight under the Arch. The armoured column moves down along the Champs Elysees, mops up the adjacent streets and takes the barricades.

'At the same time Rouvillois attacks Tour Mauborg Barracks. The Quai D'Orsay will bear for many years the scars of the tank battle which caused a fire in the Record Office. At the end of the afternoon we welcome General de Gaulle at Montparnasse. He walks in front of the German officers from Von Choltitz headquarters. On a table belonging to the French Railways covered with maps, General Leclerc reports the improvement of the situation. But before he starts, he has the great pleasure to embrace his son, Ensign 1st Class in our Marine Armoured Regiment.

'I try to reach my parents by telephone, they live in Versailles and I am so delighted to hear my father's voice after four years . . . my mother can't speak!

'During the night 25/26 August, we transfer the Divisional Headquarters to La Tour Mauborg Barracks, while the units count their prisoners of war (more than 12,000) and end the occupation of Paris. Indeed, during this historic day, we have limited our actions within the quadrilateral – Porte d'Oleans – Hotel de Ville – Place de L'Etoile – Porte de St Cloud.

'We must now prepare for the official entrance of General de Gaulle into the liberated capital. But to do this with safety we must have some additional units, however, General Gerow, under whose command we are, finds it difficult to release them due to the fluid battle situation. Doubtless, he has also received explicit instructions from the Supreme Allied Commander to organise an official entrance into Paris by all the three Commanders of the Allied Forces.

'But De Gaulle feels that he must enter alone and be the first Chief of State in his own capital. After some protracted discussions between the officers of Gerow's and Leclerc's headquarters and a busy meeting at La Tour Mauborg Barracks, it is decided that for several hours some more units of the 2nd French Armoured Division will be taken off their combat mission to help in Paris, whilst

Left: Gen von Choltitz being taken from the Prefecture de Police to Montparnasse Railway Station./*Gen A. Gribius*

79

the 4th US Infantry Division will be positioned in the Bois de Vincennes, where the Germans are counter attacking, and Roumiantzoff with the most of our Spahis Recce Regiment will move forward to the north of Paris.

'I was not present at the Te Deum inside Notre Dame and I did not participate in the glorious march along the Champs Elysees . . . General Leclerc had given me permission to meet my parents in Versailles which had also just been liberated'.

Troyes – an Armoured Attack

In his book *War as I knew it* General Patton tells how, on 26 August 1944, the Signal Corps sent a group of army reporters and photographers to record *A Day with General Patton*. In a few terse sentences he outlines a typical hectic day in the life of an operational army commander. Towards the end of the account he writes:

'I returned to Fontainbleau (HQ XX Corps) and flew to the XII Corps which was situated on the Sens-Troyes road. While there General Wood came in to state that the 4th Armored had just captured Troyes. This capture was a very magnificent feat of arms. Colonel, later General, Bruce C. Clarke brought his combat command up north of the town, where a gully or depression gave him cover, at about three thousand yards from the town. The edge of the town was full of German guns and Germans. Clarke lined up one medium tank company, backed it with two armored infantry companies, all mounted, and charged with all guns blazing. He took the town without losing a man or a vehicle'.

This is the story of that 'magnificent feat of arms' as told by two officers who took part – Brigadier-General Arthur L. West, Jr, who was then a major commanding Task Force West and Colonel Crosby P. Miller, whom we have already met in an earlier chapter, commanding C Company of 35th Tank Battalion. The story, written at the request of General Bruce Clarke, is based on the notes of the task force commander as jotted down on the day after the fight:

'After the fall of Orleans, the 4th Armored Division continued its drive to the east. As part of XII Corps, the division seized Sens and crossings of the Yonne River on 21 August 1944, and Montargis on 23 August. Combat Command A (CCA) 4th Armored Division, commanded by Colonel Bruce C. Clarke, received orders on 24 August to seize Troyes, and secure crossings of the Seine River in that locality. The combat command was ordered to move out in two columns at first light the next morning. The northern column, Task Force Oden (Lieutenant-Colonel Delk M. Oden), was given the mission of crossing the Seine River north of Troyes and seizing the high ground north and east of Troyes, while the southern column, Task Force West (Major Arthur L. West, Jr) was to seize Troyes itself and secure crossings of the Seine River within the environs of the city proper. For this operation, the task force composition was as follows:

Task Force Oden
35th Tank Bn (less one company)
C Co, 10th Armd Inf Bn.
66th Field Artillery Bn
Plat, Co A, 24th Armd Engr Bn
Plat, Co D, 25th Cav Recon Sqn

Task Force West
10th Armd Inf Bn (less one company)
C Co, 35th Tank Bn
94th Armd Field Artillery
Plat, Co A, 24th Armd Engr Bn
Plat, Co D, 25th Cav Recon Sqn

'Early on the morning of 25 August the task forces moved out abreast toward Troyes to a point about 10 miles west of the city. During the march of Task Force West, a tank from C/35 periodically left the column, knocked down a telephone pole, and broke the telephone wires with its tracks to ensure that no warning of the approach of US Forces would be received in Troyes by telephonic means. This practice was SOP (Standard Operating Procedure) in the 4th Armored Division. In the vicinity of the town of Pavillon, the Combat Commander ordered that the main highway approaches to Troyes be avoided and the remainder of the march be executed cross-country and/or on secondary roads. At the same time, Colonel Clarke ordered the immediate seizure by Task Force West of the high ground in the vicinity of Montgueux, four miles west of Troyes, as a base of operations prior to assaulting the town. Task Force West moved rapidly and by 1500 hours had occupied, without opposition, the high ground of Montgueux which dominated the entire city of Troyes. Up to this point, with no Germans in evidence, the question as to the enemy's whereabouts was uppermost in everyone's mind. However, ten minutes after the Task Force occupied the high ground, sporadic artillery fire began to fall on the forward slopes of the hill mass. Thus, it was evident that Troyes was still held by the enemy and the Combat Commander ordered the city assaulted with a minimum of delay. Reconnaissance elements were promptly dispatched by the Task Force Commander, Major West, to ascertain the degree of resistance to be expected, the best routes of approach, minefields, barriers and the like. Company and platoon leaders engaged in a hasty reconnaissance, the artillery forward observers registered in, and all of the minute details in preparing for an attack were attended to. The units under the command of or in support of Task Force West to carry out this attack were:

Task Force West
10th Armd Inf Bn (less Co C) – Major A. L. West Jr
HQ Co – Capt Howard Seavers
A Co – Capt T. J. MacDonald Jr
B Co – Capt Julian Newton
Svc Co – Capt Robert Bryan
Medics – Capt Isadore Silverman
Co C, 35th Tank Bn – Capt C. P. Miller
94th Armd Field Arty Bn – Lt Col Alex Graham.
Plat, Co A, 24th Armd Engr Bn
Plat, Co D, 25th Cav Recon Sqn

'The Combat Command S-2 relayed forward an estimate of 500 enemy troops in the city composed of rear echelon elements left behind to prepare demolitions and attend to the last minute evacuation matters. Estimates of enemy opposition filtered in from patrols which indicated an aggressiveness that portended more than rearguard delaying tactics on the part of the enemy. Liaison planes reported heavy anti-aircraft fire in the vicinity of the city. The 25th Cavalry and the I & R (Intelligence and Reconnaissance) Platoon of the 10th Armored Infantry Battalion both reported heavy small arms and mortar fire on both main approaches into Troyes approximately two miles distant from the city proper, indicating an outer perimeter defence. By 1600 hours the enemy artillery fire was beginning to increase in volume and accuracy on the Montgueux hill causing 15 casualties. Colonel Clarke, CCA Commander, arrived at the Task Force Command Post and made a rapid estimate of the situation. He then ordered a co-ordinated assault on Troyes to jump off at 1700 hours. His concept of the attack was a typical "desert" type attack directly into the city across the broad flat plain, which stretched for three and one-half miles between the base of Montgueux hill and the city, using the tanks in conjunction with the infantry mounted in half tracks, moving at maximum speed to attain the highest possible shock impact on the enemy. Last minute preparations were rapidly completed and

Below: Paris is liberated! Excited Parisians throng around one of Gen Leclerc's tanks, as it motors slowly along Avenue Victor Hugo on its way to the heart of Paris./*IWM*

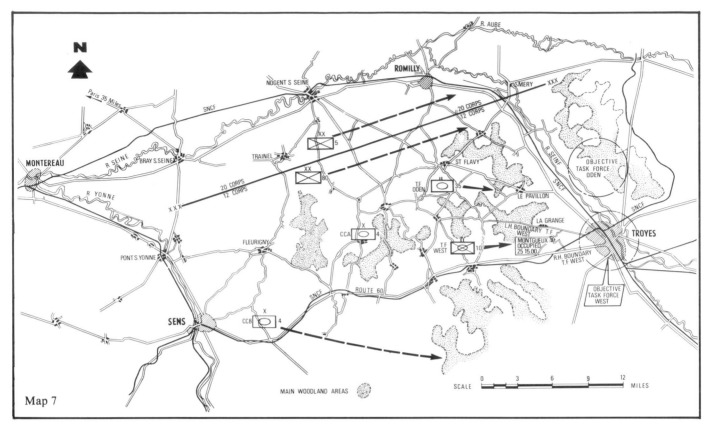

Map 7

Major West issued the following oral order to his commanders [see Sketch Map 7]: "This force attacks Troyes at 1700. Line of Departure forward edge of this hill (Montgueux hill mass). Boundaries: left boundary is road A (pointing to the road which runs through La Grange to the north of Montgueux into Troyes), right boundary is road B (Route 60). Formation is column of companies – companies in line. C/35 (tanks) will lead, followed by A/10 (Infantry) with machine-gun platoon attached. Engineer platoon with mine detectors ride in A Company half tracks. Following A Company will be Battalion Headquarters, B/10, Mortar Platoon and Medics. Assault Gun Platoon (75mm Howitzers) and Reconnaissance (jeeps) Platoon will cover right flank keeping inside (left) of road B hugging our artillery fire. This is a mounted attack. We will stay in our vehicles until forced to dismount. 94th Armored Field Artillery Battalion covers road B (pointing to Route No 60) with time fire commencing 1700 and will sweep up road B as we advance, firing on targets of opportunity on call. We can get 155s on call as well. Maintenance/10 remain vicinity of Montgueux until called forward. Battalion CP behind C/35. Radio silence until 1700. It is now 1615. We will maneuver any place across the open ground that we see fit, keeping the whole force together at all times, and pushing the A/10 half tracks right up with the tanks. Now for the city itself. All we have is the 1/50,000 map, but you can see from here the general outline

of the city. We will establish three phase lines where we can regain control when we get into town. The first phase line – first buildings (pointing). Second – the railroad line that runs through town parallel to the river. Third – in the vicinity of that church steeple on the Seine River. In case anything prevents our co-ordination at each of the lines, push right on to the Seine River and get the bridges. When we initially enter the city, do not use the roads (main streets). Go in between the blocks, through yards, houses etc, until you reach the railroad track in town. Then we will take a main road and the whole force will attack down this one road. If the Germans are there in strength, we will get in behind them and then attack their rear. Are there any questions? Move out!"

'The leading assault companies moved down around the hill into their jump-off positions by 1700 and moved out on the attack. The medium tank company, C/35, deployed with its three platoons abreast in line with the exception that the right flank platoon, commanded by Lieutenant Grice, nearest road B, was echeloned right with orders to watch the right flank and road B. A German armoured car was encountered and quickly eliminated. As the attack gained momentum, the artillery increased in intensity, seeking out the apparently lucrative targets which were sweeping across the open ground toward the city. The enemy artillery observers must have gloated to themselves over the shambles they expected to create because in

front of the advancing US Forces were two major obstacles: a railroad on a high embankment running diagonally across the plain, and between that obstacle and the city, an anti-tank ditch of no mean proportions. However, the tanks and half tracks went up and over the railroad embankment without a pause and again began to pick up speed. Engulfed in enemy artillery the Americans could hardly see in any direction without facing the flame of an exploding shell. Two tanks received direct hits. One was hit on the front slope plate without harming the tank and the crew continued to push forward despite their ringing ears. The second tank, that of Lieutenant Cline, 2nd Platoon leader, was hit by an HE round on the left rear of the turret. The blast slammed the open turret hatch leaf down onto his head, peppered his neck with small fragments and smashed him down on the floor of the turret in a semi-conscious condition – but the tank crew continued on in the attack (Lieutenant Cline was up and fighting again by the time the city was reached). To escape the accurate artillery fire, the Task Force Commander ordered the entire force to move more rapidly and to move into the bursting concentrations, so that, as fol-

lowing concentrations fell (30 seconds or so later), they fell to the rear and flank of the particular group of vehicles which had driven into the prior burst. As Task Force West moved across country, it took up "marching fire" from the tanks and half tracks to force unseen enemy gunners and panzerfaust (anti-tank) gunners to keep their heads down and reduce their accuracy. This fire was extremely effective. Later Captain Miller, C/35, claimed it was too much so – a .50 caliber machine-gun slug from a half track behind him penetrated his bedroll on the rear deck of his tank and punctured his air mattress.

'As Task Force West attacked across country it employed the technique of reconnaissance by fire from the tanks and infantry half-tracks. This fire is extremely effective as was learned earlier in the hedgerow fights in Normandy. The expenditure of machine-gun and tank-HE may appear expensive, however, the shock effect gained was tremendous. This technique was employed effectively many times throughout the war by elements of the division.

'During this part of the attack the Task Force Commander's jeep was hit by artillery fragments and Major West was thrown out and fell into a foxhole occupied by an enemy soldier whom he killed. A warning was quickly flashed to the following vehicles, and it was discovered that the entire field was occupied by German infantry in partially covered foxholes. The first platoon of A/10 dismounted from their half tracks and killed or captured over 100 Germans as they lay in their holes.

'At the anti-tank ditch, the last major obstacle, many of the tanks, already running at their top speed in 5th gear, literally leaped the ditch, clawed at the far edge and finally churned their way out onto level ground. In some cases, the grinding tracks gouged out a precarious passage for a few of the half tracks. Capt Miller's tank landed on the far side of the ditch with such a jolt that from then on the main gun would not fire and they had to travel the rest of the way to the edge of Troyes with only machine-guns firing. Once they reached the main square his gunner found that a cleaning rag left on the gun mount, had been thrown up into the recoil mechanism when the gun was jolted out of battery at the anti-tank ditch. They cleared the jammed gun by putting the muzzle against a tree in the square and pushing the gun back out of battery by driving the tank forward and thus freeing the rags! Leaving the foxhole in which he had been thrown Major West ran to the anti-tank ditch, and after a quick search, managed to find a passageway, so the remainder of the force crossed it in single file. In the process several Germans with radio sets were discovered hiding in well-camouflaged holes dug into the

side of the ditch. They were field artillery forward observers and all were effectively dispatched. An immediate reaction was noticeable in the lessened accuracy of the enemy's artillery fire.

'Small arms fire was being received from both flanks, but, due to the efficient work of the US Artillery Forward Observers with the tank and rifle companies, friendly time fire was falling on both flanks and to the front. The time fire succeeded to a large extent in rendering the enemy counter fires ineffective.

'Enemy anti-tank guns along road B, pinned down by artillery shells bursting in the trees overhead, were overrun and their crews knocked out. Thus, as Task Force West approached the city of Troyes, it became more and more evident that the German force was no 500-man rear guard demolition detachment, but a well-entrenched and well-equipped defending force. After crossing the anti-tank ditch, the attack became somewhat disorganised and lost its cohesiveness due to the necessarily piecemeal crossing of the ditch and the mopping-up operations in its vicinity. Nevertheless, the assault was pushed vigorously and the outskirts of town were reached. At the edge of the built-up area, radio orders

Below: Halftracks of the French 2nd Armd Div line up in front of the historic Arc de Triomphe during ceremonies at the Tomb of the Unknown Soldier, following the liberation of the French capital./*IWM*

Bottom: French and American troops, FFI and gay Parisian girls are intermixed in a joyous crowd making up part of the Paris Victory Parade 26 August 1944. The pavements and flag-decked windows are jammed with cheering civilians who watched General Charles de Gaulle, President of the French Committee of National Liberation, lead the column of French armoured troops and patriots./*IWM*

were issued to continue through the city and secure the bridges over the Seine River with a secondary purpose of getting behind the Germans. The Task Force was split into two attacking groups; one under the 10th Armd Inf Bn Executive Officer, Major Leo Elwell, consisting of two tank platoons and one infantry platoon; the other under the Task Force Commander, consisting of one platoon of tanks and the remaining two companies of infantry. This splitting of the force was by accident and confusion – not by design. Both forces advanced independently of each other toward the river. As both groups moved out, all contact between the two was temporarily lost. The group under Major Elwell moved in a northerly direction on a back street for a short distance then turned east on a main thoroughfare and drove straight through to the river. One tank was rocked by a panzerfaust hit on a bogie wheel, but was able to limp slowly along behind the column. A German anti-tank gun, firing blindly at the flank of the passing column from a narrow side street, eventually so irritated their intended targets that a squad of infantry stopped and knocked it out.

'The column continued to roll until it entered a large square with a park-like area in the centre and a large auditorium or concert hall at the east end. The rear end of this concert hall overlooked the Seine River. A perimeter defense was set up in the square with tanks and infantry covering every street which debouched onto the square. Patrols were sent out to locate the bridges. A tank, which attempted to move around the rear of the concert hall onto the street running along the river bank, was driven back to cover by a tremendous blast and a shower of shattered brick masonry. It was later determined that this was the result of direct fire from a German artillery howitzer across the river. At the moment, however, the blast cooled down the tanker's curiosity.

'The infantry turned their attention to clearing out the considerable number of snipers who were harassing the force from the buildings surrounding the square. The elements under the Task Force Commander advanced slowly but surely against determined opposition until the railroad station was reached. At this point, no town plan being available, the force was lost among the buildings, both as to location and direction, with increasing enemy fire harassing it. Fortunately, radio contact was regained with the Executive Officer's group and, by the simple method of firing .50 calibre tracers into the air, the positions of both forces were determined. Major West's group then reorganized and began to fight its way through to effect a link-up with the Executive Officer's group. Shortly thereafter physical contact was

established between the two forces and a four-block square perimeter defence was set up. Coincident with link-up, bridges were seized intact across the Seine River, and the engineer and reconnaissance platoons moved across to outpost and secured them. The Task Force command post was established in a French house on the square.

'Apparently many Germans failed to get the word that Americans were on the river and in the square – a tiny French car occupied by two Germans wheeled into the square from a small alley and skidded to a halt behind a 32-ton Sherman tank. The surprised look on the faces of the Germans was almost ludicrous.

'Two German trucks pulled out of an alley into a street leading from the square and leisurely moved away down the street. Unfortunately for them that street was outposted by the assault gun tank (105mm) of C/35. The tank fired one round on delay fuse which passed through the trailing truck and burst in the leading truck, knocking them both out. The sniper fire was dying out, although one sniper in a church steeple continued to fire and inflict casualties despite all efforts to dislodge him. Finally Lieutenant Grice, 1st Platoon C/35, elevated his tank's 75mm gun

Below: Victory Parade in Paris, 29 August 1944. American infantrymen in mass formation march down the Avenue des Champs Elysées with the Arc de Triomphe in the background. /*IWM*

and effectively silenced the sniper. Just as things seemed to be quietening down a little, a column of enemy trucks was observed in the early darkness moving along a street from the northwest leading into the square. The column was halted and the first truck set on fire by one round from a tank in the square. Half tracks from A/10 moved around behind the column, knocked out the last vehicle and trapped the whole convoy. The trucks must have been an ammunition convoy – the burning truck exploded and continued the chain reaction. Burning trucks exploded periodically during the night, making a shambles of the street, and causing Major West to say a few well-chosen words as each blast threatened to smash the glass in the tall French doors of his CP. Medical attention, by this time, had become a vital need for approximately 30 wounded men requiring immediate care. Repeated attempts had been made to contact the Medical Detachment by radio, but to no avail. As the enemy fire indicated that the Germans had closed in behind the Task Force elements at the square, it was now assumed that the Medical Detachment had either been intercepted and captured or had halted to await relieving forces before attempting to get through. However, Captain Seavers contacted the local French authorities with a view to securing French medical assistance. By midnight a small group of French doctors and nurses were functioning and caring for the wounded.

'Meanwhile, the Battalion S-2 Lieutenant Abe Baum, later Major and Commander of Task Force Baum of Hammelburg fame, had been busy contacting local French authorities and through them had discovered a baker who daily delivered his bakery products to the German garrisons. With the baker's information, and a town plan surprisingly supplied from the baker's office, a plan of attack was formulated to break out and regain physical contact with the remainder of the Combat Command. At 2000 hours a platoon of infantry, supported by one platoon of tanks, moved out to establish that contact. After an advance of approximately one mile against sporadic resistance there was imminent danger of their being cut off and surrounded in the rapidly fading daylight. Consequently, they were recalled and a decision was made to hold fast for the night. At 2300 hours the Combat Commander, Colonel Clarke, called by radio and requested information as to the existing situation and what assistance, if any, was needed. He was given the situation and a plan was formulated which involved the launching of an attack at first light by a CCA relieving force of one medium tank company. This tank company was to fight towards the centre of the city while elements of Task Force West were to simultaneously fight back from the

river to effect a junction with the relieving force.

'Secondary attacks were planned by the Task Force Commander, utilising four tank-infantry teams, which were to assault such various centres of German resistance as were known from information supplied by the French townspeople and the baker. These attacks were designed to further disrupt the German garrison and to break the back of the enemy defence from within. The first of these secondary attacks was to be launched simultaneously with the main link-up effort of the Task Force, while the other three were to jump off spaced 15 minutes apart, dependent upon the success of the main link-up operation. With the plans completed for the early morning attack, the Task Force waited for dawn. Intermittent clashes occurred throughout the night caused mainly by Germans, unaware of the exact location of the Task Force, blundering into the US perimeter. However, some elements of the German force knew the location of the Reconnaissance and Engineer Platoons which had seized and outposted two bridges across the Seine River. The Germans attacked during the night and forced the outposts back to the bridges, but were unable to take the crossings. Here the US troops held until morning. It should be pointed out here that there were *two* sets of bridges involved – the Seine River split within the city and formed a small island so that the US troops held the western set of bridges to the island and the Germans held the island and the eastern bridges. The island was shelled intermittently by division artillery during the night. The Reconnaissance Platoon was ordered to attack and seize the island at daylight coincident with the main Task Force attack. Upon receipt of this order Lieutenant Stan Lyons (now Lieutenant-Colonel), the platoon leader, turned to the Task Force Commander and stated, "What do you think I am, a G...D... Combat Commander?" As the time for the planned attacks approached, information came in on what was purported to be the command post of the enemy 51st SS Brigade. Through the dim half light of early morning, enemy trucks were observed lined up along a street near the square. Major West quickly dispatched armoured vehicles to block both ends of the street. Further action then was held up until better light.

'Promptly at 0600 hours the planned attacks were launched. The Reconnaissance Platoon, moving rapidly, overran two German artillery batteries in the process of displacing and eliminated eight howitzers and accompanying personnel. The tanks and armoured vehicles covering the trucks of the suspected German command post opened fire and knocked out these vehicles. The buildings on both sides of the street erupted Germans as the firing started. These individuals were either killed or captured. Among the captured was a German general officer, the commander of the 51st SS Brigade.

'The main attack jumped off and immediately established radio contact with the relieving tank company, A/35, and by 0800 hours a link-up between the two forces had been realised within the city. A platoon of A/35 was promptly dispatched to assist the Reconnaissance Platoon in its effort to clear all the enemy from the island. Shortly after the link-up with A/35 (tanks) the three planned secondary attacks were initiated. All of these were successful and unvarying in design and execution, so the relating of one will suffice. From information received from the French the previous evening, the location of the Gestapo Headquarters and the size of the local Gestapo force had been ascertained. The location of this headquarters was approximately eight blocks away from the Task Force perimeter. The designated attacking force was one platoon of armoured infantry supported by a platoon of C/35 tanks. The assault force moved out and traversed the eight blocks without opposition until they came to the large school building housing the Gestapo headquarters. The tanks took up firing positions, and, upon signal, commenced to pour round after round of HE, AP, and WP into the building followed by .30 and .50 calibre machine-gun fire. The building became a holocaust within a matter of minutes.

'The tanks ceased firing and the armoured infantry moved in with rifle, grenade, and bayonet to complete the mission. In fifteen minutes, the fight was ended with 58 German dead counted, 50 prisoners and no casualties to the assaulting infantry-tank team. At approximately 1100 hours, 26 August, the Task Force Commander received word that his force would be relieved by the 53rd Armored Infantry Battalion. By early afternoon the relief was accomplished and Task Force West moved out to rejoin the remainder of CCA northeast of Troyes.

'One mine was hit while leaving the city which killed the Battalion Operations Sergeant, Sergeant Cook, and wounded several others including the Battalion S-3, Captain J. J. J. Shea. Also, the bodies of the Battalion Surgeon and several medics were found this day. The medics had been murdered, each with a bullet through the red cross on his helmet. It was difficult to accurately estimate enemy casualties, however, the 51st SS Brigade plus attached troops, probably lost over 1,100 men – half killed and half wounded and/or captured. As to equipment they lost at least 53 vehicles, 72 machine-guns, 10 artillery and anti-tank guns, plus masses of small arms. The total American losses were 3 vehicles, 15 killed, 55 wounded and evacuated, 10 wounded and remained.

'It will be of interest to those who participated in this battle that the city square around which Task Force West established its perimeter was, as of 1960, for the most part a parking area; that the concert hall still stands; and that in the square stands a large stone monument on which is carved scenes depicting the Germans in occupation in Troyes, the fighting in the city and the Germans in flight.

'Before this carved slab are two stone figures showing a French civilian grieving over the body of an American soldier. Apparently the French of Troyes have not forgotten.'*

*An account of this battle, written by Brigadier-General West and Colonel Miller, appeared in the Nov/Dec edition of *Armor* magazine in 1963. This account is substantially the same, however, I have been able to add in extra details which have been kindly provided for me by the authors.

Below: The Command Group of 37th Tank Bn, 4th Armd Div, strung out over the snow covered fields near Conthil, France, preparing to launch a new offensive, 14 November 1944. The centre tank belongs to the battalion commander Lt-Col Creighton W. Abrams (later Chief of Staff, US Army). /*US Army*

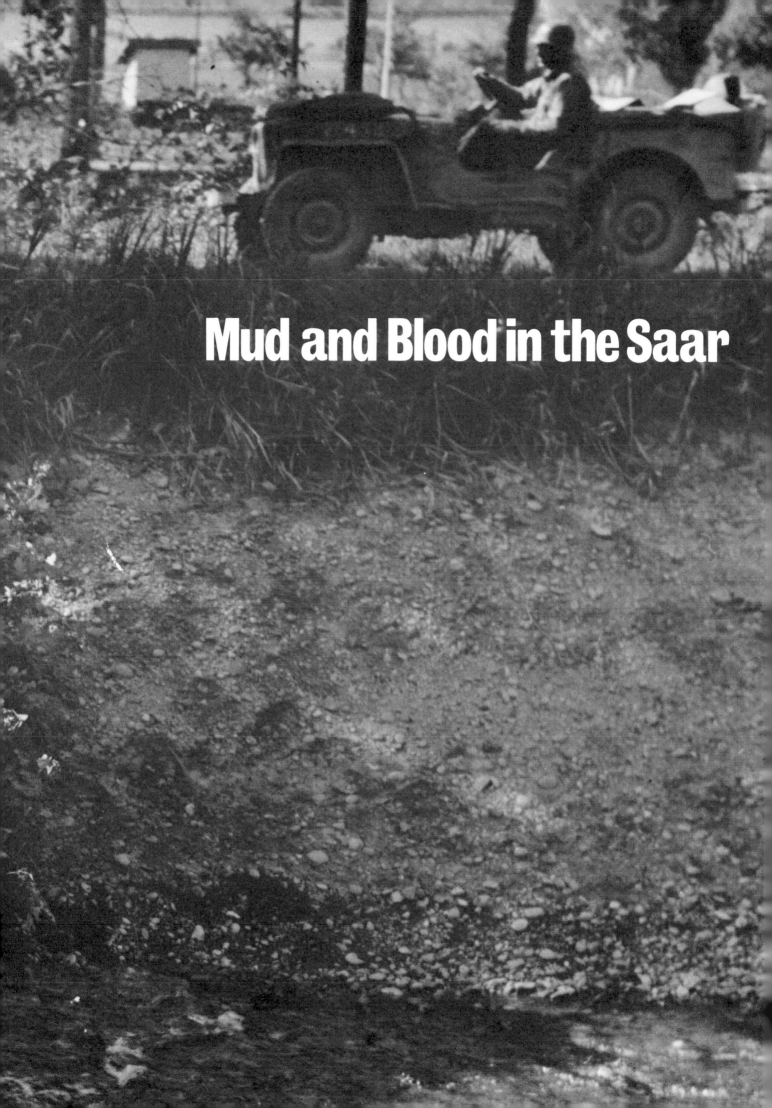

Mud and Blood in the Saar

The Nancy Bridgehead

In early September 1944 Combat Command A of the 4th Armored Division, led by Colonel Bruce C. Clarke, later to become famous for his heroic action at St Vith in the Ardennes battle, fought what was described by Major General Eddy, commander of XII Corps, as one of the finest operations of the war, when they re-established a vital bridgehead over the Moselle River at Nancy. Before their action 35th Infantry Division had carried out a forced crossing of the five tributaries of the Moselle, south and southeast of Nancy, whilst 80th Infantry Division crossed to the north of the city. This double envelopment was followed by the encirclement of Nancy to the east as far as Chateau Salins, by 4th Armored, which caused such confusion far behind the German lines that they hastily evacuated the city and 35th Infantry was able to occupy it with little opposition. General Eddy likened CCA's 'ride around Nancy' with Jeb Stuart's ride around Richmond in the American Civil War, with the difference that 'Clarke's ride' had played a key part in causing the fall of the city. Indeed, in the two week operation CCA amassed a truly remarkable list of achieve-

ments. They re-established a bridgehead that was in imminent danger of being lost; breached a strong enemy position and penetrated to a depth of 45 miles behind German lines; destroyed the command installation of the unit charged with the defence of the Nancy sector; blocked the retreat of the German forces driven out of Nancy by the attack of the 35th Infantry Division; engaged in mopping up operations over a wide area centring around Arracourt; fought one of the bitterest tank battles of the entire war; and for a period of eight days fought an aggressive defensive action against superior forces to hold the Arracourt salient of the Nancy bridgehead from which the Third Army was to launch its winter offensive early in November. Whilst accomplishing all this, great damage was inflicted upon the enemy with comparatively light losses to the Command. A summary of enemy casualties for this 14-day period included: prisoners of war – 1,884; counted killed – 589; tanks counted destroyed – 107; self-propelled guns destroyed – 30; other large calibre guns destroyed – 32; other vehicles destroyed – 491. During this period the division, in its advance east of Nancy and in its active defence of the bridgehead, met and defeated elements of three enemy infantry divisions, one panzer division, two panzer brigades and five separate battalions including anti-aircraft, engineer, armoured and paratroops.

It Really Happened

In any major operation of war such as this one, there are always many acts of individual heroism. Here are a few, gathered from eye witnesses and checked from official reports by Brigadier-General Hal C. Pattison, whose full account of this classic action is now used for instructional purposes at the US Armor School, Fort Knox, Kentucky. Brigadier-General Pattison served throughout the campaign with 4th Armored, he was the Executive Officer of CCA and later the Assistant Divisional Commander.

Baptism of Fire

On the afternoon of 11 September five replacements joined the headquarters of the combat command. Among them was Private Sewing, whose civilian occupation had been that of policeman in his home town of Sioux City, Nebraska. During much of the day on the 13th the headquarters was under artillery fire and on occasions small arms fire, from stragglers hidden along the route of advance. In the bivouac area on the evening of the 13th a lone German gun had forced the CP to move three times in the space of an hour, before settling down for the night in a wide re-entrant that ran through the town of Fresnes. Private Sewing had been outspoken in his

Previous page: A well camouflaged Sherman of the 8th Tank Bn, 4th Armored Div, fording a canal, as it follows up the retreating German forces, 9 December 1944. The steepness of the bank gives an excellent, if unusual view of the top of the tank, in particular the commander's .50cal Browning machine gun – but can you see the commander?/*US Army*

Below: Infantrymen of XII Corps pass a sign pointing to Saarbrücken, Germany, as they advance along a debris-covered street in the French town of St Avold, captured on 27 November 1944./*IWM*

resentment at being shot at so much without getting a chance to shoot back. So he was put on guard duty for the night and promised that before morning he would probably have a chance to shoot. And sure enough, at about four in the morning Private Sewing was heard to challenge sharply and then to fire his rifle once. Investigation at daylight proved that with his one shot he had hit a member of a German patrol squarely between the eyes at a range of about 100 feet. Private Sewing's first shot set off a small skirmish that lasted for half an hour or more, in which three Germans lost their lives and 11 were captured.

Beyond the Call of Duty

As the leading elements of the combat command entered the town of Valhey on the afternoon of 14 September 1944, Sergeant Joe Sadowski's 'dozer tank of A Company of the 37th Tank Battalion was second in column. The lead tank had swung north around a corner as Sadowski's tank clattered into the village square. A German anti-tank crew 100 yards down the road had time to lay its gun and an armour-piercing shell ripped into the Sherman's flank. The flaming tank lurched to a stop against the town watering trough. The tank commander ordered his crew to dismount. They raced through a shower of machine gun and rifle fire to the shelter of a building. There Sadowski discovered that his bow gunner was still in the flaming tank. He ran back to the tank, clambered up the smoking front slope plate, and tried to pry open the bow gunner's locked hatch with his bare hands. Bullets snapped and ricocheted off the tank as he tugged and beat at the hatch. He stood on the smoking tank and strained at the hatch until he had been hit so many times he could no longer stand. He slid from his medium and died in the mud beside its tracks. His father and mother were given his posthumous Congressional Medal of Honor. After the town was cleared of the eight 88mm guns and 300 infantry that defended it, the force was turned east towards Moncourt, so that it was four days later before a party could return to recover Sgt Sadowski's body. It was discovered then that the population of Valhey had buried Sgt Sadowski in the local cemetery, with all the honours they could provide. His grave was heaped with flowers. The following day, in pouring rain, the entire population of the village stood by the cemetery in mourning and in tribute as Sergeant Sadowski's body was removed for transfer to a military cemetery.

Infiltration

During the hours of darkness of the nights of 15, 16 and 17 September many bands of Germans attempted to escape through the screen established to gather them in. No doubt some did find their way through, but hundreds were captured, and in the process many strange things happened. For example, the commander of the 53rd Armored Infantry Battalion had his command post concealed near a road, one of five that converged on high ground at what was to become known as 'The Five Corners'. During one of these nights he heard a 'klup . . . klup . . . klup' issuing from the pitch darkness and evidently close by. Sending a sentry to investigate he waited, puzzled as to what it might be. Soon the sentry returned prodding a German prisoner and carrying a German machine gun. The odd sound the battalion commander had heard had been the sound of a pick the German was using to dig in his gun. He had been sent to set up an outpost to cover the escape of a large group of his companions. The now thoroughly alerted 53rd Armored Infantry Battalion had good pickings that night. The same night a strange fracas began which at first seemed to be a fire fight between the 66th Field Artillery Battalion and A Company of the 126th Maintenance Battalion. The areas occupied by these two units were only three to four hundred yards apart, with a shallow valley running between. Across this valley was one of the rare wire fences to be found in France. About 400 yards beyond was a 'cage' containing more than 1,000 prisoners of war. At about 2200 hours some scattered firing began, soon reaching the intensity of a small attack, with both the commanding officer of the 66th and Captain Walter Donnelly of the maintenance company reporting that the other unit was getting trigger happy and they wished it would stop. Both stated they had no enemy contact. To make the circumstances more strange, both were fine combat officers noted for their coolness. Each was instructed to get the firing stopped before any further damage was done. By now a couple of radiators had been riddled in the ordnance area and an ammunition trailer set afire in the artillery area. But the firing continued in the ordnance area, and soon Captain Donnelly called for military police to come to take some prisoners off his hands. It now appeared that a group of more than 150 Germans under the command of a lieutenant-colonel had attempted to infiltrate through the valley between the two units. In so doing one of their number blundered into the wire fence and accidently discharged his weapon, thus starting the shooting. The score from this fracas amounted to more than 100 prisoners, with several more dead. The capture of the German officer was a story in itself. In the ordnance company was a warrant officer, of whose name there seems to be no record. Up until this night he had not fired a shot in anger. To say that he did so now would be to embroider the truth, but he did put forth a valiant effort. Asleep in his slit trench under his pup tent he was awakened by the sound of firing. He lay still, gripping his carbine. Then someone stumbled over his tent rope and, peering out, he saw a tall booted figure silhouetted against the light of the gunfire. Knowing there were no shiny boots to be found on Americans, he stealthily raised his carbine and pulled the trigger. Only the click of a misfire resulted. Hearing the click the German spun round and wrested the carbine from the astonished warrant officer's hands. But he was a resourceful lad and, tackling the German about the ankles, brought him down with a thud, causing the German to lose his monocle. The German refused to surrender formally without proper assistance, and called for his adjutant and aide who appeared out of the darkness, clicked their heels, saluted smartly and handed over their weapons in surrender. The request of the German that a light be brought so that he might search for his monocle was refused.

Devotion to Duty

At about 0700 on 19 September Captain William Dwight, liaison officer for the 37th Tank Battalion, was returning to his battalion area near Lezey from combat command headquarters, which was in the vicinity of Arracourt. It was very foggy, limiting visibility to about 50 yards. As he approached Lezey from the southwest he heard firing ahead. As he continued he heard tanks moving, and soon saw them looming up ahead of him through the fog. They were German tanks! He called into his battalion and found that it was under attack by the panzer unit which he had been following through the fog. Being armed with nothing larger than a pistol, he returned to combat command headquarters, where a platoon of tank destroyers was made available to send to the assistance of the 37th. Captain Dwight started on the return journey to his battalion, leading his four tank destroyers. Near Bezange he ran head on into another panzer column and lost one tank destroyer in the fire fight that began at once. He secured a position on high ground west of Bezange as the fog began to lift and engaged the enemy in a fight that lasted for nearly two hours, during which nine enemy tanks were destroyed while Captain Dwight lost two more destroyers. In spite of being reduced to one tank destroyer and a few dismounted crewmen, Captain Dwight held his position, first against the enemy tank attack and later against an attack by enemy infantry, until the situation cleared enough to permit a limited objective attack by the 37th to extricate his small force from its exposed position. This was an example of the tenacious devotion to duty of all personnel that brought the battle of that day to a successful conclusion.

'Bazooka Charlie'

Major Charles Carpenter, by profession a teacher of history in the Moline, Illinois, High School, was the commander of the Cub artillery liaison planes of the division. Almost abnormal in his complete lack of fear he would and frequently did, go almost anywhere in his light, slow plane. In the division he had earned the nickname of 'Bazooka Charlie' because he had equipped his plane with three standard infantry anti-tank rocket launchers under each wing. He had wired them up so that he could discharge them one at a time or all six together, by means of push buttons in his cockpit. Before a serious illness removed him from action, he destroyed five German tanks and several trucks, but it was about noon on 19 September that he rattled down out of the sky with his queer fighting craft to the surprise and consternation of a German tank company and the gratitude of the whole command, but most particularly the water point crew. Because it was the only place in the area where water was to be had in sufficient quantities, the water point with its crew of six men had been set up near Rechicourt. Soon after the tank battle of the 19th began, Carpenter appeared over the battlefield in his Cub, but the fog was too thick for observation. However, he remained over the area and at about noon, passing over Rechicourt, he observed a company of German tanks moving in the direction of Arracourt. As he watched them they attacked and overran the water point installation. He reported their position over the artillery radio net and moved into the attack. Diving sharply he fired two rockets and missed with both of them. Climbing rapidly he dived again at such a steep angle the wings of his plane quivered

Below: A Weasel of 6th Armd Div. This small tracked vehicle replaced many jeeps in November 1944, because of the thick mud and terrible going. */6 Armd Div Assoc/George F. Hofmann*

and shook, but this time one of his two rockets found its mark, damaging a tank and causing the crew to bail out and run. A third time he attacked, and for a second time was successful. The German company commander was apparently at a loss to meet such a situation, for the undamaged tanks hesitated and then withdrew to attack later in the day. The warning that this pilot gave of the force aided materially in stopping its attack later on. And his interference saved the lives of the water point crew, for when first attacked by the plane, the German tank commanders were firing at the crew with machine guns. In the confusion the crew escaped into the stream, where they remained hidden in the water until rescued soon after dark.

Leadership

During the days of heavy tank fighting around Arracourt, outstanding performances of duty on the battlefield became routine for officers and men. From the outset on 19 September the troops defended and counter-attacked around the clock against superior numbers. An example of the outstanding leadership which made this possible was the part played by Captain William Spencer, company commander of A Company, 37th Tank Battalion. On 19 September, when the enemy first attacked, Captain Spencer and his company were at Luneville, part of a small force led by Major Hunter and dispatched the day before to assist the reserve command. This force was recalled early on the 19th and arrived in the Arracourt area about 1300 hours that day. At this point enemy tank forces had penetrated in the south through Bures, Coincourt and Rechicourt to the outskirts of Arracourt. Plans were immediately made for Major Hunter to counter-attack with A and B Companies of the 37th Tank Battalion through Rechicourt to Coincourt. This attack jumped off and proceeded as planned, accomplishing its mission as darkness fell. In the counter attack Captain Spencer was conspicuous at the head of his company, engaging enemy tanks at close range with his own tank and directing the movement of his platoons. In the final phase of this counter attack three tanks of A Company were knocked out, one of them Captain Spencer's. At this point, the enemy tanks having fled, Major Hunter's force was ordered to join the remainder of the battalion at Lezey. Major Hunter offered to take Captain Spencer, who was superficially wounded, on his tank. Spencer declined. Instead he sent the remainder of his company with Major Hunter and he proceeded on foot in the dark to gather his men, some wounded, from the knocked-out tanks. Having gathered some eight survivors of the destroyed tanks together, Captain Spencer proceeded on foot across country, through scattered enemy troops, leading his men back to the battalion area and arriving there with all of them about 2200 hours. The following day, 20 September, A Company, with Captain Spencer in the lead, took part in the vicious fighting around Ley and culminated in the day's operations with a successful night assault on Moncourt. A Company held Moncourt the night of 20/21 September. Two days later Captain Spencer led his company alone (strength, seven tanks) in an attack against 22 enemy tanks. A Company lost one tank, and destroyed 17; only five enemy escaped. Despite most difficult fighting, despite the necessity for constant attack against superior numbers, despite the loss of two thirds of the company, Captain Spencer's

Below: Three knocked out German tanks near the German frontier 25 November 1944. They are all PzKpfw Panther Ausf Gs and were destroyed by 4th Armd Div Shermans like the one in the foreground which may or may not be bogged./*US Army*

intelligent, courageous, and aggressive leadership maintained in A Company throughout this period a high state of morale and efficiency which was maintained to the end of the war. For this action, Captain Spencer was awarded the Distinguished Service Cross.

The Advance is Halted

The operations of Third Army during the latter half of September underwent an abrupt change, as the dazzling pace of their August gallop through France slowed to a canter, then a trot and finally came to a virtual standstill. This dramatic reversal of fortunes was in no way due to increased enemy activity, on the contrary, the Germans were still thoroughly disorganised and falling over each other to escape Patton's fast moving armoured spearheads. Not only were Third Army's patrols able to penetrate right into the main square of the fortress city of Metz on 6 September, finding virtually no enemy there, but also, on the same day, other patrols entered Germany and pierced the Siegfried line defences in two places. Later it would take many weary, bloody weeks before these successes could be repeated. The advance was halted for a number of reasons, the main ones being a lack of supplies, particularly of petrol and oil, a lack of foresight in planning at the highest level and a rapid deterioration in the weather. As far as the lack of supplies was concerned there was not really any shortage at the invasion beaches and ports, but the problem

Below: Taking cover at a street corner in Metz, this XX Corps soldier watches others advance with a Sherman at the next corner, 18 November 1944. /*IWM*

was getting it forward to the advancing troops along the inadequate road network. As General Eisenhower, the Allied Supreme Commander, explained in his book *Crusade in Europe*:

'All along the front we felt increasingly the strangulation of movement imposed by our inadequate lines of communication. The Services of Supply had made heroic and effective effort to keep us going to the last possible minute. They installed systems of truck transport by taking over main-road routes in France and using most of these for one-way traffic. They were called Red Ball Highways, on which the trucks kept running continuously. Every vehicle ran at least 20 hours a day. Relief drivers were scraped up from every unit that could provide them and vehicles themselves were allowed to halt only for necessary loading, unloading and servicing'.

Because of this strangulation it was necessary for SHAEF to impose priorities and this they did, favouring the British and Canadian thrust in the north to Third Army's advance in the south. This brings us to the second main factor, namely planning. None of the top level planners had foreseen the enemy collapse happening so quickly or so completely, therefore they were not prepared, as Liddell Hart put it: 'either mentally or materially to exploit it by a rapid long range thrust'[*]. General Patton was frustrated beyond belief as first one, then another and another of his armoured columns ran out of fuel and halted. Quite correctly he protested to SHAEF and was understandably annoyed at Eisenhower's apparent penchant to favour Montgomery at his expense. However, as Martin Blumenson explains in the *Patton Papers*: 'There was no plot, no conspiracy ... the breakout and pursuit had simply moved too fast to allow the logisticians to set up an orderly and adequate system of support. Even Patton in his darkest moments realised this'. Finally of course, the weather played its part too. October and November were the rainy season in that region of France and day after day there was an almost continuous downpour of cold, drenching rain.

'Pools of water lay everywhere, some of them like good-sized lakes, and the mud was almost unbelievable. It was deep, slimy and slippery. Leather and clothing mildewed and got musty, metal began to rust. Entirely aside from fighting the enemy, there was a constant battle to keep equipment clean and usable

[*]*History of the Second World War* by B. H. Liddell Hart.

and to keep oneself as dry as possible. It was a thoroughly miserable time for everybody.'*

There were shortages of adequate clothing and footwear, so, when the weather turned cold, feet began to freeze and there were many cases of 'trench foot' reminiscent of the early days of World War I. Patton, a firm believer in adequate comforts for his men, spent a great deal of time and effort getting galoshes, overshoes, woollen socks and long woollen underwear for them.

The Fortress of Metz

The period of 'aggressive defence' lasted from 25 September until 7 November, when the restraining order was lifted and Third Army was allowed to get on the move again. Of course the planning staffs had not let the time pass unfruitfully, so all was ready for 'jump-off'. However, the Germans also had not been idle. This heaven sent breathing space had enabled them to regain control of their scattered forces and to garrison properly such fortresses as the old city of Metz. The city, on the east bank of the Moselle, was ideally situated for defence and had withstood many attacks during its 1,500-year history. Barbed wire and earth fortifications had been built around the city to supplement the water barriers which the river and its tributaries

Patton and his Third Army by Col Brenton G. Wallace.

provided to the west, north and south. Perhaps the strongest defences lay in the hills which surrounded Metz on all sides. Over the years many underground forts had been built, connected by underground passageways with concrete and steel doors which had been designed so that they could not be seen from ground level, making direct artillery observation and fire impossible. They were also relatively impervious to aerial attack. There were some twenty forts, but the strongest of all were Fort Driant, south of the city on the west bank of the river, Fort Jeanne d'Arc opposite it on the east bank and Fort Verdun. Most of the forts had been built originally during the Franco-Prussian war of 1870, improved at the time of World War I and again when the Maginot Line was constructed, and finally, of course, the Germans had themselves improved the defences. The larger forts had 150mm guns and 105mm howitzers, mostly of French origin. Many had steel and concrete tops buried under thick layers of earth, concrete embrasures, ditches and moats, barbed wire and minefields. All were manned by special Fortress Battalions and the Gestapo guarded the only escape route to the east, to see that all would stay to fight to the finish! XX Corps surrounded the city, with 95th Infantry Division crossing the Moselle north of Metz on 8 November, whilst the 5th Infantry Division crossed to the south. Elements of 90th Division went over in the vicinity of Thionville also, to help surround

Below: An infantry patrol moves cautiously through Metz, clearing out the last of the German snipers./*US Army*

Metz to the south. Throughout the attack the bombers of the 8th Air Force pounded the city in support of the 19th Tactical Air Command. The weather was wet and gloomy, the defence tenacious. The enemy were dug into the cellars of shops and houses as well as in the forts and had to be blown out block by block, with grenades and point blank tank gunfire. By the 18th the last avenue of escape had been blocked, but the city did not surrender until 22 November and even then some forts actually held out until mid December. Third Army suffered over 7,000 casualties in the battle for Metz and in a nearby hospital Patton asked one of them if he had heard that Metz had fallen. The soldier smiled and said yes. Patton grabbed him by the hand, smiled back and said, 'Tomorrow, son, the headlines will read "Patton Took Metz", which you know is a goddamn lie. You and your buddies are the ones who actually took Metz.'*

The Offensive Continues – a Perfect Tank Attack

Third Army continued its Saar campaign on into early December. Typical of their hard-fought actions is the following account of a tank attack by 4th Armored Division on the village of Singling 5-6 December 1944, which first appeared in *Army in Europe* a magazine for the USAREUR soldier and civilian, published in December 1962 and is reproduced here by kind permission of the editor.

'The General with the Iron Cross nodded his head in grudging approval as three platoons of Sherman tanks with armoured infantry mounted on their decks, topped the ridge some 1,000 yards away and roared towards the village with all guns blazing. As they neared the outskirts, the two leading platoons fanned out to the right and left while the reserve platoon shot forward into the gap. At the village edge the tanks halted, seeking defiladed positions while the infantry scrambled off the decks and began the dirty job of clearing the houses – room by room and floor by floor. "A perfect panzer vorstoss", muttered the General as he mounted his command car and gestured to his driver to move out smartly. "Wish they were mine. Driver, let's get the hell out of here!" As General Fritz Bayerlin, commander of the crack Panzer Lehr Division, made his hasty departure from the tiny French village of Singling in Lorraine, troops of the 4th Armored Division sped him on his way with a fusillade of small-arms and tank cannon fire. The "perfect tank attack" which had just been unfolded under his professional observation was no "canned" training exercise. Team B of Combat Command A, 4th Armored Division, had just demonstrated the

tactical skill and flexibility which, in just five months, had made it one of the most formidable forces on the European battlefield. The General, fighting with his back to the border of his homeland, would try to shore up his defences, knowing all the while that the "Spearpoint of the Spearhead" had irreparably ruptured them. The date was 6 December 1944 – eve of the third anniversary of Pearl Harbor. American men and metal were nearing the borders of the Third Reich. And in the vanguard of General George S. Patton, Jr's pace-setting Third Army, was the 4th Armored Division. Guarding the frontiers of the Reich was the vaunted West Wall or Siegfried Line, extended westward in depth by the reversed fortifications and pillboxes of a still-formidable Maginot Line. Designed for all-round defence, and capitalising on heavily wooded and compartmented terrain of Lorraine, these Maginot fortifications would require some five months of arduous, deadly, day-by-day slugging before the Allies could burst through and revert to a war of movement. But, early in December 1944, the front was still fluid and hopes were high that the momentum which had carried the armoured columns from Normandy to the French-German border, would also carry them through the fortified belt.

The Attack [see Sketch Map 8a]
'On 5 December the 4th Armored was attacking on two axes; Combat Command A on the right via Saare-Union-Rahling-Bining and Combat Command B on the left on the axis Oermingen-Singling. Final Division objective, assigned to Combat Command B, was the high ground in the vicinity of Rimling. Combat Command A had cross-reinforced its tank battalion (the 37th) and its armoured infantry battalion (the 51st) into two task forces each consisting of two tank companies and two infantry companies, supported by a company of tank destroyers and an armoured field artillery battalion. The task forces, according to 4th Armoured Standard Operating Procedures (SOP) bore the names of the two battalion commanders, and both had been further divided into two balanced teams each consisting of a tank and armoured infantry company. The two task forces (TF) were to jump off abreast, with TF Oden reverting to a supporting role after seizing Rahling. Combat Command A was to side-slip to the north east, take Rohrbach, and support CCB's drive to the divisional objective. CCB, however, had experienced trouble crossing the Eichel and was unable to make the Line of Departure (LD) on time. It is with Task Force Abrams that we are concerned, for it was Team B of that task force which launched the impromptu attack and wrung the reluctant accolade from the commander of the defending

The Patton Papers by Martin Blumenson.

forces. Since it was CCB's objective, CCA's initial attack plan had disregarded the innocent looking hamlet of Singling, a cluster of some 50 houses almost due east of intermediate objective Bining-Rohrbach. Around Singling's austere, weather-beaten church, brownstone schoolhouse and market square were clustered tile-roofed houses whose pastel coloured walls provided a relieving splotch of colour against the drab countryside. As in most villages in Alsace-Lorraine, the stables were integral with the houses, with manure piled in the front yards. The bucolic, innocuous appearance of the buildings concealed some harsh military realities. Some of these farm houses had three-foot reinforced concrete walls; garden walls were high and thick. And concrete pillboxes guarded the approaches to the town from all four points of the compass.

'Task Force Abrams had jumped off about mid-morning of 5 December, and by dusk was still several thousand yards short of Rohrbach, nursing a bloody nose. 14 Sherman tanks had bogged down in the ooze, and heavy anti-tank fire from Singling had left them all in flames. Lieutenant Colonel Creighton W. Abrams recommended that he be permitted to reduce Singling on the morrow to preclude again running the fire gauntlet en route to Rohrbach. In the absence of approval of this plan, Abrams assumed that his original mission remained unchanged, and he kicked off in the morning of the 6th in a column of teams, Team A leading, counting on supporting fires from the artillery and his attached tank destroyer platoons to neutralise Singling until it came under attack by CCB.

Pinned Down

'Because of the soupy nature of the terrain, the half-tracks were unable to manoeuvre cross-country so the infantry mounted the decks of the tanks. Team A, under Captain William Spencer, waddled forward through the goo, and again came under intensive direct and indirect fire from Singling when they swung eastward. Despite intense smoke and direct fire concentrations, the anti-tank guns in Singling continued to pin down Team A. Vehicles bogged down in the rain-soaked ground, and, as had been true for the past month, the tanks became sitting ducks for accurate heavy artillery barrages and direct fire from Singling and beyond. Corporal John "Swede" Nelsen, tank driver of Company B, 37th Tank Battalion, was sitting in his medium tank *Bottle Baby* in the scant concealment of an apple orchard. "I had the motor off so we could hear the enemy shells come in", said the tanker from Brooklyn. "I had just finished cleaning my periscope and had stuck it back in place when – wham! It sounded and felt like our gun firing, but it wasn't. A shell had hit our turret. I looked back and saw smoke behind me. I was thinking of getting out when – wham – again! And I'll be damned if I didn't have a German armour-piercing shell in my lap. It came through in front of me and must have had just enough force to get through the armour plate and drop. I looked at the slug in my hands. I remember thinking that it felt heavy. It was so hot it burned my gloves. I didn't look at it long, though, I can tell you. In exactly two seconds I was out of that driver's seat. As I slid out of the hatch, another shell clipped the

Below: Map 8a The attack on Singling 5-6 December 1944.

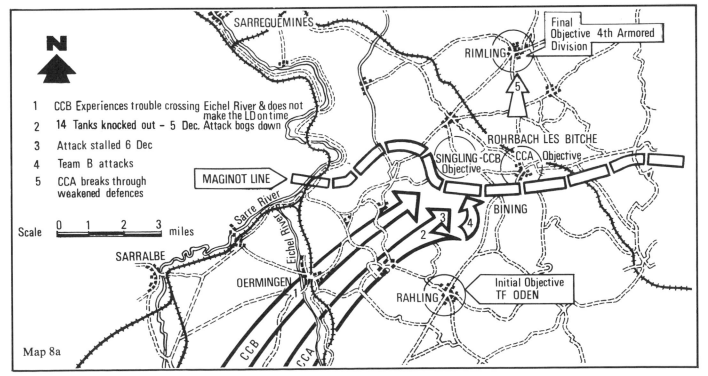

Map 8a

N

1 CCB Experiences trouble crossing Eichel River & does not make the LD on time
2 14 Tanks knocked out - 5 Dec. Attack bogs down
3 Attack stalled 6 Dec
4 Team B attacks
5 CCA breaks through weakened defences

Scale 0 1 2 3 miles

SARREGUEMINES
RIMLING
Final Objective 4th Armored Division
ROHRBACH LES BITCHE
SINGLING -CCB Objective
CCA Objective
MAGINOT LINE
BINING
Sarre River
Eichel River
SARRALBE
OERMINGEN
RAHLING
Initial Objective TF ODEN
CCB
CCA

tank inches from my legs. I dropped into the mud, did some fast crawling until I got to a building, and took time out to find that I wasn't hurt. Of course my gloves weren't much good". Colonel Abrams, deciding that fire alone could not neutralise Singling, decided to eliminate the town and its defenders. Team B, which consisted of the B Companies of the 37th Tank Battalion (Captain James H. Leach) and the 51st Armored Infantry Battalion (1-Lt Daniel M. Belden), was ordered to attack from column to seize and hold the village, which it was later learned to have been defended initially by two infantry companies, three tanks, and five anti-tank guns. Captain Leach was given the order to attack; he informed Lt Belden but, as the infantry was already mounted on the tanks, Lt Belden could not pass the word on even to his platoon leaders. Captain Leach deployed his tanks, putting the 2nd Platoon under 2-Lt James N. Farese on the left; the 1st Platoon, commanded by 1-Lt William F. Goble, on the right; and the 3rd Platoon, under 1-Lt Robert M. Cook, in support. The command tank moved between the 2nd and 1st Platoons in front of the 3rd. As the 2nd Platoon tanks carried no infantry, the three infantry platoons were mounted on the remaining 11 tanks (5 in the 1st Platoon, 4 in the 3rd, the commanding officer's tank, and the artillery observer's). The infantry platoons were widely dispersed; the 11 men of the 2nd rode on four tanks. Before the attack at 1015, Batteries A and B of the 94th Field Artillery Battalion put 107 rounds of HE on Singling. The assault guns of the 37th Tank Battalion took up the smoke mission and continued to fire north of the town until the tanks got on to their objective. Company A of the battalion turned east and throughout the day fired on the Singling-Bining road and to the north. One platoon of tank destroyers, in position to support the attack, actually did little effective firing during the day because heavy enemy artillery fire forced the guns back. The other platoon remained in an assembly area and was moved into Bining the next day.

'As far as the tankers noticed, there was no appreciable return fire from the enemy. As the company approached the town, the 1st and 2nd Platoons swung east and west respectively, and the 3rd Platoon moved in through the gap to come up substantially on a line. The effect then was of an advancing line of 13 tanks on a front a little less than the length of Singling, or about 600 to 700 yards. Only Lt Farese's tank was notably in advance. Leading the tanks of S/Sgt Bernard K. Sowers and Sgt John H. Parks by about 50 yards, Lt Farese moved up the hillside south of Singling and turned left into an orchard. As his tank topped the crest of a slight rise just south of a stone farmyard wall, it was hit three times by armour-piercing shells and immediately was set on fire. Lt Farese and his loader, Pfc William J. Bradley, were killed. The gunner, Cpl Hulmer C. Miller was slightly wounded. The rest of the crew got out. Sowers and Parks backed their tanks in defilade behind the rise and radioed the others not to come up. The shells that hit Lt Farese were probably from a Mark V tank which was parked beside a stone barn, though they may have come from a towed 75mm anti-tank gun in the same general vicinity. In any case, what Lt Farese had run into was a nest of enemy armour and defensive emplacements – a perfect defensive position which the enemy used to the full and against which Team B fought and plotted all day without even minor success. In this area were at least three Mark V tanks, two SP guns, one towed anti-tank, and one machine gun (German .42 or possibly an American .50cal) which successfully blocked every attempt at direct assault or envelopment, and during the day fired at will at all movements across or along the main street and to the south and southeast. Sgt Sowers and Sgt Parks found that if they moved their tanks only so far up the slope as to bare their antennae masts they drew armour-piercing fire. For some time, however, Parks and Sowers were the only ones who suspected the strength of this thicket of enemy defensive armour. They knew that they could not advance, but they had seen only one tank and one gun. The destruction of Lt Farese's tank was, of course, reported to Captain Leach, but Captain Leach at the moment was preoccupied by another more immediately pressing problem, an enemy SP fifty feet in front of him.

The Infantry Attack
'When the two tank platoons carrying the infantry reached a hedge just south of Singling, they slowed up to let the infantry dismount. Lt Belden got off ahead of his platoon leaders. First to reach him was 2-Lt William P. Cowgill, whose platoon assembled most rapidly because the men happened to be riding on tanks relatively close together. Lt Belden told Cowgill to take the left side of town, disregard the first three houses on the south and move in; 2-Lt Theordore R. Price was ordered to take the right side. Belden said to 1-Lt Norman C. Padgett, "Follow up after Cowgill". Padgett commented drily afterwards, "I was in support". That was the plan. Neither leaders nor men had any knowledge of the town or of the enemy. They were to clean out the houses, splitting the work as circumstances dictated. Though all the platoon leaders and a good percentage of the men were recent replacements, they had all had combat experience and had fought in towns before. The enemy facing Team B was

in fact stronger and better armed (particularly in respect to heavy weapons) than the attackers. Nevertheless, before the battle was joined some of the enemy troops had been warned by their own officers that they were facing the 4th Armored Division, "one of the best divisions in the American Army". This they had a chance to discover for themselves in both Singling and Bining as the day wore on. Lt Cowgill (3rd Infantry Platoon) with Pfc John T. Stanton, his radio operator acting this day as runner, came into town ahead of his platoon. They made their way nearly up to the main square before spotting an enemy self-propelled gun (SP) parked beside No 44 [see Sketch Map 8b]. The building, burning from shell fire, clouded the square with thick smoke. Cowgill turned and shouted back a warning to the tanks not to come up. Padgett with two men of his 1st Squad was nearby. He had not waited to assemble his platoon as they were trained to watch him, when they dismounted, and to follow. This they did, though the 2nd Squad was actually held up most of the morning by some house-clearing. At Cowgill's shouted warning, Captain Leach dismounted and advanced along the street ahead of his tank. The SP up to this point was apparently unaware of them, though the commander's head was out of the turret. Padgett, Leach, Cowgill, and the two men started firing to make him button up. Then the SP moved. It backed across the street to the church preparatory to heading west. In the meantime more infantry had come up

from the south. When Lt Belden approached, the street was crowded. Annoyed, he shouted at the men to clear off and fan out into the houses on either side. His shout was less effective than a burst of machine gun fire from the SP which followed the shout by a matter of seconds. The 1st Squad of the 3rd Platoon (Lt Cowgill), which, for the first half hour or so that it remained together, was under command of Cpl Ralph R. Harrington, ducked into houses on the west side of the street. The 2nd Squad, under Sgt John McPhail, retreated hastily into No 45 on the east, and the street was nearly clear. Belden could not see the SP. He stopped a soldier to ask what they were getting ahead. The answer was: "Machine gun". "If it is a machine gun nest", said Belden, "we'll bring up a tank". In the mysterious pathways of rumour, this remark travelled rearward, lost its "if", and resulted in the ordering of the last tank under Sgt Kenneth L. Sandrock of the 1st Tank Platoon to clean out an enemy machine gun nest. Sandrock moved west from his platoon which had driven into the orchard east of town, fired pot shots at the church steeple on the chance that it might be an enemy OP, went on up the south street, and found no machine gun nest. Then, meeting Captain Leach, Sandrock drove his tank in behind No 6, where he remained separated from his platoon for the rest of the day.

'In the meantime the enemy SP at the square had completed its turning and headed west along the main street. Leach continued

Below: Map 8b The fight in the village of Singling 6 December 1944.

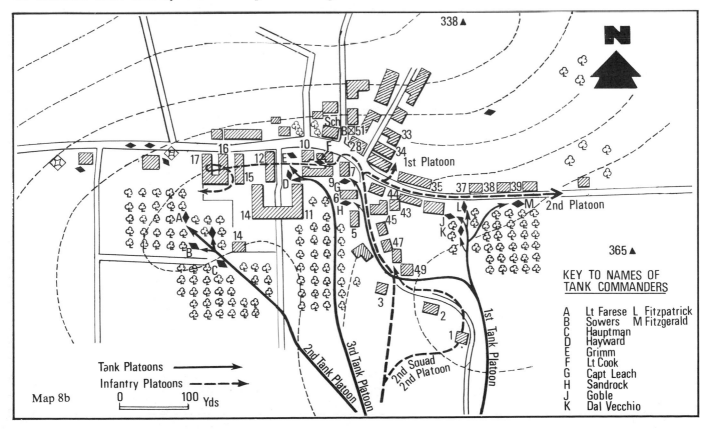

Map 8b

Tank Platoons ⟶
Infantry Platoons ⟶

0   100 Yds

KEY TO NAMES OF
TANK COMMANDERS

A   Lt Farese   L Fitzpatrick
B   Sowers   M Fitzgerald
C   Hauptman
D   Hayward
E   Grimm
F   Lt Cook
G   Capt Leach
H   Sandrock
J   Goble
K   Dal Vecchio

to fire his tommy gun at it. But in so doing he blocked the line of fire of his own tank behind him and the SP escaped. Leach did not attempt to follow. He had received the report about a tank that had knocked out Lt Farese, and decided that it would be wiser to attempt to get the escaping SP from the flank by moving the 3rd Platoon tanks through the west end of the town. He therefore had his own tank back between buildings No 6 and No 7, where he was covered from the west and could command the square, and called Lt Cook. Cook's three tanks, his own, the one commanded by Sgt Giles W. Hayward, and the 105mm assault gun, commanded by Sgt Robert G. Grimm, were advancing on the town between the two southern trails. In front of them the large farm building (No 11) was on fire and clouds of smoke reduced visibility to the north to a few feet. Cook led his tanks to the right of the burning farm with the idea of .cutting across the main street in pursuit of the enemy SP. As they approached, Pvt Charles R. McCreer, Cook's loader, saw Farese get hit in the orchard to his left. He may have informed Cook, or may have assumed that Cook had seen it too. In any case, Cook did not absorb the information and made his next moves in ignorance of the existence of enemy tanks on his left flank. He drove his tank between the corner of the burning barn and the house north of it, No 9. Between these buildings, invisible in the smoke was a low stone retaining wall and about a two foot drop into the walled garden in front of No 11. Hitting this unseen barrier at a 45-degree angle, Cook's tank teetered dangerously on its left tread. For a moment it threatened to overturn, then lumbered on, righting itself. Grimm and Hayward, following, had little trouble as the first tank had broken down the bank. The garden in which the three tanks found themselves was enclosed on the north and west by a four foot concreted stone wall, stepped up to six feet high around the north-west corner. Despite this enclosure, they felt, on emerging from the smoke pall, as naked as if they had suddenly come up on a skyline. In fact, their position was seriously exposed from the north, for the continuous slope of the ground northward for several hundred yards cancelled out the wall as a screen. Immediately across the street were two smaller gardens with low stone walls, and a dirt trail leading down into the valley. Originally, Cook had no intention of staying there. He planned to cross the road, then work around to the west still intent on trapping the SP which he knew was somewhere on his left. He did not know that its gun now commanded the street, and he would have found out too late if Lt Cowgill had not appeared at that moment to warn him. Cowgill's platoon had set out immediately after the escape of the SP from the square to move into the west side of town. Cowgill, himself, with two men of his 1st Squad (Harrington and Pvt Grover C. Alexander), moved along the south side of the street (The other four men of the squad stayed behind near No 7 from which later on they undertook an independent mission to the north). Cowgill, Harrington and Alexander made their way to No 10 and from there could see two German SPs parked on either side of the street 200 yards to the west. It was then that Cowgill, coming around No 10 into the garden into which Cook's tanks had just driven, found Cook and warned him of the enemy. Cowgill said, "There is a Kraut tank behind the third building down to the west". Cook got the impression that the "tank" was located behind a house which he could see on the north side of the street. He therefore, had his tank and Grimm's 105mm chop down the corner of the wall in front of them. This fire probably nettled the enemy into replying, and a round of 75mm struck the northwest corner of No 10 not far from where Cowgill was standing. Cook dismounted and with Cowgill walked around to the east side of the building which had been hit.

'In the meantime the 2nd Squad of Cowgill's platoon under Sgt McPhail had moved on from No 45 into which the SP's machine gun at the square had driven them. Satisfied that there were no enemy in No 45 the seven men crossed the square and entered No 28 a handsome low-lying stone house set back from the street and surrounded by a two foot wall, surmounted by an iron railing. In this house McPhail and his men discovered 12 civilians sheltering in the cellar. A few minutes were consumed in searching them, then the squad set out to continue the sweep of the north side of the street. McPhail and Tech 4 Ben A. Todd emerged through the front door of No 28 and made a dash to the schoolhouse. A third man tried to follow but ducked back when machine gun bullets spattered in the front yard. Then, and for the rest of the day, No 28 was under direct fire from the enemy tanks on the west. McPhail and Todd reached the school; the rest of the squad stayed in No 28. Lt Cowgill, standing on the other side of the street, shouted across to ask McPhail whether he could see the enemy's SPs. He could. Cowgill ordered him to fire. Lt Cook, having seen the true location of the SPs, returned to his tank, and backed it into an alley between No 9 and No 10, just wide enough to let him through. He told Grimm and Hayward about the enemy SPs, asked Grimm whether he thought he could get out of the garden if necessary, and Grimm thought he could. Cook then called Captain Leach and asked whether tanks could be sent around to hit the enemy guns from the south-west. Leach radioed orders to Sowers (2nd

Tank Platoon) to try to go through the burning barn (No 11) and find a way to attack the SPs. Sowers tried, but got only a few yards. Just beyond the wall, the nose of his tank, exposed through the gate to the west, was shot at. Convinced that advance was impossible, Sowers returned to the orchard. Every attempt to deal with the enemy so far had been made in ignorance both of the layout of the town and of the enemy position. This Lt Cowgill set out to remedy and, while Cook manoeuvred his tanks, Cowgill and his two men started on a devious exploratory journey through the houses to the west. At the same time McPhail and Todd, who had fired a few rounds at the SPs, discovered what seemed to them more profitable targets in enemy infantry in the valley to the north. This enemy was also occupying the attention of two other groups of men in town. The four men of Cowgill's 1st Squad (Pvt Joseph C. Bridges, Pvt William M. Convery, Pfc Frank M. O. Asplud, and Pfc L. W. Battles) who had stayed at the square when the squad leader, Harrington, had accompanied Lt Cowgill, spotted 15-18 Germans near a pillbox in the valley. They crossed the street, took up firing positions in the yard of No 28, and shot into the Germans. They thought two were hit before the group dispersed. They continued to fire until an officer across the street by the church shouted at them to stop. The officer was Lt Price (1st Platoon), whose men had come last into town because they had stopped at two small pillboxes south of Singling to take and disarm 11 unresisting Germans. Although Price's mission had been to occupy the east end of town, when he arrived at the square he could see Lt Padgett's (2nd Platoon) men already moving along the houses to the east. Lt Cowgill's men were on the west. Price decided to go north. Tech/Sgt Lovell P. Mitchell with four men cleaned out the houses on the southeast corner of the square while S/Sgt John Sayers and six men took over No 35. Price with the rest of his platoon crossed the street to the back of the church, moved along the hard-surfaced alleyway between the church and No 35. Posting Pvts Rudolph Aguilar and Randall S. Brownrigg at the northeast corner to watch in that direction, Price and four men followed the alley around the north side of the church. At the corner they could see the Germans at the pillbox who had already been spotted by the four 3rd Platoon men. A burp gun was firing from somewhere to the northwest. The steep drop of the Singling ridge to the north made it possible for Price's men to return fire over the roofs of the houses back of No 28. Under cover of this fire Lt Price and Sgt Elmer White planned to work their way into the valley behind the northeast row of houses. But they were checked at the outset by a heavy wire fence which, hooked to the corners of No 34 and No 35, enclosed the alleyway. It was at least six feet high and too exposed to enemy observation to be scaled. It would have to be cut. The platoon wirecutters, however, had been entrusted to a man who two days before had been evacuated, taking the cutters with him. White went into No 34 to look for tools. While he was in there, the Germans in the valley were getting ready to give up. They were encouraged in this not only by the continuing small arms fire of Price's men and the four men of the 3rd Platoon, but also by machine gun fire and HE fire from Lt Cook's tanks. Sergeant Grimm started it by dispatching a lone German a few hundred yards away with 100 rounds of .30cal. Minutes later, Grimm saw six Germans jump up and run into the valley pillbox. In his own words he "closed the door for them with HE". All three tanks also periodically fired HE at the ridge 1,200 yards to the north, more to register the range of the skyline on which German tanks were likely to appear than to engage specific targets. The total effect, however, was to throw a large volume of fire in the direction of a handful of enemy, and shortly Lt Price saw white cloths wave from the pillbox. It was then that he ordered the men across the street to cease fire. 12 Germans walked up the hill and surrendered to Price. One who spoke some English reported that there were five more in the valley who were anxious to surrender but were afraid to come out. After all the Germans had been disarmed, Price sent one back down the hill to corral his comrades. At that moment, however, a volley of enemy mortar and artillery struck the square. One shell hit No 34 and Sgt White inside was wounded in the head by fragments and wood splinters. Sayers and Pvt Randall S. Brownrigg outside and Cpl Frank B. McElwee in No 43 were slightly wounded. Price and his men ducked back from the alley, and began occupying houses on the square where they were to remain all day. Although Price believed that the enemy held the houses to the north, he decided not to attack them, because by advancing north he would move out of contact with the platoons on his flanks. No more was seen of the German emissary or the five volunteers for capture. The 11 still in the possession of the 1st Platoon were sent down the road south. Just as these started off, two more walked up the hill to the schoolhouse, and surrendered to McPhail and Todd. McPhail escorted these two across the square to the street south. There, seeing Price's 11 walking down the street, he motioned to his two to fall in with them and, himself, returned to the school. He and Todd then climbed to the second storey, and resumed the business of shooting at the enemy in the valley. The four men of the 1st Squad decided then to go down to the pillbox to get whatever Germans might still be in it. They found none, but did draw machine gun fire from the direction of Welschoff Farm. Battles was wounded in the leg and the squad was pinned in place for several hours.

'From the east end of town, Lt Padgett (2nd Infantry Platoon) had also seen the enemy infantry in the valley, but he had seen two other things which worried him far more – a rocket launcher firing from about 800 yards west of Welschoff Farm, and seven enemy tanks on a ridge northeast. Padgett was in No 39, which he had reached with his 1st Squad without difficulty after going through the three small houses to the west. These houses were occupied only by a few scared civilians who were rounded up and sheltered in No 39. House No 39 was a fine place to be. Outwardly just another farm house, it was actually a fortress, with walls of three foot concrete reinforced with steel girders. Nevertheless, Padgett was still worried. Protection enough from artillery and the rocket launcher (which Padgett decided was shooting short anyway), the house would not be of much avail against the enemy tanks. More reassuring were the four tanks of the 1st Platoon (Lt Goble) which pulled into position in the orchard opposite No 39 about the same time that Padgett arrived there. The enemy armour, though threatening, was still too far away for direct action. Padgett sent his runner to report the situation to Lt Belden and also to find the 2nd Squad of his own platoon and bring them up. When the runner failed to return in what seemed to Padgett a reasonable time, he sent out another man, Pvt Lonnie G. Blevins, on the same mission. Blevins left on his run under the impression that the infantry company CP was at No 3 where it had first been set up by Belden on entering the town. Actually Belden had stayed in that house less than half an hour, only long enough to set up the radio and notify the 51st Infantry Battalion that he was in town. He then moved to No 28. Blevins reached No 44, where he met a man of Price's platoon and was warned not to cross the square which enemy guns to the west covered. Blevins went around No 44 and on up the road south to No 3. Finding no one, he returned along the west side of the street and got as far as No 5. A tanker, one of Sandrock's or the forward observer's crew, waylaid Blevins and told him to take charge of a prisoner who had just walked up to the tank and surrendered. At No 7 Blevins with his prisoner met Battles who had not yet started for the valley pillbox. Battles took temporary charge of the prisoner while Blevins dashed through a burst of machine gun fire across to No 28. In a few minutes he re-appeared in the door and motioned to Battles to send the prisoner over. Half his

mission accomplished, Blevins still had to find the 2nd Squad. By luck he met them near No 44 and delivered his message to Pfc Phillip E. Scharz in charge.

'Scharz's squad had already with little effort accomplished one of the most notable successes of the day. Investigating the southernmost house of the town, which the rest of the infantry, entering between No 2 and No 3, had bypassed, they found a Frenchman and asked whether there were any Germans inside. He shook his head, but Scharz's men, noticing a radio antenna thrusting out of a cellar window, were suspicious Four of them surrounded the house, and Scharz and Pfc Lewis R. Dennis went in. In the cellar they found 28 German enlisted men and two officers. None offered any resistance. They were frisked and evacuated. A search of the house then revealed large stores of small arms and ammunition. When the squad emerged, they met on the road the 13 prisoners sent back by Lt Price and McPhail. Having discovered enemy in one house, they searched with slow caution the others along the street, and so arrived late at the square where Blevins found them. When Blevins had completed his mission of telling Scharz to take his squad east, the enemy artillery and mortar which had wounded four of Price's men was falling around the church. Blevins crossed the street to No 7 to "see Battles". With Battles now was 1st Sgt Dellas B. Cannon who was on his way to the CP. Cannon sprinted across to No 28, Blevins followed, and then worked east back to No 39. Cannon had not been in the CP long before a round of 75mm hit the building, Pfc John E. Tsinetakes was scratched by dislodged plaster but there were no other casualties. The fire had quite possibly been drawn from one of the enemy SPs by the recent activity in the street. In any case the

Below: GIs of 5th Infantry Division clearing the former German SS barracks in Metz. */IWM*

shot decided Cannon to go west to where the SPs were and "get a closer look". He invited McPhail who had just come over from the school to go along. The two set out, taking almost exactly the route that Lt Cowgill, unknown to them, had already followed twice. Sgt Grimm had started Cowgill on his first journey from the garden, which the 3rd Platoon tanks occupied, by blasting open the door of No 12 with a burst of .50cal. Cowgill and his two men entered and climbed to the attic. They found that, although they could see the two enemy SPs through the damaged tiling on the roof, they could not see beyond. They continued exploration westward. For one reason or another they were unable to reach the roofs of the next three buildings. In the last (No 17) they found their progress blocked by the lack of an opening of any kind in the west wall. They backtracked through the courtyard between No 16 and No 15 and then walked through an opening in the south wall out into a garden-orchard walled with concreted stone like all the Singling gardens. They crawled to a gap in the wall and found themselves within spitting distance of the two SPs. Beyond, in an arc or line not more than 200 yards distant, they saw the outlines of three enemy tanks. They returned at once to Lt Cook's position to report. Cowgill sent word to Lt Belden that there were "five enemy tanks on the west" and then he took Lt Cook back to the OP at the wall. Harrington and Alexander were left at No 12 which Cowgill decided was the most suitable spot he had seen for his platoon headquarters. When Cook returned from his reconnaissance, he was impressed with both the strength of the German position and the difficulty of dislodging them. Their command of the main street and of the nose of the ridge west of town made it impossible for tanks to attack them.

Artillery, it seemed, despite the proximity of our own troops, was the most logical answer, and Cook therefore went to look for the observer, 1-Lt Donald E. Guild. Guild was in the infantry company CP with Lt Belden and Capt Leach. When Cook joined them, the four officers discussed the problem. Lt Guild felt that artillery could not be brought down without unduly endangering friendly troops. Mortar fire would be fine, but the infantry had brought no mortars because they had too few men to man them and carry ammunition. The mortar squad, down to three men, were armed with a bazooka. Lt Cook suggested that the street might be smoked with grenades and the tank mortars. Behind that screen the tanks might cross the street and attack the enemy from the northeast. Actually he felt that the smoke alone would be enough to force the SPs to withdraw. The proposal was not seriously considered because Captain Leach preferred to try the infantry bazooka. This was the decision and the job was given to Lt Cowgill. He sent back to ask Belden for a bazooka, and riflemen to protect it. His plan was to shoot at the Germans from the attic of his CP. Lt Guild advised that it would take the SP about two minutes to elevate its gun to fire, and that was considered ample time to launch the rockets and move out. Belden sent Pfc Kenneth L. Bangert and Pvt Frank LeDuc down to Cowgill with the headquarters bazooka. Headquarters runner, Pfc Melvin P. Flynn, went over to No 7 occupied by seven men of the machine gun and mortar squads. His message apparently was, "Lieutenant Cowgill wants some riflemen to protect his bazookamen". What happened was that S/Sgt John W. Herring, the two men of his mortar squad who carried the second bazooka of the company, and S/Sgt Patrick H. Dennis, leader of the machine gun squad,

Below: German prisoners march out of Fort Jeanne d'Arc following its capitulation to Third Army on 13 December 1944./*US Army*

went down to No 12; the other three men of the machine gun squad remained all the rest of the day at No 7 where, having no field of fire, they were unable to set up their gun.

Stalemate in Singling

'While Cowgill's men got ready to attack the German tanks on the west, a series of incidents occurred to suggest that enemy armour might be forming up on the north for a counter-attack on Singling. Tanks to the north were observed moving east; prepared artillery concentrations were laid on the town; the enemy on the west renewed his interest in our tanks in that sector (2nd Platoon); and finally, tanks came into the east side of town. The enemy tanks (three to five) moving on the north apparently along a road were spotted and reported by Sgt Grimm, but as the range was extreme, he did not fire. Furthermore, Grimm's gun was trained through the gap in the wall to the northwest against the SP threat. Sgt Hayward had adjusted on the north ridge and Grimm left that zone of fire to him. Lt Cook moved his tank into the courtyard of the cluster of buildings (No 8 – No 10) where he could observe north. Suddenly just west of town a white signal flare shot upward. Almost immediately a short, intense artillery concentration rocked the town. Mixed with shells of light or medium calibre were some rockets and some mortar. The tankers' later estimate was that the fire was about equivalent to a battalion concentration of five minutes' duration, that at times as many as 20 shells hit in the same instant. In the 2nd Tank Platoon sector the shelling followed by only a few minutes an incident to which the tankers paid little attention at the time. A dismounted German suddenly appeared on the rise in front of them and walked across the orchard less than 50 yards away. Before the tanks could adjust fire on him, he had gone. The intense shelling, which started almost immediately, forced the tanks to back a few yards to a cabbage patch beside the orchard trail. When the artillery fire broke off, they stayed where they were, and there by a curious freak Sgt Hauptman a few minutes later lost his tank. A German AP shell hit the crest of the rise 100 yards in front of him, ricocheted off the ground, and ploughed into the right side of Hauptman's turret. His loader, Pfc William J. McVicker, was killed. If the German tanks west of town aimed that shell to carom into the tanks parked where they had been observed by the lone infantryman, the accuracy of this shot was most remarkable. The reaction of the tankers at the time, however, was that they were still not defiladed from the enemy northwest. Lt Cook, to whom Hauptman reported his loss in the temporary absence of Captain Leach, ordered Sowers and Parks (the remaining tanks of the 2nd Platoon) to get their tanks into shelter. Both drove up behind the 3rd Platoon in the lee of No 11. They were moving when Grimm casually turned his field glasses to a pillbox on the ridge 1,200 yards north where he had seen a few enemy infantry minutes previously. He got his glasses on the spot just in time to see the long gun tube of the German tank's 75mm flame and fire directly at him. The round hit nearby, and Grimm had a split second to decide whether to shoot back or run for it. He figured that his 105mm without power traverse could not be laid in less than 20 seconds. That was too long. He threw his tank in gear and backed out of the garden. He had just started when a second round hit Hayward's tank on the sprocket, crippling it. In the next few seconds Hayward was hit four times and the tank began to burn. Gunner Cpl Angelo Ginoli and the bowgunner Pvt John H. Furlow were killed; Hayward and his loader, Pfc Vern L. Thomas, were wounded. Grimm made good his escape through the opening between No 9 and No 11. Outside, the tank bogged down in the heavy mud, and the crew evacuated while Grimm got Sowers to pull him out. The 2nd and 3rd Platoons, Sgt Sandrock of the 1st Platoon, the command and the artillery observer's tanks were now all bunched and immobilised in the area southwest of the square which, covered on three sides by buildings, was the only relatively safe place in town for tanks. It was becoming increasingly apparent to both infantry and tanks that, with the small forces at their disposal and against an enemy who had at least equal strength and every terrain advantage, they could not hope to secure their position in town by attack. They had, instead, to make such dispositions as would complement the enemy's stalemate and wait it out. They were expecting momentarily relief by units of Combat Command B. Colonel Abrams had already called Captain Leach to tell him the relieving companies were on their way. In the meantime there was no point in incurring needless casualties. Lt Price, after having four men lightly wounded by artillery, gave strict orders to his platoon to stay inside unless the Germans counter-attacked. Lt Padgett's men holed up in the cellar of their fortress house and the lieutenant himself found a bed which, as long as there was no place to go, he made his personal headquarters. While the enemy tanks, however, on the north still threatened to attack, Padgett was very busy trying to find ways to deal with them. He sent his runner, Blevins, across the street to warn the 1st Platoon tanks (Lt Goble) in the orchard. (Goble's vision to the northeast was obstructed by a 6-7-foot brush and apple-tree hedge, and by houses and brush on the north side of the road). Lt Padgett himself then set out to find the artillery observer to see whether a concentration could not be put on the enemy to discourage if not destroy him. He tried four times to walk down the street to the company CP; three times he was turned back by spurts of machine gun bullets on the west side of No 37. The fourth time he got through to report to Lt Belden, but he could not find Lt Guild. It was late in the afternoon when Padgett returned to his own CP.

'While Padgett had been trying to get to Belden, Lt Guild, the observer, had already spotted the enemy tanks himself from the roof of his OP, No 33, and had informed Captain Leach. Leach took the warning personally to Lt Goble. Goble, figuring that if the Germans attacked they would come either down the road or in back of the houses opposite, had Sgt Robert G. Fitzgerald on the right move his tank down the hill to within 15 yards of the edge of the road, where he could observe better to the northeast. Fitzgerald kept his gun sights at 1,400 yards, the range to the northerly ridge where the enemy was reported. The first tank to appear, however, drew up behind No 37 and No 38

less than 150 yards away, heading towards the church. The enemy Mark V and Fitzgerald saw each other at about the same time, but neither could immediately fire. While the enemy started to traverse his turret, Fitzgerald brought his gun down. He shot first, and at point-blank range, put the first round into the Mark V, setting it on fire. One man jumped out and ran behind one of the houses. Fitzgerald fired two more rounds into the burning tank. Later, on warning by Lt Padgett's infantry that more enemy tanks were approaching from the northeast, he drove his tank through the hedge and east along the road almost to the bend where observation north and east was clear. He saw an enemy tank, but before he could adjust his sights the German fired smoke and in a few seconds disappeared as effectively as an octopus behind its self-made cloud and escaped. Rockets then began to fall close to Fitzgerald's tank. Whether this was aimed fire from the battery near Welschoff Farm or simply a part of the miscellaneous area concentration on the town, Fitzgerald did not stay to find out. He

Below: Maj-Gen Walton H. Walker, CG XX Corps, leaves a building in Metz with French Army officers after a ceremony in which he formally returned the liberated town to the French residents./*US Army*

retired westward to the concealment of the hedge, and there, leaving his tank, crossed with Lt Goble to Padgett's CP. From the house they could see a Mark V in the valley northeast, apparently parked with its gun covering the road east, facing, that is, at right angles to the tankers' observation. Fitzgerald went back to try a shot at it. Again he moved his tank east, getting a sight on the enemy between two trees. The second round was a hit; one more fired the tank. He then shot a round or two at another Mark V facing him about 800 yards away, at which Sgt Emil Del Vecchio on the hill behind him was also firing. Both 75mm and 76.2mm shells, however, bounced off the front armour plate of the enemy. Fitzgerald decided to move back to his hedge. Back in No 39 again he saw an enemy SP moving east in the vicinity of Welschoff Farm. Rather than risk exposing his tank again by moving it out to the east, Fitzgerald decided to wait until the SP came around behind the farm and emerged into his field of fire. But the SP did not emerge. Whether concealed among the farm buildings, it fired into the 1st Platoon tanks cannot certainly be determined. But in any case, a short while after it had disappeared, two rounds of AP hit Lt Goble's tank in quick succession. The first round set it on fire and wounded Goble and his gunner, Cpl Therman E. Hale. The second round penetrated the turret, then apparently richocheted inside until its momentum was spent and finally landed in the lap of the driver, Tech 5 John J. Nelsen. Nelsen dropped the hot shell, scrambled out, and with the loader, Pvt Joseph P. Cocchiara, ran from the burning tank. In the excitement they headed the wrong way and high-tailed up the main street into the centre of town. There they paused long enough to ask some infantrymen where the tanks were. Directed southward, they eventually came on Sgt Sowers' tank and got inside. As soon as Lt Goble was hit, S/Sgt John J. Fitzpatrick took command of the platoon and ordered them to back over the ridge behind them into defilade from the enemy north. As they backed, a round of HE exploded in front of Del Vecchio's tank, splattering it with fragments. The enemy continued to fire at Goble's tank, but the others reached the cover of the hill without loss.

'On the other side of town Lt Cowgill's bazookas in the attic of No 12 were getting ready to fire at one enemy SP. (One of the two guns in the street had withdrawn by this time). In the garden east of No 12 Sgt Hayward's tank was burning. McPhail, leader of the 2nd Squad, and Company 1st Sergeant Cannon were on their way westward to have a look at the SPs, unaware that the reconnaissance had already been made and action taken as a result of it. They sprinted past the burning tank, picked up Harrington at the chapel, and followed Lt Cowgill's previous route to the wall beside No 17. Through the same gap Cowgill had used to observe, the three men fired at Germans standing near the tanks and pillboxes. They hit one who rolled down the slope. After half a dozen rounds, they moved back. Cannon and Harrington went to the basement of No 12, where they found S/Sgt Patrick H. Dennis and S/Sgt Harold A. Hollands, both with rifles, preparing to cover from the basement windows the bazookamen, then getting set to fire through the roof. One of the two bazookas with old-type firing mechanism failed to go off. From the other, the three men in the attic, launched five rounds in turn at the SP. Only the last hit and it did no more than knock a fragment off the right side of the turret. It did, however, cause the crew to jump out, and two were shot by the four men in the basement. Hardly had this happened when a Mark V drew up alongside the damaged SP and sent a round crashing into the side of No 12. At about the same time another shell from the north struck the building at its foundations, showering the men in the cellar with plaster. It was a narrow escape on both scores, but no one was hurt. Cowgill moved his men to No 13, which turned out to be another of Singling's thick-walled fortress-farms. Here the 3rd Platoon sat out the second of the enemy's short, sharp artillery concentrations, which scored three hits on the building but did little damage.

Singling is Cleared
'Combat Command B, relieved Team B in Singling that night, and elements of the 12th Armored Division took over the mission the text day. With Team B's attack attracting the bulk of the enemy's attention and available troops to Singling, Task Force Oden of Combat Command A bypassed to the east and overran the single enemy rifle company remaining in defence of Bining and Rohrbach. The stubborn enemy defence had been breached by an audacious attack by two understrength companies.

'The Fourth was the only one of the Army's World War II armoured divisions which did not adopt an official nickname. Newsmen and headline writers supplied such noms-de-guerre as "Crack", "Rolling", "Rip-Roaring", "Phantom", "Hard-Hitting", "Patton's Pace Setters", and "Spearpoint of the Spearhead".

' "They shall be known by their deeds alone!" said then wartime Commander, Maj-Gen John S. Wood, when asked to designate a nickname for the 4th. For 4th Armored troopers, this has always been name enough'.

Below: Pfc Walter Dabic, a medic with 9th Armd Inf Bn, samples his outfit's first fried egg of the year, near the Siegfried Line, 18 February 1945./6 Armd Div Assoc/George F. Hofmann

Left: American artillerymen relaxing in a bivouac area in Germany, after hard fighting inside enemy territory. Despite the peaceful scene there is a slit trench with substantial overhead cover behind the pup tents just in case it's needed. /*IWM*

Below: Private Leslie Couglas liked the protection of slabs in a cemetery where he dug his foxhole near Arracourt, France, but I doubt if he managed to persuade anyone to share it with him!/*6 Armd Div Assoc /George F. Hofmann*

Bottom: When you are tired enough you can sleep anywhere! Two worn out GIs share a foxhole somewhere in France. Note the equipment packs, pouches, water bottles, ammo and grenades close at hand around the edges of the foxhole. (The grenades are the standard Mk2 A1 Fragmentation Grenade.)/*IWM*

A Pictorial Miscellany

As in my other books on British and German formations, I am including a pictorial miscellany of soldiers' memories, this time featuring the GIs of the United States Army in North West Europe, taken between July 1944 and the end of the war. The photographs do not deal with the bloody business of making war, but rather the basic mechanics of living 'in the field', with all its attendant hazards. The pictures show GIs making the best of the difficulties which beset civilised man, unaccustomed as he is to living rough, when he has to improvise and make do with whatever comforts he can scrounge. I have included pictures of doughboys with the local people, particularly the girls they met en route to Germany and eventual victory. I have also shown, all too briefly, some of those wonderful people who followed the troops, for example the Red Cross girls, with their inexhaustible supplies of hot coffee and doughnuts; the entertainers, who travelled the world performing in barns and fields, on improvised stages and in the backs of trucks. Lastly, I have included just one of the splendid newspapers and magazines produced for the armed forces, which kept them in touch with home and with the rest of the world outside their immediate combat area. I'm afraid that I have made my selection purely on subject appeal rather than always sticking rigidly to photographs of actual Third Army soldiers. However, as I explained in the opening chapter of this book, the pictures are, I'm sure, representative of life throughout the victorious Allied armies as they liberated Europe from the Nazi yoke.

Left: This GI has pitched his pup tent in the mud and water of an unfinished German tank trap – what a place to choose! /*IWM*

Below: Infantrymen take a brief respite from battle in the taproom of a deserted public house in Tessy sur Vire, 3 August 1944./*IWM*

Right: Smoke and chunks of rockhard earth fill the air, as GIs blast a foxhole for a dugout in the frozen, snow covered ground somewhere in Belgium. The bitter winter weather produced many problems, for example, 6 Armd Div found it was so cold, that the only way to get the grease and oil out of the gun barrels of their new Shermans (armed with 76mm high velocity guns) was to pour petrol into the barrels and strike a match, which melted the grease sufficiently to clear the bores! Howard McNeill of A Company 68th Tank Battalion was surprised that 'we weren't blown to hell and back!' (Taken from *The Super Sixth* by George F. Hofmann.)/*US Army*

Above right: An explosive couch. Private Herbert Reffne, an ammunition bearer with 76th Infantry Division, catches up on a little sleep atop some ammunition boxes./*US Army*

Right: A soldier's best friend is his rifle. A GI inspects the barrel of his carbine as he sits on the edge of his snow covered foxhole. No matter what the living conditions might be that was one item of personal gear which was always kept clean!/*US Army*

Left: Sgt John Opanowski, a member of the 10th Armd Div, emerges from a dugout built under the snow in the Bastogne area, where his unit was taking cover from heavy German artillery fire./*US Army*

A Roof Over One's Head

Like the soldiers of the American frontier army who, towards the end of the last century, fought the Indian wars in the 'Wild West', half a 'pup' tent (a two-man shelter) was normally home for most GIs, but it was combined in this war with the inevitable slit trench, with or without overhead cover. Sometimes it was possible to find more exotic places to shelter, such as the 'tomb with a view' or the cellar abounding with liquid refreshment which I have featured.

An Army Marches on its Stomach

Along with booze and broads the subject of food was never far away from soldiers' thoughts in this as in any other campaigns, so I have included a few scenes of GIs at 'chow', plus one of the inevitable 'KP' or 'cookhouse fatigues' as they are known in the British Army. There were five types of rations in the US Army, viz: A – all fresh or frozen food. This was usually only served in permanent quarters or camps, so the GIs of Third Army mostly said goodbye to Scale A when they left the UK. B – sometimes called 'Ten in One' as it consisted of enough food for three meals for ten men for one day. This pack contained powdered eggs, powdered milk, cereals, coffee, canned butter, canned

Right: You can't escape 'KP' even in the front line! Last night these soldiers of A Company, 9th Armored Infantry Battalion, 6 Armd Div, were routing the Germans from their forts in the Siegfried Line, today they are peeling potatoes on KP, 22 February 1945. */6 Armd Div Assoc/George F. Hofmann*

Below: Stray cows were always fair game!*/IWM*

Bottom: Stanley Moore, James Martin and Warren Tilkins of 6th Armd Div receiving coffee from Red Cross Clubmobile worker Natalie Fullan./*6 Armd Div Assoc/George F. Hofmann*

roast beef and other meats, canned fruit, dried vegetables, crackers (ie biscuits), jam etc. Two hot and one cold meal could be served from this ration pack. C – small cans of mixtures of meat, vegetables, beans, jam, crackers, powdered drinks, sugar, cereal etc. D – an emergency ration of solid rich chocolate. K – these were done up in neat, waterproof cardboard packages about the thickness of an average book, but narrower. The outside was camouflaged so that if it was left on the ground it would not be seen from the air. Each package contained one meal for one man and was marked either breakfast, dinner or supper. Breakfast contained a fruit bar, Nescafe, sugar, crackers and a small tin of ham and eggs. Dinner and Supper contained a can of cheese or potted meat, crackers, orange or lemon powder, sugar, chocolate or other sweets and chewing gum.

Both C and K rations could be eaten cold or heated if preferred (and battle conditions permitted!) and each man carried one or two meals on his person whilst all vehicles had more K rations on board. Many GIs carried paraffin pocket heaters or candles, and small gasoline stoves were issued to outposts, wire crews (signallers who repaired telephone lines) and other small groups. All units had large two-burner gasoline ranges and whenever possible, kitchens were set up where hot meals could be cooked and the men were then either rotated back to them or the hot food sent up in insulated cans. Frequently in the preparation of hot meals, a mixture of the various rations was used. All, particularly

K rations, were said to be well balanced and rich in vitamins.

'Shifting troops, the press of campaign – but the men seldom go hungry. The mess sergeant tries to send forward two hot meals a day; cereal, hotcakes, coffee for breakfast; meat, potatoes, two vegetables, bread and butter or jam, dessert, more coffee for supper. The food is placed steaming hot in Marmite cans – large tri-sectioned, thermos-type containers – enough food in one can for fifty men. The sergeant, a couple of cooks, and if possible the mail orderly, go along with the mess truck. Mail to the front-line soldier is voted as vital as calories and ammunition. Each vehicle tries to get as near its own company as possible; an area behind a protecting hill is an ideal spot. Marmites are placed about ten yards apart and the doughboys infiltrate for their mess kits and chow, eating in as dispersed locations as possible lest they make a target for jerry. After the meal the kits are returned to the kitchen, to be brought out clean on the next trip. Often the food is prepared on as little as ninety minutes' notice. But there are no epicureans in combat, only toiling humans who have learned every trick of bodily privation short of extended thirst and hunger. . . .'

That was how the unofficial history of the 76th 'Onaway' Infantry Division described 'chow time'. Sometimes, however, things didn't go so smoothly, as George F. Hofmann explains in his splendid history of the 6th Armored Division entitled *The Super Sixth*: 'It was Thanksgiving in the mud of Lorraine. All units who were fortunate to have kitchens had turkeys – others would get it later. Headquarters Battery, 231st Armored Field Artillery Battalion, was in position just south of Leyviller. Their kitchen crew prepared a dinner of turkey with all the trimmings and began serving the artillerymen who eagerly filed past the chow line with mess kits in hand. Just as the Headquarters Battery personnel started to dig into the turkey and dressing, a German round came screaming in and burst a short distance away. Mess kits went flying everywhere, and in quick order the artillerymen were flat on their bellies face deep in the Lorraine mud. The only casualties were a few spilled mess kits, the worst case being Sergeant John P. Moylan's, known as the 'mouthpiece'

Below: An American Red Cross worker passes out the doughnuts and coffee at an Army rest camp in Belgium./*IWM*

because of his legal expertise. "The first time in my Army career that I ever got the drumstick. My mouth was watering at the thought of tearing into its luscious meat when that shell came whistling over. I fell flat on my face and my mess kit went flying. When I finally picked myself up the coveted drumstick was lying (sic) in a manure pile". No doubt Moylan had a few other choice words to say.'

Mail from Home
One of the biggest morale boosters in any army is an efficient mail service, and as one might expect the US Army mail service was invariably excellent. Third Army's Postal Services dealt with enormous quantities of letters and parcels in both directions, first class mail normally coming in by air. 'The day ended on a happy note for some of the combatants, especially B Company of the 25th Armored Engineer Battalion. Seven bags of mail arrived with some of the first Christmas parcels, giving the morale of the company a great boost. Everyone seems to be answering letters this evening.'*

The Super Sixth by George F. Hofmann.

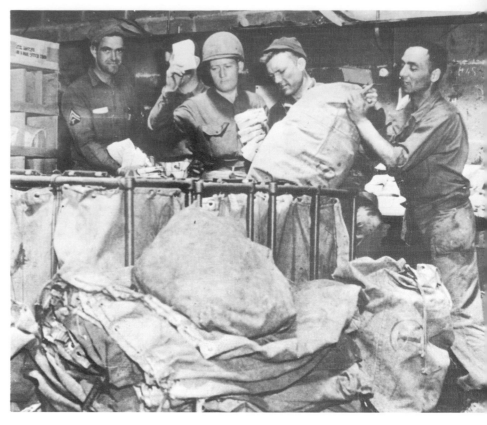

Above: Letters from home 1. Mail for front line troops being sorted in an Army Post Office, somewhere in France./*IWM*

Left: Letters from home 2. The crew of a General Stuart light tank with 5th Infantry Division, read their mail in Schwanheim, Germany, March 1945./*US Army*

Below left: Gathered around a camp fire, behind the front lines, soldiers read mail from home./*US Army*

Various Comforts

Hard liquor was not always easy to obtain but occasionally there were windfalls, such as when Combat Command A of 6th Armored Division captured the German communication headquarters for the Brest peninsula, which was located at Pontivy – 1,000 cases of cognac and champagne, over 100,000 litres of red wine stored in large wooden casks, and hundreds of bottles of assorted wines. It did not take long for the word to get out. Charlie Barbour of the 86th Recon drove his CO back to Pontivy and loaded up the jeep with liquor. Others opened their 10-in-1 rations and drank wine. Others left with as much liquor as they could carry. When Corps heard about the cache of liquor, they immediately investigated and before long most of it was removed, except for the 100,000 litres of wine which were given to the French and a number of bottles that were left with Lt Hughes' Civil Affairs Section. 'We kept what we thought would do our small detachment for the duration of the war. In sixty days our supply was gone.'*

* *The Super Sixth* by George F. Hofmann.

Other 'pleasures of the flesh' were equally hard to come by and even then, subject to problems not experienced in civilian life, as is evidenced in this amusing quote from *The Super Sixth*:

'Other members of the 6th Armored Division had reasons for not moving out for the attack on the 8th, but not the same reason as expressed by the Division Commander. A couple of starved studs from C Company, 44th Armored Infantry Battalion, found refuge in Nancy with some local "ladies of the night". The platoon sergeant told Corporal Bob Brooke to go to the "cat house" and get them out. Being in a most comfortable position between the sheets and not willing to trade sex for combat, the reluctant infantrymen told Brooks to "go to hell and move out without us". The CO alerted the MPs who spurted for the comfortable residence and knocked on the door through which a soft reply came: "Come in quickly, honey, and quietly shut the door". "Come in, honey, hell" replied the MPs; and the armoured infantrymen from C Company gazed out from under the sheets which were quickly replaced with fatigues and the environment of military combat and a possible date with one of Patton's "Valkyries"!'

Below: Vive Uncle Sam! GIs received a real welcome at the little village of Montcuit, where they were met by farmers on the hot, dusty road, and given a cool drink of wine./*IWM*

Right: 'How you gonna keep 'em down on the farm now that they've seen Paree?'/*IWM*

Below: How to learn French 1. These two GIs are trying hard to concentrate on their French phrase book, but I think 'teacher' must have been quite a distraction./*IWM*

Left: How to learn French 2. *Avez-vous une jolie jeune fille madame?/IWM*

Below left: French girls show their gratitude to liberating GIs in the nicest possible way!/*IWM*

Below: A young French girl wields a skilful needle as she makes a Star Spangled Banner to wave during liberation celebrations in her village. /*IWM*

Right: Wash, rinse, sterilise. 777th Anti-aircraft Battalion soldiers washing their mess kits after three days of rain in a bivouac area near Nancy. */6 Armd Div Assoc/George F. Hofmann*

Below right: Washboard Blues. Private Harold 'Professor' Shepherd, washes clothes on a quiet day at the front, near Nancy. He was a school teacher back home./*IWM*

Above: GIs ride 'liberated' horses they captured from the Germans in Chambois after Third Army had liberated the town, 21 August 1944. */US Army*

Right: American soldiers help French farmers in the St Malo area to harvest their bumper crops, which for the first time in four years will be all theirs. */IWM*

Below right: Doing his smalls. A GI gets some advice on how to beat the dirt out of his underwear at a communal laundry post in Cherbourg. */US Army*

Other forms of relaxation, just as satisfying, were, however, allowed. Nothing could have been more wonderful than the luxury of a hot shower as this soldier of 76th Division remembers:

'The hill was quiet now. Only the broken trees and churned earth were reminders of the hell that had broken loose there. From the scattered pillboxes which a few days ago had sheltered Nazi troops came the voices of tired men relaxing after their ordeal. Christmas mail and packages had just reached them and were being opened in weather that was almost like a Spring day back home. Farther away in an open field near a small Luxembourg village, several hundred grimy, mudcaked fighters had been trucked to a Quartermaster shower unit, the first hot showers since the division had left England. "I had to travel through France, Belgium and most of Luxembourg to get a chance of hot water and soap", said S/Sgt Philmon A. Erickson, "but boy, it was worth it".'

Left: An ambulance driver, somewhere in France, gets his first opportunity to shave in four days. The rear view mirror of his vehicle provides a handy shaving mirror./*IWM*

Top: A small French stream provides comfort for the 'Barking Dogs' of these two infantrymen./*IWM*

Above: Seated on a petrol can, feet in a canvas bucket, this GI really looks at peace with the world, as he washes off some of the battlefield grime./*IWM*

USO Operations

All those who served with the American Armed forces will remember the magnificent work done by the USO (United Service Organisations) who not only provided camp shows all over the world, but ran clubs, mobile canteens and special services for troops in transit. The last function could reach enormous proportions when one remembers how many thousands of men were being transported within the United States alone. Typical of this transit problem was the town of Sayre, Pennsylvania, where the local USO committee offered to feed troops on trains when they made a brief stop there. By the end of the war they had served over half a million soldiers, all satisfied customers. One day, early in the war, they were told to expect three troop trains, however, by 4am the next morning not three but seven trains had stopped. They had fed 30,000 men. When the last train pulled out there was not a drop of milk, a bottle of coke or a crust of bread left in the entire town! There was no typical USO club and such unusual structures as churches, log cabins, a museum, a castle, a barn, railway sleeping cars and many other strange places were used. The USO programme varied greatly from club to club depending on the needs and circumstances of their potential customers. Dancing and meeting girls was rated as the most popular activity at USO clubs, with eating a fairly good second. However, when asked what they did the last time they were in a USO, the list in order of frequency was: write a letter, read a magazine, listen to the radio, talk to girls, listen to records, play games, meet buddies, see a movie, take a shower. At the peak in March 1944, there were a total of 3,035 USO clubs, lounges and mobiles all over the world, serving 12 million US Servicemen. As with the clubs there was no standard USO theatre, camp shows entertained huge audiences numbering as many as 15,000 GIs seated on the ground, as few as 25 men in jeeps stationed

Below: Standing on the back of a truck Bing Crosby sings to a group of GIs on the 'Cow pasture' circuit in France. /USO Inc

at a lonely outpost, or beside the hospital bed of a single wounded soldier. Many big names were among the hundreds of entertainers who gave freely of their time and talents. One of the first performers to go overseas, and one of the few to complete four overseas tours and later to set a record of 25 years continuous service, was Bob Hope. The troops loved him. He could walk out on a GI stage and recite Mother Goose and break up the audience. From its inception in February 1941 to the end of 1947, Camp Shows Inc gave a staggering 428,521 performances to a total audience of 212,974,401! At the height of production, immediately following VE-Day, its curtain rose 700 times a day. Camp Shows enlisted and co-ordinated the greatest number of entertainers performing to the largest audiences, playing the most locations and travelling the greatest number of miles in the history of show business.

Above: Glamour at the Front. Marlene Dietrich who also helped entertain the troops with USO road shows, is pictured here with a crowd of GIs in Normandy in 1944. /*USO Inc*

Above right: A seven day furlough to 'Blighty'. The first contingent of US troops on leave from the Western Front arrive in England. They are at liberty to spend their seven day leave in any place in the UK with the exception of Northern Ireland./*Associated Press*

Left: Santa Claus rehearses. Pfc Nathan Teasta found this Santa Claus costume in Eschweiler. He is presenting K rations to his buddies Pte James McDermott and Pfc Earl Heinmann./*IWM*

No Brass Allowed!

No Brass Allowed!
From Iwo Jima to Salerno, from Bataan to Berlin – everywhere the Americans fought, they carried *Yank* with them. For it was their own voice, their very own magazine, written, illustrated and edited by enlisted men only. The highest rank of anyone on the staff of *Yank* or as a contributor, was Sergeant. As a result the pages of *Yank* gave a refreshingly blunt and informative view of the war, often ironically humorous and boldly amusing, always profoundly moving. Army men loved it and were proud of it. Even the Navy, Marines and Coastguards admitted it was terrific. As for the American civilian, when he got a glimpse of *Yank* he was crazy about it ... but circulation was confined entirely to the Armed Forces, although soldiers could arrange to have copies sent to their home addresses for a modest two dollars for 52 issues.

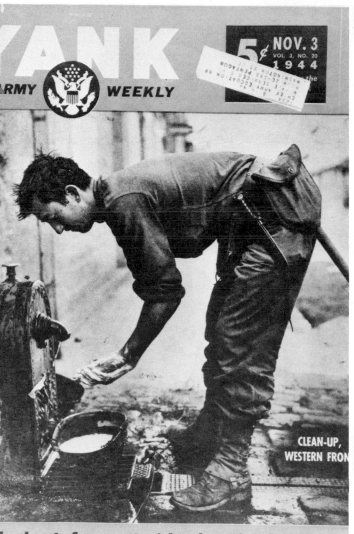

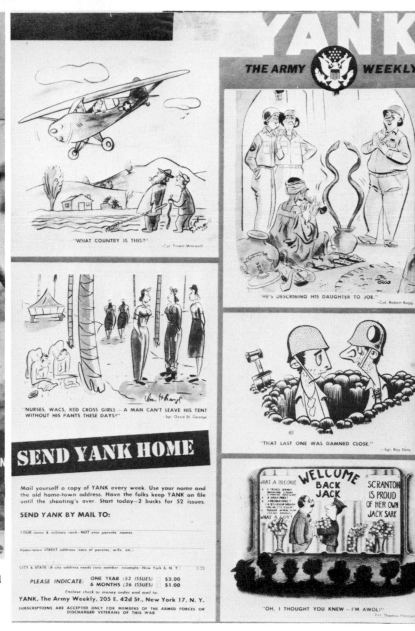

Right: Cover and cartoon page of the Army weekly paper *Yank*, which together with *Stars & Stripes* were widely read and enjoyed by the other Allied armies as well as the US Forces./*Office of Public Affairs US Army*

123

Below: Operation Christrose in action. German troops rush across a Belgium road, blocked by knocked out vehicles and armour, during the initial stages of their Ardennes offensive. /IWM

The Bulge

The Ghost Front

To the north of Third Army, within the First Army sector, lay the Ardennes Front. In December 1944 it was popularly known as the 'Ghost Front', a cold quiet place where the artillery of both sides fired only when they wanted to register possible future targets and where patrols probed enemy lines more to keep in practice than for any aggressive reason. German watched American and American watched German within small arms range of one another. For over two months now each side had strenuously avoided irritating the other along the whole of the 85 mile front. It was here that Adolf Hitler, chose to stage his final all out gamble designed to smash the Western Allies and drive them back to the sea. Operation Christrose (also called 'Watch on the Rhine') was undoubtedly one of the best kept secrets of the war. Three armies – the 6th SS Panzer under Colonel-General Joseph 'Sepp' Dietrich, the 5th Panzer under Baron Hasso von Manteuffel and the largely infantry-composed 7th Army, commanded by General Ernst Brandenburger, were secretly assembled into Army Group B under Field Marshal Walther Model. The plan was to break through on the Ardennes front between Monschau in the north, and Echternach in the south (see Sketch Map 9). The attack would brush aside the weakly held American positions, aim to cross the Meuse between Liege and Namur, bypass Brussels and reach Antwerp within the week. The Western Allies would never recover from such an onslaught and would have to sue for a separate peace. That was the brilliant, if risky plan, which the Führer himself had devised. And along roads and tracks spread with straw to muffle the noise, over 250,000 troops, nearly 2,000 pieces of artillery and 1,000 tanks and assault guns, moved slowly and quietly into their attack positions. H-hour was to be at first light on 16 December 1944. In addition to the frontal attack, picked men, masquerading as Americans, in US army uniforms and vehicles, were to be employed to get behind the front lines, seize vital points such as the bridges over the Meuse, spread rumours, give false orders, create panic and confusion.

'If Georgie's coming we have got it made'

Christrose was still in the final stages of preparation whilst, in early December, Third Army continued its Saar operations. Methodically and relentlessly they advanced against stubborn German opposition, until, by 15 December, they were close to the German border and to the pillboxes and tank traps of the Siegfried Line. Little did they realise that within a few hours they would be changing direction completely and soon be writing a new and splendid chapter in their history. Space does not permit me to go into detail in order to recount the 'Battle of the Bulge' as the Ardennes offensive is popularly called. In

Below: Map 9 The Battle of the Bulge.

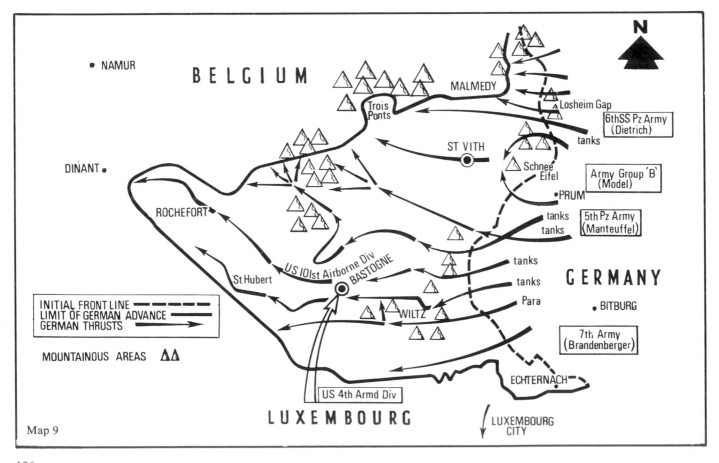

Map 9

Left: Follow me! A squad leader waves his men forward past a burning halftrack. Note his rolled up Shelter Quarter, camouflaged jacket, entrenching tool and map/dispatch case (*Meldekartentasche*). The latter was mainly worn by platoon and squad leaders or dispatch riders. He is carrying a *Maschinen pistole* 43/1./*IWM*

Below: The infamous Obersturmbannführer (SS Lt-Col) Jochen Peiper compares his map with the sign posts as he thoughtfully chews his cigar. His Kampfgruppe made the first deep penetration into the Ardennes sector, leaving a trail of murdered civilians and American soldiers in its wake. Sentenced to hang for the Malmedy atrocities at the Dachau trial in 1946, his sentence was first commuted to imprisonment and finally he was released in 1956 despite protests from the American Legion. The vehicle he is leaning on is a *Schwimmwagen* (an amphibious Volkswagen)./*IWM*

any case, as this book is primarily about the Third Army it would be incorrect to do so. Third Army really only got into the act when, at a conference at Verdun on 19 December called to discuss the worsening situation, General Eisenhower asked Patton to 'pull the chestnuts out of the fire' and to counterattack from the south. Patton calmly replied that he could do so with three divisions in only three days time. This caused consternation, as the difficulties of executing a 90 degree turn with an entire Army can well be imagined. (Patton did not let on that some days earlier, on 12 December, he had made his staff study just this problem, namely what the Third Army would do if called upon to counterattack an enemy breakthrough in the First Army sector.) It was another highspot in Patton's career and the resulting epic relief of the beleaguered 101st Airborne Division at Bastogne, fully vindicated his confidence in his own ability and in that of Third Army. This confidence was undoubtedly shared at soldier level even if SHAEF had some misgivings. When for example, Colonel (later General) Bruce C. Clarke, told the sergeant in command of one of his forward infantry positions in that other beleaguered garrison of St Vith (see Sketch Map 9) that he had heard that General Patton's Third Army had turned north and was attacking the south side of the Bulge. 'The sergeant thought for a minute and said "That's good news. If Georgie's coming we have got it made". I know of no other senior commander in Europe who could have brought forth such a response.'

A Prayer for Dry Weather

Before telling of 4th Armored Division's relief of Bastogne, I would like to recount an anecdote of an incident which took place about this time at HQ Third Army. In his notes to General Patton's book *War as I knew it* Colonel Paul D. Harkins, Patton's deputy Chief of Staff throughout the war, explains in some detail how the now famous prayer for dry weather came to be written. He explains:

'On or about 14 December 1944, General Patton called Chaplain O'Neill, Third Army Chaplain and myself into his office in Third Headquarters at Nancy. The conversation went something like this:

Gen Patton: "Chaplain, I want you to publish a prayer for good weather. I'm tired of these soldiers having to fight mud and floods as well as Germans. See if we can't get God to work on our side".

Chaplain O'Neill: "Sir, it's going to take a pretty thick rug for that kind of praying".

Gen Patton: "I don't care if it takes the flying carpet. I want praying done".

Chaplain: "Yes, sir. May I say, General, that it usually isn't a customary thing among men of my profession to pray for clear weather to kill fellow men".

Gen Patton: "Chaplain, are you teaching me theology or are you the Chaplain of the Third Army? I want a prayer".

Chaplain: "Yes, sir".

'Outside the Chaplain said, "Whew, that's a tough one! what do you think he wants?" It was perfectly clear to me. The General wanted a prayer – he wanted one right now – and he wanted it published to the Command. The Army Engineer was called in, and we finally decided that our field topographical company could print the prayer on a small-sized card, making enough copies for distribution to the Army. It being near Christmas, we also decided to ask General Patton to include a Christmas greeting to the troops on the same card with the prayer. The General agreed, wrote a short greeting, and the card was made up, published, and distributed to the troops on 22 December. Actually, the prayer was offered in order to bring clear weather for the planned Third Army breakthrough to the Rhine in the Saarguemines

Above: A captured photograph shows German soldiers taking boots and equipment off American dead in Housfeld, during Kampfgruppe Peiper's advance./*IWM*

Top left: Attack! Standing beside a disabled American half track a German soldier indicates an enemy position. He is wearing a waterproof coat, while his companion's belt with the other rank's buckle (the officer's buckle was circular) is plainly visible. Also, under his right arm can be seen the edge of his field canteen (*Feldflasche*)./*IWM*

Bottom left: Stuck in the mud! American soldiers struggle to reposition their 57mm M1 anti-tank gun in a forward area on the German-Belgium border, in order to try to stem the German offensive, December 1944./*US Army*

129

area, then scheduled for 21 December. The Bulge put a crimp on these plans. As it happened, the Third Army had moved north to attack the south flank of the Bulge when the prayer was actually issued. It read as follows:

'Almighty and most merciful Father, we humbly beseech Thee, of Thy great goodness, to restrain these immoderate rains with which we have had to contend. Grant us fair weather for Battle. Graciously hearken to us as soldiers who call upon Thee that, armed with Thy power, we may advance from victory to victory, and crush the oppression and wickedness of our enemies, and establish Thy justice among men and nations. Amen.

'And on the reverse side:
'To each officer and soldier in the Third United States Army, I wish a Merry Christmas. I have full confidence in your courage, devotion to duty, and skill in battle. We march in our might to complete victory. May God's blessing rest upon each of you this Christmas Day.

G. S. PATTON, Jr
Lieutenant General
Commanding, Third United States Army

'Whether it was the help of the Divine Guidance asked for in the prayer or just the normal course of human events, we never knew; at any rate, on the 23rd, the day after the prayer was issued, the weather cleared and remained perfect for about six days. Enough to allow the Allies to break the backbone of the Von Runstedt offensive and turn a temporary setback into a crushing defeat for the enemy. We had moved our advance Headquarters to Luxembourg at this time, to be closer to the battle area. The bulk of the Army Staff including the Chaplain, was still in Nancy. General Patton again called me to his office. He wore a smile from ear to ear. He said, "God dam! look at the weather. That O'Neill sure did some potent praying. Get him up here. I want to pin a medal on him". The Chaplain came up next day. The weather was still clear when we walked into General Patton's office. The General rose, came from behind his desk with hand outstretched and said, "Chaplain, you're the most popular man in this Headquarters. You sure stand in good with the Lord and the soldiers". The General then pinned a Bronze Star Medal on Chaplain O'Neill. Everyone offered congratulations and thanks and we got back to the business of killing Germans – with clear weather for battle.'

4th Armored to the Rescue

Brigadier-General Hal C. Pattison was the executive officer of Combat Command A 4th Armored Division, when the Ardennes offensive took place. He writes:

'For me memories of Bastogne begin at dusk of 18 December 1944 as I stood beside the road in front of the house which sheltered the Command Post of Combat Command A of the 4th Armored Division. I was the executive officer of CCA as I had been for over a year and would continue to be throughout the remainder of the fighting in Europe. We were expecting, momentarily, to receive word of D-day and H-hour for our participation in a Third Army attack, a copy of the plan for which reposed in my shirt pocket. The mission of the division was, in general terms, to attack in zone in conjunction with other divisions of the XII Corps to, "penetrate the Siegfried Line and drive to the northeast to establish a bridgehead over the Rhine River in the vicinity of Worms-Mainz-Darmstadt." Since we were, at the time, in Corps reserve and our units were busily

Above: A C-47 cargo transport Dakota crash lands safely after dropping supplies to the 101st US Airborne Division defending Bastogne against heavy German attacks./*IWM*

Top left: GIs clearing expanded and split jerricans off the road near Stavelot, where a fuel dump was set alight to form a very effective road block during the German advance./*IWM*

Bottom left: Bastogne, December 1944. Looking gaunt and exhausted two of Bastogne's gallant defenders exchange a few words. The soldier on the left is carrying an M1 carbine, universally known as the Garand./*IWM*

engaged in a heavy maintenance programme, I had nothing better to do than to keep an eye on the road for the expected messenger from Division. Physically, our command post was located in a set of farm buildings on the main road between Dieuze and Fenetrange on the Saar River. As the Division had recently been withdrawn from action, and with the knowledge that it would soon be recommitted in the same zone, Division Headquarters had remained in place at or near Fenetrange while all troop units were put into assembly areas to its rear. Corps Headquarters was farther to the west. As I stood in front of the CP that winter evening the division commander, Major-General Hugh Gaffey, with his military police escort, suddenly appeared out of the dusk from the direction of Corps Headquarters. Catching sight of me he signalled for me to come to the road where he stopped only long enough to say, "Pat, we have a change of orders. You will be ready to move early tomorrow. Send your liaison officer to Division and we will get him back to you with your instructions before midnight". The 4th Armored Division was a proud and confident unit but at the moment it was sore in body and spirit, figuratively licking its wounds to both. It had entered combat in July shortly before the St Lo breakout and participated in the later stages of that action and was the instrument of First Army that opened the door to Brittany by capturing Avranches and the bridges intact, over the Selune River. Thereafter it had cut the Brittany Peninsula before leading the Third Army across France until it was stopped logistically in Lorraine in September. It had wreaked great damage to the German Army with minimum damage to itself in personnel and equipment. By the time of the September halt, however, many

of its combat vehicles had in excess of 2,000 combat miles on their odometers. During the November campaign to cross the Saar the going had been tough. Robbed of its favourite tactic of manoeuvre by the constant rains, flooded streams, deep mud and a restricted road net, Division losses of men and equipment had mounted. On top of that two of its most respected commanders had been taken away: Colonel Bruce C. Clarke, the commander of CCA on the first of November, to go to the 7th Armored Division for promotion to Brigadier General and Major-General John S. Wood for "rest and recuperation" on the third of December. At the same time, Colonel Clarke's successor had been replaced for inefficiency and was, in turn replaced by an officer from Third Army Headquarters. Neither General Wood's replacement, General Gaffey, or the new CCA commander, Brigadier-General Herbert Earnest, had yet been fully accepted by the Division. When it went into reserve about 12 December the first order of Division business was maintenance and absorption of the few available replacements – none of whom were trained tank crewmen. Tank engines and tracks were in special need of replacement and there were not enough

of either to go around. On the evening of 18 December much work remained to be done, especially in CCA which had come out of the line after CCB. As General Gaffey's little convoy of two jeeps sped eastward, I hurried into the CP to get the liaison officer on his way to Division Headquarters, to contact General Earnest and acquaint him with the new situation and to get word to the units of the imminent move.

'For the past 48 hours we had been hearing of a German offensive to the north of us and had disquieting news only that day about the success the Germans were having along with rumours of new highly effective weapons they were employing. As a consequence, it took no great amount of imagination to guess we were being shifted north to help deal with the situation there. But the magnitude of the whole thing was, at the moment, beyond our expectations. When, around 2300 hours, our liaison officer returned with orders we were not much enlightened. Essentially, we knew only that we were to move north to the vicinity of Longwy in Belgium. We were to move at 0900 on the 19th (CCB which was located to the north of us was to move at midnight), on a route that took us northwest past Metz and

Above: A weapons carrier vehicle stands snowbound during a blizzard somewhere along the Belgian front and awaits digging out by shovel crews./*US Army*

Above left: This excellent aerial photograph shows armour and infantry of 6th Armd Div advancing through the snow near Bastogne, a typical village in the Ardennes./*US Army*

Left: Shermans of 712 Tank Bn, 90th Division move up to firing positions outside Bavigne, Luxembourg./*US Army*

Right: Halftracks of Third Army advance towards Bastogne./*IWM*

across the flooded Moselle. We would receive further instructions en route. We moved on schedule and, shortly before dark, somewhere southeast of Longwy, we were met by a messenger from Division with instructions to bivouac for the night and were given a "goose egg"* to use. We went into an assembly area around a farm and got busy with servicing the vehicles and feeding the troops. Within an hour we were told we had stopped prematurely and were ordered to move at once to Longwy. En route we were again met with destination orders and a "goose egg" for our assembly area around a village to the north-east of Arlon. We arrived at the designated area well before daylight of the 20th and established ourselves in the local school house but soon had instructions to move again – this time to a village a few miles north of Arlon

*'Goose Egg': an oval drawn on a map around an area allocated to a unit as a leaguer/harbour area/hide.

on the Bastogne highway. By noon we were in place and had established a screen to the north on what turned out to be our line of departure for the advance on the 22nd. The march itself holds some vivid memories. A sense of apprehension resulting from the dearth of information coupled with the knowledge that such a move could mean a real emergency existed. Pride in the businesslike professional conduct of the troops during what was turning out to be an epic shifting of direction of a field army; columns of troops were moving north, others east and still other logistic units were moving west as we got nearer Luxembourg. These columns were crossing each other at road junctions with never a pause by either crossing column; MP control so perfect that vehicles of crossing columns passed through the intervals of the other with the precision of trained horsemen in a dressage in the riding hall. Exasperation at the seeming confusion as to destinations and assembly areas. The murmur and beat

of the sound of artillery fire and the lightning-like shimmer of the flashes on the northern horizon as we drew nearer to Arlon – the necessity to discipline the imagination as to the meaning of it all. The relief of arriving at our destination and getting some "good information" as to the situation. As I look back with the realization of the magnitude of the troop movement, the speed with which it was arranged and carried out and the efficiency of it all, I cannot help but be proud to have been a part of one of the great military operations of history. From our standpoint at the time we were chagrined at the number of combat vehicles which we lost on the march

for it meant we would be going into action brutally short of firepower. The ordnance people, however, did herculean work in getting the cripples back to us. Most of them had joined their units before the final relief of Bastogne took place on the 26th. 21 December was taken up seeking information and getting ready for the attack which was to take place at dawn of the 22nd. Our column was to attack north on the Arlon-Bastogne highway and the other, CCB, to the west of us. The mission

was, of course, to relieve the 101st Airborne Division in Bastogne. Our advance got off on schedule in a heavy snowstorm which, fortunately, stopped about mid-morning. We soon began to pick up stragglers from units which had been overrun in the early momentum of the German attack. All of these men were wet, hungry and cold and some were wounded and many were without weapons. It was heartening to hear most of them ask to join us and fight again but the several hundred we recovered that day were sent to the rear for a rest, dry clothes and food and eventual return to their own units. By mid-afternoon we had reached Martelange where Corps engineers had destroyed the bridge as a part of the barrier plan. This was to hold us up for more than 24 hours. The current of the Sure River and the gorge through which it ran made a treadway bridge out of the question, so the engineers constructed a Bailey bridge about 90 feet in length. This operation was hampered by freezing rain which had begun and a company of German paratroopers, but during the day of the 23rd we got a company of armoured infantry across and secured the far bank of the river. Once across early on the 24th, we expected to make rapid progress towards Bastogne but a regimental headquarters of the German 5th Parachute Division was located in Warnach and it took nearly 24 hours of nip and tuck to drive the Germans out of the warm village into the cold. General Patton had told us to attack all day

and all night and not stop till we got to Bastogne but the Germans dictated otherwise. We had to call off the attack about midnight for lack of infantry and regroup. In any case tanks can't keep on going on courage alone – they need gas. Early on Christmas Day we did drive the Germans out and continued the advance to the next hard nut – Tintange which was also cleared on Christmas Day. On the 26th we advanced another five or six miles and captured Hollange after another hard fight with a battalion-size defence force.

'Meanwhile our companion CCB had fairly fast going until it hit Chaumont where it suffered heavily from anti-tank fire with the result that its tank battalion was close to non-effective for a 24-hour period. To bolster the attack Division, on Christmas Eve, moved the Reserve Command from the right flank, where it had been committed on the 23rd, on a 60 mile march around the left flank of the division zone to attack northeast towards Bastogne. Late on the 26th elements of the 37th Tank Battalion commanded by Creighton Abrams, the greatest of several great soldiers of the 4th Armored, broke through on the Assenois road to enter Bastogne. While this was the psychological victory two more days of hard fighting were required to widen the corridor into Bastogne. By evening of the 28th, CCA had cleared the length of the Arlon-Bastogne highway and elements of the 35th Division had moved up to hold the shoulder. Access to Bastogne was secure.

'We experienced a good bit of hard fighting during the campaign in Europe but none to equal the relief of Bastogne. In addition to battling the bitter cold and wet the German paratroopers were fanatical fighters and driven out of a position they counter-attacked or infiltrated the rear and had to be cleaned out to the last man. They fought like tigers for any place that protected them from the bitter cold. We were hampered greatly from the effects of the attrition of the November offensive for the crossings of the Sarre and the subsequent vicious fighting in the Siegfried Line; armoured infantry companies were at no more than 50 to 60% strength in riflemen – tank companies of as many as 10 tanks (of a TO&E strength of 17) were the exception. Tank crews were in many instances short of one of their number and there were no replacements to be had. This shortage increased the physical exhaustion as well as the combat efficiency of the crews, since it caused greater demands on the remaining members for the arduous work of servicing and maintaining the vehicles as well as providing for close in security during the night bivouacs. Trained infantry replacements had not been available for some time. Early in the advance towards Bastogne the 51st Armored Infantry Battalion had received approximately 70 replacements who had been drawn from anti-aircraft units and the headquarters of logistical units. There had been no time to give them the refresher training that Third Army had planned – the urgency

Above: German dead litter a field near Bastogne, killed during their unsuccessful attacks on the beleaguered garrison of 101st US Airborne Division./*IWM*

Top left: German POWs, captured in the battle of Bastogne, are marched to the rear by Private Frank Kelly, an MP 4th Armd Div, past a well laden halftrack (note the M1917 .30cal Machine Gun sticking over the side). /*US Army*

Bottom left: Infantrymen of 4th Armd Div approach the outer perimeter of Bastogne./*IWM*

of the situation dictated the really unwise policy of putting them directly into front line units with dire consequences. Not only were they a drag on the veteran soldiers, but by the time we reached Bastogne every one of those 70 unfortunates had become a casualty; killed, wounded or evacuated as psychologically unfit. There were many memorable incidents – sad, tragic, funny, prosaic. On the day before Christmas a truck load of Christmas packages was delivered to the CCA headquarters. The major casualties thereafter to the members of the headquarters were gastro-intestinal as a result of over indulgence in the rich fare of home made sweets. On Christmas Day General Patton visited all the units in contact. As he approached our headquarters from the direction of Arlon a fighter plane (American without markings of any kind) strafed his small convoy of jeeps. As any other mortal, General Patton found refuge in the roadside ditch. After his departure and since only his dignity was harmed, we had a good laugh at his expense. After Warnach we got a surge forward when our light tank company with a section of AAA quad 50s attached attacked a German position in a wood an hour before dawn. The unexpected result – a paratroop battalion destroyed. Nearly 300 killed were counted including the battalion commander and his staff in their sleeping bags. A day later an attached battalion of our 318th Infantry Regiment was leading our attack in a wooded area. The leading company reported itself in position for the assault and called for the artillery preparation. At the battalion commander's insistence the artillery forward observer was with him at his CP instead of with the assault company which had, in fact, reported its position improperly. As a consequence the artillery preparation fell directly on the assault company which had so many casualties that it had to be withdrawn from action. General Patton directed that at the stroke of midnight on New Year's Eve every artillery piece in Third Army would fire on a likely target as a New Year's salute from Third Army to the Wehrmacht. Our division artillery selected as its target a road leading from Viller-le-bon-Eau to our right flank which was being held by elements of the 35th Division supported by our 51st Armored Infantry Battalion. At midnight all 17 battalions of organic and supporting artillery fired 10 salvos onto a mile stretch of that road. Shell shocked captives reported that a panzer grenadier regiment had been on an approach march on the target road for a dawn attack when hit by the midnight salute. The German regiment was decimated and the attack on our position failed to materialise. On the afternoon of the 29th an artillery spotter plane watched a disorientated German tank company of 13 tanks heading towards one of our positions in

140

broad daylight and in column. Our tank battalion commander was alerted, put one of his companies in a flanking position and destroyed all 13 of the German tanks in a matter of one or two minutes. Our part in the Battle of the Bulge ended early in January when we were suddenly pulled out of an attack and sent southeast into Luxembourg as Army reserve to be prepared to deal with a German attack brewing in the Sarre-Moselle Triangle. The Bulge had been a new experience for us. Heretofore we had attacked on a narrow front, penetrating and cutting off German positions and forcing their evacuation or surrender. Stragglers and remnants of enemy units were dealt with by following infantry informations. The Bulge was a different story. We could have made a typical armoured run into Bastogne at almost any time but that would not have secured the road. Every kilometre of the way had to be cleared of persistent German defenders as we advanced. We were back to the conventional, "Leavenworth Solution".

Sequel

'After a period in Luxembourg of battalion size operations in support of other units, the 4th Armored Division crossed the Our River into the XII Corps bridgehead late in February and advanced on Bitburg. By 1 March we had closed on the Kyll River east of Bitburg and were ready for further work. During the first week of March the Division crossed the Kyll through a 5th Infantry Division bridgehead and headed for the Rhine River which

was reached at Andernach less than two days later. A short period of relative inaction was followed by an attack south across the Moselle towards Bad Kreuznach and Worms. By 20 March the Division had captured Worms and gone into an assembly area west of Oppenheim on the Rhine. On the 23rd orders were received to cross the Rhine at Oppenheim on the 24th through a bridgehead established by the 5th Infantry Division. On that day I destroyed the Third Army plan to pass through the Seigfried Line, advance to the northeast and secure a bridgehead over the Rhine in the vicinity of Worms-Mainz.

Darmstadt

'Three months later and by a far different route than he anticipated, General Patton had his XII Corps across the Rhine in the precise area he had wanted to be all along. By midnight of 24 March the 4th Armored Division was passing through the outskirts of Darmstadt on its way to seizing the bridges of its own and establishing bridgeheads over the Main River at Hanau and Aschaffenburg. For its operations from 22 December 1944 to 27 March 1945 the 4th Armored Division was awarded a Presidential Distinguished Unit Citation – only the second complete division ever to do so.'

First into Bastogne

As Brigadier-General Pattison has explained, it was the 37th Tank Battalion who were leading on the final run into Bastogne. Here is how the privately published Divisional

Above: A Panther (PzKpfw V Ausf G) abandoned in the snow by the Germans when their Ardennes offensive failed, is inspected by US soldiers from the 3rd US Armd Div. /*US Army*

Top left: Alles Kaput! A Sturmgeschutz III Ausf G in ruins near Bastogne, forms a not unattractive piece of modern sculpture./*IWM*

Bottom left: An upturned Panther near Bastogne./*IWM*

history tells of the last dramatic moments:
'The final assault was launched from the far edge of Assenois, the last village before Bastogne. In the lead was Company C of the 37th Tank Battalion, followed by Company C of the 53rd Armored Infantry Battalion. Lieutenant-Colonel Creighton W. Abrams, then commander of the 37th Tank Battalion, clinched a cold cigar in the corner of his mouth and said, "We're going in to those people now". With that, he swept his arm forward and the charge was on. The command tank of Company C, 37th Tank Battalion moved out first. In the turret was First Lieutenant Charles Boggess, Jr. "The Germans had these two little towns of Clochimont and Assenois on the secondary road we were using to get to Bastogne" he recalled later. "Beyond Assenois the road ran up a ridge through heavy woods. There were lots of Germans there too. We were going through fast, all guns firing, straight up that road to bust through before they had time to get set. I thought of a lot of things as we took off. I thought of whether the road would be mined, whether the bridge in Assenois would be blown, whether they would be ready at their anti-tank guns. Then we charged, and I didn't have time to wonder". Meanwhile, four American artillery battalions were slamming barrages into enemy-held Assenois and the edge of the woods beyond it. The 22nd, 66th and 94th Armored Artillery Battalions of the 4th Armored dropped in 105mm shells

Above: The camouflaged 75mm ATk Pak 40 in the foreground fired point blank to score a direct hit on this halftrack of 90th Armd Inf Bn, 6th Armd Div, near Wardin, Belgium, 16 January 1945./*6 Armd Div Assoc/George F. Hofmann*

Left: This 6th Armd Div Sherman was put out of action in the Belgian town of Mageret, east of Bastogne, 15 January 1945./*6 Armd Div Assoc/George F. Hofmann*

and a supporting battalion lobbed 155mm howitzer rounds. Under the artillery support, Lieutenant Boggess' medium tanks advanced through shell bursts to the enemy positions. The ground pitched, and houses spilled into the street, but the undaunted American forces kept going. "I used the 75mm like a machine gun", said Boggess' gunner, Corporal Milton Dickerman. "Murphy (Private James, the loader) was plenty busy throwing in the shells. We shot 21 rounds in a few minutes and I don't know how much machine gun stuff. As we got to Assenois an anti-tank gun in a halftrack fired at us. The shell hit the road in front of the tank and threw dirt all over. I got the halftrack in my sights and hit it with high explosive. It blew up". Dirt from the enemy shell burst had smeared the driver's periscope. "I made out okay, although I couldn't see very good", explained Private Hubert Smith. "I sort of guessed at the road. I had a little trouble when my left brake locked and the tank turned up a road we didn't want to go. So I just stopped her, backed her up and went on again". The armoured infantry was also in the thick of the fighting, and one of the infantrymen distinguished himself gallantly enough to become the third Congressional Medal of Honor winner in the 4th Armored Division. He was Private James Hendrix, a 19-year old rifleman with Company C, 53rd Armored Infantry Battalion. His citation read: "Private Hendrix dismounted and advanced upon two 88mm gun crews, and by the ferocity of his action compelled the German gun crews first to take cover and then surrender". Hendrix, a red-haired, freckle-faced farm boy from Arkansas, later explained, "We ran up on them yelling 'come out' but they wouldn't. One poked his head out of a foxhole and I shot him through the neck. I got closer and hit another on the head with the butt of my M-1. He had American matches on him. Others came out then with their hands up". The citation continues: "Later in the attack this fearless soldier again left his vehicle voluntarily to aid two wounded soldiers threatened by enemy machine gun fire. Effectively silencing two enemy machine guns, he held off the enemy by his own fire until the wounded men were evacuated". "I just shot at the machine guns like all the 50s on the halftracks were doing" Hendrix said. "A halftrack had been hit pretty bad and these fellows were wounded and lying in a ditch. Machine gun fire was mostly toward them, but some bullets were coming my way". Continuing the attack, Hendrix again endangered himself when he ran to aid still another soldier who was trapped in a burning halftrack. Braving enemy sniper fire and exploding mines and ammunition in the vehicle, he pulled the wounded man from the conflagration and extinguished his flaming cloth-

ing with his body. Hendrix explained it so: "Grenade exploded between his legs and everybody got out. But he was hollering for help. I pulled at him and got him out on the road, but he was burned bad. I tried to find water to put out the fire, but the water cans were full of bullet holes so I beat out the flames as best I could. He died later".

'The four lead tanks in Boggess' column drew ahead as the halftracks were slowed by German shells and debris. The tankers rolled along, sweeping the wooded ridge with machine gun fire. Finally, they burst through the German defences and into the 101st Airborne perimeter. Lieutenant Boggess ordered the roaring Sherman tank down to a crawl. In the open fields beyond the pines he saw red, yellow and blue supply parachutes spilled over the snow like confetti. Some of the coloured chutes, caught in the tall pines, indicated where ammunition, food and medicine had been dropped to the besieged troops. The column halted. Standing up in his turret, Lieutenant Boggess shouted, "Come here, come on out" to khaki-clad figures in foxholes. "This is the 4th Armored". There was no answer. Helmeted heads peered suspiciously over carbine sights. The lieutenant shouted again. A lone figure strode forward. Lieutenant Boggess watched him carefully; "I'm Lieutenant Webster of the 326th Engineers, 101st Airborne Division" the approaching figure called. "Glad to see you". The time was 4.45pm 26 December.'

Below: A frostbound 88mm gun abandoned by the retreating German forces, somewhere in the Ardennes./*IWM*

Across the Rhine

Operation Christrose, the End

January 1945 saw the enemy trying desperately to stem Third Army's advance northwards from the Bastogne area. Having failed, they were forced to carry out a costly withdrawal into the Siegfried Line positions. Striving to hold back Third Army's inexorable advance the Germans also endeavoured to disengage their battered panzer divisions. By the end of the month the Ardennes offensive was over. Operation Christrose had proved a disastrous and expensive failure from which Germany would never recover. They had been driven right back to their starting points and were forced to take refuge in the forts and strongpoints of the 'West Wall'. Third Army losses in the Ardennes campaign were the heaviest they ever suffered. In under six weeks they had lost nearly 5,000 killed, 22,000 wounded and just over 5,000 missing. On the other side of the coin they had inflicted tremendous losses on the enemy. The estimate of the havoc wrought by Third Army alone was a staggering 143,818 enemy casualties. Third Army had moved further and faster and engaged more divisions in less time than any other Army in the history of the United States.

A New Offensive

On 29 January 1945, the 13 divisions of the four corps which made up Third Army were abreast the Moselle, Sauer, and Our Rivers, ready to take on the Siegfried Line defences, from Saarlauten in the south, to St Vith in the north. By the end of February all four corps had breached the Siegfried Line and were exerting unrelenting pressure all along the front. However, it had not been a walkover. The terrain and foul weather had proved once again to be just as formidable enemies as the Germans. The advance was across very rugged terrain, cut by numerous flood swollen, swiftly flowing rivers. Typical of the engagements fought is this account of the crossing of the Sauer River by the 76th Infantry

Division, which had only recently joined Third Army.

The 76th Infantry Division Attack the Siegfried Line

Attack! the long awaited order had come at last. Less than 90 days earlier the men of the 76th 'Onaway'* Infantry Division had been training against a simulated enemy in the peaceful hills of Wisconsin; only two weeks ago they were champing at the bit as VIII Corps reserve in the area of Champlon, Belgium, now they were to undergo one of the most gruelling tests modern war could devise. Combat Team 417** was to be attached to the 5th Infantry Division for an attack, on 7 February 1945, north across the Sauer River into Germany. The immediate objective was to seize the high ground in the vicinity of Ferschweiler and Ernzen (see Sketch Map 10), CT 417 was to take part of

*'Onaway' the battle cry of the 76th, was adopted during their training in Wisconsin. It was the 'alert' signal of the Chippewa Indian warriors over whose wild hunting grounds they had often exercised.

**CT 417 was based upon the 417th Infantry Regiment, one of three in the 'triangular' infantry division. The other two were the 304th and 385th and together they made up roughly 2/3rds of the divisional strength. The remaining 1/3rd consisted of: four artillery bns (three with 105mm Hows and one with 155mm Hows) an engineer bn, signal coy, QM coy, reconnaissance troop, ordnance coy light maintenance, div HQ coy, MP platoon and the divisional band.

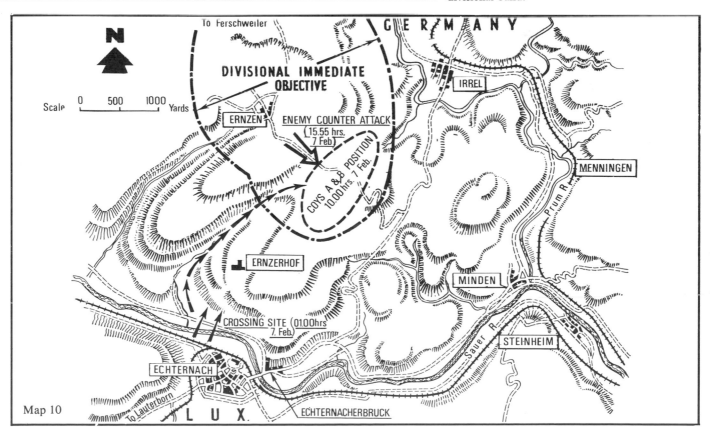

Map 10

this initial objective and then revert back to 76th Division control. The enemy positions were some of the most formidable in the world – the Siegfried Line. The name is misleading because it was not a line, but rather a series of pillbox studded positions arranged in depth. Where the terrain favoured the attacker then there were masses of positions, but where the going for tanks and infantry was difficult the defences were correspondingly thinner. They were designed more to slow up and weaken the attacker, rather than to actually stop him, so that counter-attack forces, lying in wait in large well protected bunkers, could emerge at the critical moment, and deal with the assaults. All approach routes were mined, roads blocked and tank traps abounded. 'So help me' said one doughboy a few days after the initial assault, 'the job at first seemed just too much for human beings to accomplish'. And he was not far wrong, as the pillboxes and bunkers, some descending three floors below ground, had been ingeniously camouflaged with netting, painting and natural foliage so as to resemble haystacks, barns or even summer homes. Construction was of reinforced concrete, with walls ranging from three to nine feet thick!

Above: 'Blockbuster'. The Command tank and crew of B Company 37th Tank Battalion, 4th Armored Division (Capt James H. Leach in turret) camouflaged for winter warfare. /*Col James H. Leach*

Left: Onaway cross the Sauer River. Infantrymen of Combat Team 417, 76th Infantry Division, advance down to the River Sauer through the rubble strewn streets of Echternach, 7 February 1945./*US Army*

Above right: Eight direct hits from 6 Armd Div's 75mm tank guns failed to pierce the six inch armour plate on the front of this Mk VI Tiger tank, during fighting around the Belgium town of Moinet. /*6 Armd Div Assoc/George F. Hofmann*

Right: General Patton's 'Mighty Midgets'. The Army Commander visits men of 1303rd Engineers who have just completed a bridge across the Sauer river aptly named 'General Patton Bridge', 20 February 1945./*US Army*

In each troop bunker there were at least two rooms, the living quarters and the gun room, with guns emplaced to cover the most likely avenues of approach. Built-in electric lights, ventilators, stoves, bunks and in some cases even proper kitchens, added greatly to the comfort of these fortifications. The outer perimeter was a series of foxholes, gun emplacements, carefully camouflaged communication trenches and masses of barbed wire and mines. The enemy manning these formidable defences opposite the 76th were the German 212th Volksgrenadier Division, the 23rd Penal Battalion and elements of the 44th Fortress Machine Gun Battalion. They were commanded by Lt-Gen Sensfuss and had been reformed in October 1944, after a severe mauling on the Russian front. The Siegfried Line was of course only one of the obstacles facing the GIs. Midway between the American and German lines stretched the narrow, ravine-like valley of the Sauer River, with all its bridges destroyed in their sector. In February 1945 the normally meandering stream had been swollen into a raging torrent by heavy rains and melting snow. It was now between 90 and 180 feet in width and instead of its normal placid flow there was a swirling

current of twelve miles an hour. Backing up this natural ally the Germans had covered the area with observation, fire and patrols.

This then was the formidable task which faced the men of the 76th. Zero hour was set at 0100 hours 7 February. It was to be a surprise attack, with the artillery and mortars not opening up until 0130 hours. Here is how the attack is described in the Divisional history:

'Slowly, steadily, zero hour was approaching. The 1st Battalion Command Post was at Lauterborn. Company A occupied positions just west of Echternach along high ground commanding the town, and one platoon outposted the high ground at Thoul, protecting the right flank. Two platoons of Company B were patrolling Echternach itself, with the remainder of the company southeast of the town. While Company C secured the road between Lauterborn and Echternach, the 81mm mortars of Company D were emplaced just outside of Echternach along the highway leading to Lauterborn and one platoon of the company's machine guns was located in the eastern part of the town, prepared to place fire on the village of Echternacherbruck on the river's north bank. The second machine gun platoon was on the opposite side of the town, covering the river to the west. The chosen assault crossing site was near the northwest fringe of Echternach. A road ran parallel to the river at this point, immediately adjacent to which was the railroad yard. Along railroad tracks which practically skirted the river's edge, a barrier of railroad ties had been erected. What the enemy did not have to bolster for defence, but which nature did with a vengeance, was the Sauer River, at this point approximately 150 feet wide and from six to twelve feet deep, changed by the elements from a serenely pastoral waterway to a swift, vicious military obstacle angrily overrunning

Left: Infantrymen of 90th Inf Div and tanks of 6th Armd Div move through the 'dragon's teeth' of the Siegfried Line near Heckuschied, Germany in February 1945. (Note the well laden trailer towed behind an equally well laden halftrack.) /*IWM*

Below: Probably the most photographed sign in the 6th Armd Div sector!/*6 Armd Div Assoc/George F. Hofmann*

Bottom: Dragon's teeth. Anti-tank defences stretching across the countryside near Ober-Perl, Germany. /*Col Crosby P. Miller*

its regular channel. Beyond this raging river, on the north side, was a flooded plain extending about 200 yards to the foot of a precipitous escarpment which rises almost vertically to a height of about 450 feet above the river. Leading gradually upward to the top of the escarpment is a draw which extended northeast from the left flank of the regimental zone. No patrols had been able to cross the Sauer in the vicinity of Echternach prior to the attack. From posts in the town, however, enemy movements had been under observation. During daylight hours barbed wire entanglements could clearly be seen along the river's edge. It was already known that between the river and the road there existed a dense anti-personnel minefield covered, moreover, by deadly fire from pillboxes. A prisoner had reported another minefield at the entrance to the draw. In addition the reports of visual observation were supplemented by thousands of aerial photographs.

'On the 6th the curtain rose on the real-life drama of blood and guts. A Corps Artillery 155mm "Long Tom" and two tank destroyers of the 808th TD Battalion were brought into Echternach from where they engaged a few of the pillboxes across the river. At the same time regimental anti-tank guns were whisked into the town to squelch a German tank threat should it materialise once the crossing began. The 3rd Battalion meanwhile, moved into the woods immediately south of Michaelshof. Prior to this, during the night, the 160th Engineers had hidden in Echternach 40 assault boats, which on the next night and just prior to the attack, were to be placed

150

along the town's battered street for pick-up by the infantrymen. Of the 40 boats allocated to the 1st Battalion, each of the first wave companies were to receive 16. The remaining eight boats were to be used by assault troops of Company C. After the initial wave the boats were to be returned to the near shore to transport the remainder of the battalion. Mud was ankle deep; wind-tossed rain whipped through the biting air and solid blackness covered the entire front as Onaway troops moved into attack positions on the night 6/7 February. In addition to Division Artillery, the 304th Infantry Regiment was to support the crossing by direct fire. Along the Sauer, rifles and automatic weapons of the 1st and 3rd Battalions, together with the 105s of Cannon Company and 57s of Anti-tank Company, were to lay down a blanket of fire on enemy installations. Shortly after midnight engineer guides directed Companies A and B, 417th Infantry, to the boats. A manning crew of three engineers and 10 infantrymen hand-carried each craft from the town to the river 500 yards away. Moving in a column as silently as possible from the centre of Echter-

nach along a street which led to the northwest edge of town, the portage party proceeded along the highway paralleling the railroad to form a line fronting on the river. In the meantime Lt-Col Clarence A. Mette, Jr, the Battalion Commander, moved to his observation post on the extreme northwest fringe of the town. From this point of vantage overlooking the Sauer, he directed the crossing operations. The moment had come. At a signal, Company B stole across the railroad through the tie fence and to the river's edge a few yards beyond. Here the bank dropped abruptly four feet to the churning river. In the darkness it was difficult to get the boats into the water and loaded. At 0100 Company B shoved off in the first wave. Pvt Lewis M. Gregorich was a member of the first platoon to cross the swollen Sauer. He and more than a dozen other tense comrades in the assault boat held their breath as hails of fire from enemy positions streaked the inky darkness. They hit shore and raced for the hill; struggled up the slippery incline. Suddenly they saw it. There it was, their first pillbox. "We hesitated for a second", Gregorich said, "and then we

Below: Wounded tank crewmen of 4th Armd Div chat together after the drive into Bad Kreuznach was completed, 19 March 1945./*US Army*

closed in. We didn't kill the krauts but sent them back alive to the Battalion CP. There were eight of them". 25 "supermen" in a second pillbox fought viciously until they were entirely surrounded, then surrendered meekly. A third pillbox, near the summit, with the help of a bazooka team yielded 62 krauts.

'Immediately thereafter Company A began its crossing. The assault boats were filled each with 12-16 men. Midstream the boats drew fire from Nazi pillboxes on the hill of the German shore. The boat behind the one in which rode Pvt Harry Goedde sank under a direct hit, its occupants swept downstream. His own boat started to drift towards the very spot where a Nazi machine gun was spitting fire from the bank. The men tried frantically to restrain their course by grabbing for rushes along the water's edge but swamped the gun-whales. Along with his companions, Goedde shed his equipment and plunged into the icy water. Several were immediately carried away by the current. A medic called for help and Goedde, a confident swimmer, took him in tow until they both made shore. Meanwhile, on the Luxembourg side a building had been set afire by a German shell. Wet and shivering, from under the protection of weeds, Goedde watched the warm fire. In its glare he could see the assault boats coming across and the Germans opening up on them. A shell threw up a sheet of water, a boat lurched crazily, and the men spilled into the freezing, racing river. He could see their heads bobbing and

Above: Engineers of Third Army, descending ladders to remove the German explosives seen piled against the side of a bridge over the Moselle River, south of the city of Trier, March 1945./*IWM*

Right: Two soldiers of 11th Armd Div, carry a wounded comrade to safety, as a Sherman halts at the head of a narrow street in Andernach, Germany. Just in front of the tank is a burning enemy vehicle which it has just knocked out. /*US Army*

Above: This GI has a superb view across the Moselle valley, as he keeps watch./*IWM*

arms flailing. Then they were carried out of the radius of light and he could see them no more . . . From the very start there was enemy mortar and artillery fire, but it was not yet adjusted on the crossing site. By the time Company B was midway from the shore the enemy had its flares up and was sending in small arms fire. Some boats were damaged; some were swept down-river; others capsized. Landing troops were scattered all along the enemy bank, so that reorganisation in the dark became a major problem. There were casualties; some men had failed to get across; some never gained contact after completing the crossing. When the companies regrouped, Company A had a fighting strength of 56 enlisted men and three officers; Company B 52 enlisted men and two officers.'

Having crossed the river onto enemy soil the two companies now had to negotiate the minefield in the valley floor which they did without a single casualty. Company B then swung left to deal with the pillboxes along the face of the escarpment, whilst Company A moved forward on the right. Despite heavy artillery and mortar fire they managed to locate the heavily mined entrance to the draw and by 1000 hours on the 7th were well dug-in on the

high ground southeast of Ernzen. Meanwhile, the crossing site was under very heavy fire. Assault boats were punctured, foundered or were forced into inactivity by the accuracy of the enemy fire. The rifle platoons of Company C crossed in the few boats they could salvage under withering machine gun fire. After trying unsuccessfully to screen the crossing site with smoke and in the face of the very effective enemy artillery fire, now that it was daylight, the crossing operation had to be temporarily suspended.

At 1555 hours the German counterattacked Companies A and B in their high ground position, with three tanks supported by infantry. 14 enemy were killed and the attack repulsed without giving ground. 'Pfc Lyle Corcoran was the only bazooka man with us at the time', recalled Sgt Charles Smith, 'When the lead tank turned sideways about 20 yards from us he let it have two blasts. Fire broke out and the tank went back down the road. I think the men inside were burned to death'. Another defender, S/Sgt Guida A. Fenice watched the other tank continue to advance, 'I saw it run over one of our men in a foxhole. There were about seven German soldiers riding on the outside and I saw a buddy of mine running alongside the tank

153

firing at them with a pistol. They shot him down so I grabbed his gun and continued to fire'. Then the tank got stuck in the mud and the mounted infantry scattered for their lives. Before the crew could get out, Sgt Smith and Pfc Donald E. Hall dashed forward, jumped aboard and threw grenades into the open turret. The third tank wisely retreated.

Meanwhile, back at the river, preparations were being made to get more troops across that evening. As all but one of the assault craft had been lost or destroyed in the first crossing, more had to be brought up on the 7th, including eight storm boats and six assault boats, all equipped with outboard motors. It was decided to get the 2nd Battalion across that night before the remainder of the 1st Battalion and Company G set out at 2030 hours. Four hours later three platoons and a heavy machine gun platoon only had crossed, but operations had again to be suspended through lack of serviceable boats. Whilst the amphibious crossing was taking place the 160th Engineer Battalion tried unsuccessfully once more to install a footbridge. Four times during the night cables were secured to the opposite shore, only to be ripped out by careening boats being swept downstream, or by capsized boatloads of men, who grabbed them in an effort to stop themselves from being swept away. But the river had to be crossed bridge or no bridge. By 0400 hours 18 more boats had been procured and further elements of the 2nd Battalion began crossing. Two boats were hit by artillery fire before they could even be placed in the river, two more, riddled with shell splinters, sank six feet from shore. The other twelve made it across safely, but only one returned unscathed. Dodging lead, the remainder of the

Above: A party of four infantrymen from 80th Infantry Division, Third Army, searching the war-torn streets of Wadern, Germany for snipers. /*US Army*

battalion waited for more boats, whilst the 91st Chemical Mortar Battalion tried again to screen the far bank with smoke. More boats arrived and the difficult and dangerous operation continued. The boat containing the battalion command group of the 1st Battalion went down just before reaching shore, however, Lt-Col Mette and the other occupants managed to swim to shore and were soon organising the scattered elements of both battalions into a reinforcement party for the GIs who were still stubbornly holding the high ground.

All this time the drama of the footbridge was still going on. The 301st Engineer Battalion began to tackle the construction problem on the 8th. Despite numerous abortive attempts and many casualties, after 10 hours of patient, concentrated effort on the night 9/10 February, the footbridge was finally completed and the 76th doughboys were able to march across the river. By 1830 hours on the 11th the Sauer had been licked and a treadway bridge, spanning the 180 feet of river at Echternach, had been completed, thus allowing vehicles and supporting weapons across. The 76th Signal Company worked just as hard, getting a telephone line across. They tried a variety of methods, crawling across the pontoon bridge with the wire attached to one leg, swimming it across, firing it across by bazooka, but in every case the enemy severed the wire with gunfire. Finally, by using heavy iron weights, they managed to sink it to the bottom of the 15-foot deep river, where it survived exploding mines and shellfire.

Having dealt successfully with the natural obstacles, the attackers now turned their full attention on the enemy defences. Here is how their history describes one typical operation:

'Some forts offered tenacious resistance. On the 10th the 1st Battalion was attacking north of the Sauer along a draw approach to the high escarpment overlooking Echternach. Suddenly the air was filled with the thunderous din of exploding shells. Heavy mortar and artillery fire opened up simultaneously on Company C in positions along the draw, and on the battalion command post in Ernzerhof. In the west, Companies A and B were pinned on the high ground by flanking fire coming from a pillbox overlooking the approaches from the river. Its two main firing embrasures covered a 180 degree field of excellent observation. There was only one likely approach, the wooded draw which terminated about 75 yards from the fortification. The pillbox was divided into two compartments. There was no connecting door but both rooms opened into a depressed and concealed outdoor pit at the rear of the box. The firing compartment contained two offset embrasures at slightly different elevations, but these firing positions were reached via a narrow corridor with several ninety degree turns which were so staggered as to make grenading of the defenders extremely difficult. At the rear of the pillbox, however, was a firing post which, due to its depressed position, had only a limited field of fire. Under cover of darkness on the night of the 10th, a 12-man assault squad attempted to take the position. At 200 yards, efficient machine gunnery, and then mortar fire, stopped the squad, seriously wounding one man. No further attempt was made to take the pillbox that night.

'On the morning of the 11th a combined assault was planned by Lt-Col Mette; assisted by Capt Stanley G. Maynard; Capt Charles H. Wilson, Artillery Liaison Officer from

Left: Infantrymen of the 90th Infantry Division, Third Army, pick their way through rubble and bomb debris as they advance into Mainz, Germany, 22 March 1945./*US Army*

Below: A light machine gun crew of the 65th Infantry Division, Third Army, covers a street in a small German town, near the point where units of Third and Seventh US Armies met for the first time in the Saar Palantinate, 20 March 1945./*US Army*

901st FA Battalion; 1-Lt Henry E. Gerry, Battalion Intelligence Officer and acting Operations Officer. At 1500 a 25-man assault team commanded by 2-Lt Walter W. Henderson of Company C moved up along the wooded draw toward the pillbox. Working in three sections, a group of five men under S/Sgt Roke Smiljanic protected the left flank; four men led by Sgt Vito A. Pusco flanked on the right; 16 men formed the assault group, including a demolition man toting two 18lb satchel charges. With the team was aid man Pfc Enoch Machinis.

'The kick-off was at 1515. From an observation post in an old barn at Ernzerhof Capt Wilson directed 901st FA Battalion firing at the pillbox and surrounding enemy area. The barrage lasted 15 minutes. Simultaneously Capt Maynard's men opened fire directly on the pillbox with a captured 80mm mortar set up south of Ernzherhof. Under this combined cover the assault squad carefully worked its way up the draw. At 1550 the pallid, death signal of a green flare appeared in the sky; the artillerymen understood. They ceased firing; the concluding shell a screaming echo of the whisper in their hearts, "Good luck doughboys, give 'em hell".

'Immediately two .50 calibre machine guns north of Ernzerhof opened up with crossfire on the pillbox. From the adjacent woods it also received the whooshing rockets of bazookas. Up the ridge in a staggered wedge formation came the assaulting infantrymen. An anti-personnel mine exploded, the wire tripped accidently by Lt Henderson. He and Pfc Jack W. Wardle were slightly injured, but the lieutenant continued to lead the assault. The pillbox was completely buttoned up; fire from machine guns, bazookas, automatic and

M-1 rifles completely prevented the enemy from firing. The assault group was now 25 yards from the fort. The machine gunners lifted their fire and the demolition carrier, Pfc Leslie M. Roderick, rushing forward, placed one of the satchel charges against the door of the large front embrasure. Part of the door was blown away. A second charge was placed but failed to explode, so Sgt Pusco dashed up and tossed two grenades through the hole made by the initial explosion. By this time, however, the Germans, deserting the firing compartment, had fled via the rear exit to the quarters compartment. Members of the assault team worked their way into position and grenaded the new defence point. The Germans had had enough. Out of the pillbox came a complete manning crew of 15 men led by a staff sergeant, who was made to de-activate the minefield surrounding the fortification. The entire assault operation lasted 1hr 15min with only two of our men wounded in the action. 40 pillboxes to a square mile

and this is the saga of only one. Simple wasn't it?'

At noon on 11 February Combat Team 417 reverted to 76th Division control, they were later commended by the XII Corps Commander for the vigour, power and determination with which they had pressed home their first attack.

Across the Rhine
By the end of the third week of March 1945, the Allied armies had all reached the west bank of the Rhine throughout its length. They had one bridgehead across at Remagen where on the afternoon of 7 March, well to the north of Third Army, Lieutenant Karl H. Timmermann and Company A of 27th Infantry Battalion of US First Army had captured the damaged Ludendorff Railway Bridge before it could be properly demolished. The SHAEF plan was that the main crossing operation would take place in an area just above the

Below: Smoke generators pour out a protective screen along the Rhine, as men of the 89th Infantry Division, Third Army, prepare to cross the river at Oberwesel, 17 miles south east of Koblenz, 26 March 1945. /*IWM*

159

Ruhr, on the night 23/24 March. However, some 150 miles to the south the commander of Third Army had other ideas! Third Army had been given permission to cross by General Bradley on 19 March, and, finding that German opposition was weak in the area of Nierstein and Oppenheim (see Sketch Map 11) Patton was determined that the first successful assault crossing should be carried out by his troops. An ingenious plan had already been proposed by Brigadier-General E. W. Williams, the Third Army artillery commander, which involved concentrating all the artillery observation planes (L-4s) and liaison planes (L-5s) and using them to ferry troops across the river. Each could take one passenger, so the over 200 planes would be able to ferry a battalion across in about 90 minutes. When it came to the crunch the 'Third Army Troop Carrier Command', as this novel force had been nicknamed, was not used, as the enemy had had no time to build up strength across the river. At 2030 hours on the 22 March the leading assault boats of Company K, 3rd Battalion of the 11th Infantry Regiment, 5th Division, crossed at Nierstein without a shot being fired at them and captured a party of German soldiers on the far bank. Upstream at Oppenheim, Companies A and B of the 1st Battalion crossed at the same time but were involved in a 30-minute machine gun battle with the enemy before the Germans there also surrendered. The entire crossing was achieved with only 20 casualties. During the next morning tanks and tank destroyers were ferried across and by the late afternoon of the 23rd, a Class 40 treadway bridge had been completed at Nierstein. Patton was understandably triumphant, although when he broke the news to General Bradley at breakfast time, he asked him not to make any official announcement so that the Germans would perhaps be kept in ignorance and not move against his bridgehead.

'Later that morning "Lucky's" liaison officer at 12th Army Group HQ could not conceal his smile as he announced that "Without benefit of aerial bombardment, ground smoke, artillery preparation or airborne assistance (giving a direct dig at Monty) the Third Army at 2200 hours Thursday evening 22 March crossed the Rhine River". General Patton timed his announcement to the world carefully. Just hours before Field Marshal Montgomery's crossing began he phoned Bradley again: "Brad", he shouted, "for God's sake tell the world we're across. . . . I want the world to know Third Army made it before Monty starts across!'*

*After the Battle Number 16 of 1977, edited by Winston G. Ramsey.

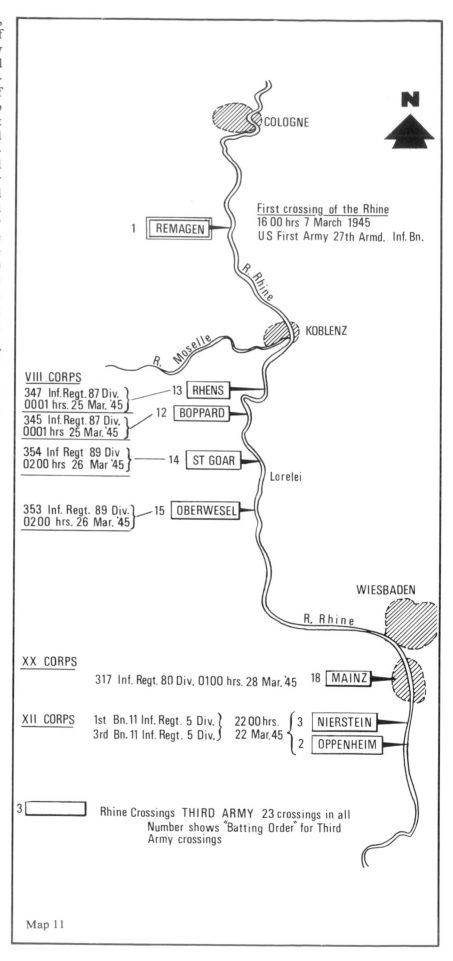

Map 11

Left: Map 11 Crossing the Rhine: Third Army crossings 22-28 March 1945.

Right: Large clouds of white smoke rise from the steep east bank of the Rhine River, 26 March 1945, as Third Army white phosphorous shells explode near a small German town./*IWM*

Below: Infantrymen in assault boats cross the Rhine near St Goar, 28 March 1945, as a GI in the foreground keeps a sharp lookout for snipers. /*US Signal Corps*

Bottom: Crossing the Rhine at Oberwesel. Loaded with soldiers of the 353rd Infantry Regiment of the 89th 'Rolling W' Division of Third Army, a DUKW hits the water on the morning of 26 March 1945. /*US Army*

Patton, arriving at the Nierstein crossing on 24 March, crossed the pontoon bridge with his ADCs. Part way over he called a short halt and, unbuttoning his flies relieved himself into the river. At the far bank, he deliberately stumbled, grabbed two handfuls of earth with the cry 'Thus William the Conqueror!' Gleefully he put in his diary that evening: '24 March. Drove to the river and went across on the pontoon bridge, stopping in the middle to take a piss in the Rhine, and then pick up some dirt on the far side . . . in emulation of William the Conqueror.'*

A hat-trick for Third Army

Third Army's second batch of crossings was made by VIII Corps, south of Koblenz in the Rhine Gorge, a difficult crossing area, with steep cliffs and a fast current to contend with. At the northernmost side near the village of Rhens, the assaulting force from 347th Infantry Regiment came under intense fire about five minutes before they were due to leave the west bank. Boats finally pushed off an hour later, but all attempts at an organised crossing were foiled by the Germans and in the early afternoon on 25 March it was decided to abandon further attempts. 10 kilometres to the south, however, the 345th did much better at Boppard, where the leading companies were soon across. Despite vigorous enemy reaction they were able to reinforce not only their own bridgehead but also to get GIs from the 347th across, who then advanced downstream to Rhens. By the evening both regiments had secured the high ground on the east bank and had begun work on a pontoon

The Patton Papers by Martin Blumenson.

161

bridge. Early the next morning 89th Division made a double assault near the famous Lorelei rocks at St Goar and Oberwesel. The enemy reacted sharply here as well, and fighting continued for most of the day. However, once the cliffs near the Lorelei had been secured, aided by an airstrike, direct enemy fire onto the bridgehead was eliminated. The hat-trick came on the 28th when at 0100 hours the 317th Infantry Regiment embarked from the Mainz waterfront, whilst the 319th crossed by the Oppenheim bridgehead to attack the enemy from the rear. All went very smoothly and Army engineers immediately began work on a 2,223-foot long railway bridge which Patton opened on 14 April, after they had worked non-stop night and day on its construction. He was offered a large pair of scissors to cut the ceremonial ribbon stretched across the bridge entrance, but he brushed them aside remarking 'What do you take me for, a tailor? God-dammit! Give me a bayonet!'

Patton and the Hammelburg Mission

Once across the Rhine there was no holding Third Army. They stormed through the Mainz-Frankfurt-Darmstadt triangle, advanced to the Main River and, on 25 March, seized bridgeheads at Hanau and Aschaffenburg. It was known from intelligence reports that a large Allied prisoner of war camp was located about 60 kilometres east of Aschaffenburg, which held some 4,700 prisoners, of which approximately 1,500 were Americans. Patton knew that the Germans had been murdering prisoners of war and therefore felt that an attempt should be made to liberate the camp. As he stated at a press conference on 30 March. . . . 'I felt that I could not sleep during the night if I got within 60 miles and made no attempt to get that place'. Patton believed that if a force was sent to liberate the prisoners it would also serve as a diversionary action to make the enemy believe he was attacking to the east toward Nuremburg instead of the north. There followed yet another controversial incident in Patton's career which those who hated him have always tried to use against him. I have been fortunate enough to secure an excellent objective account of the Hammelburg Mission written by Lieutenant-Colonel Frederick E. Oldinsky, who studied it closely at Trinity University in San Antonio, Texas, whilst reading for his master's degree. I am also greatly indebted to the editor of *Armor* magazine who first published the article in their July/August 1976 edition. Lt-Col Oldinsky writes:
'Patton's idea of a foray into enemy territory was met with very little enthusiasm. Major-General Manton Eddy, Commander of XII Corps, to whom Patton had given the mission, and Major-General William Hoge, Comman-

der of the 4th Armored Division, both disagreed with Patton's order. Additionally, according to Patton's diary, his immediate superior, General Omar Bradley, was also against the raid. For this mission, Patton had visualised a force the size of a combat command with a strength of approximately 3,000 men, 150 tanks, artillery and other supporting units. However, Patton was persuaded to send only a small task force. It is unclear exactly who or what had the dominant influence on Patton's decision to accept a smaller force for this daring venture, but the diary entry on 31 March 1945 would indicate Bradley was the dominant influence. The entry reads: "I made it (the attack on Hammelburg) with only two companies on account of the strenuous objections of General Bradley to making any (effort) at all".

'Eddy and Hoge objected because they believed the mission would fail and that Patton would be severely criticised for the attempt. Patton felt this was a very weak reason for not trying to save hundreds of Americans from being murdered by the Germans. It is also known that General Eddy, after failing to dissuade Patton from the mission, insisted on a small force instead of a combat command. General Hoge, on the other hand, was in favour of a large force, as was Lieutenant-Colonel Creighton W. Abrams, Commander of Combat Command B who had to actually provide the force. Both Hoge and Abrams were convinced that a small force would never make it, but Eddy would not yield.

'Colonel Abrams created a task force consisting primarily of Company C, 37th Tank Battalion and Company A, 10th Armored Infantry Battalion. Additionally, there was one platoon of light tanks from Company D, 37th Tank Battalion, and the assault gun platoon and a part of the reconnaissance platoon of the 10th Armored Infantry Battalion. Vehicle strength of this task force was 10 medium tanks, six light tanks, 27 halftracks, three 105mm self propelled assault guns, six jeeps and one Weasel for a total of 53 vehicles. Personnel strength was 293 officers and men. The man chosen to lead this battle-weary group (the men had slept only one night in four days of fighting) was the combat experienced S-3 (operations officer) of the 10th Armored Infantry Battalion, Captain Abraham J. Baum. This composite unit then became known as Task Force Baum.

'In order to cover Baum's departure, Colonel Abrams decided to attack the small town of Schweinheim just east of Aschaffenburg with CCB. The attack was launched on the evening of 26 March, and after three hours of fighting, CCB managed to punch a hole in the German defences. In the confusion created by the attack, Task Force Baum departed swiftly for Hammelburg. Accompanying Task Force Baum on this raid was Major Alender Stiller, one of General Patton's aides. Stiller's presence would

Above: Third Army engineers of the 80th Infantry Division, built the 'Sunday Punch' pontoon treadway at Mainz, the longest assault bridge across the Rhine (1,865 feet). */US Signal Corps*

Top left: Third Army GIs raise the Stars and Stripes on top of the Lorelei rock, overlooking the Rhine Gorge./*US Army*

Bottom left: Patton opens the 'President Roosevelt' bridge beside the demolished Mainz - Gustavsburg bridge. Offered a pair of scissors to cut the tape he is reported as saying 'What do you take me for, a tailor ? Goddamit! Give me a bayonet!' */US Army*

163

eventually be used by Patton's critics to accuse him of mounting the raid for personal reasons. Once on the road, Task Force Baum moved swiftly toward its objective. Their orders were to move to Hammelburg as quickly as possible, liberate the POWs and then return. They were to stop for nothing. For the first 20 miles, Baum encountered little opposition – only sporadic small arms and bazooka fire which did little damage to the task force except for the loss of some infantrymen riding on the tanks. Baum kept the losses to a minimum by firing on suspected enemy positions as they entered a town and by his fast movement. After passing through Lohr, the task force encountered a target that was too tempting to ignore. This target was a train loaded with multi-barreled anti-aircraft guns. Baum stopped just long enough to have his men destroy the guns with thermite grenades, and a single round from a tank gun destroyed the locomotive.

'Seven miles east of Lohr was the town of Gemunden. This was one of the more critical points of Baum's line of march since it was the location of a bridge across the Saale River. As Baum entered Gemunden, he spotted about a dozen trains preparing for departure. Without stopping, the tanks began firing at the trains and destroyed about half of them. As the column moved farther into town, Baum's force encountered the first significant resistance. Gemunden was well defended and Baum lost three tanks to bazooka fire. Baum himself was wounded in the hand and knee. The tank company commander was also wounded and had to be placed in a half-track. Baum's men rushed the bridge in an

Above: Men of a heavy weapons platoon of Third Army set up an M1917 machine gun in Saarlauten, Germany, during heavy fighting./*IWM*

Left: Infantrymen of the 6th Armd Div, dash through a burning street in a small German town east of the Rhine River, 2 April 1945, as walls of the buildings begin to collapse. /*US Army*

attempt to seize it intact, but the bridge was blown in their face, killing two of Baum's infantrymen who had made it onto the bridge. Baum called CCB on his radio and requested air support to assist him in crossing the stream, but after receiving approval of his request, Baum decided he could not wait and backed out of Gemunden to find another crossing.

'Baum elected to go north to search for another crossing even though the northern route would place another water obstacle in his line of march – the Sinn River [see Sketch Map 12]. It was in their search for a bridge over the Sinn that the task force entered the village of Rieneck, approximately four kilometres north of Gemunden. In Rieneck, a German paratrooper home on sick leave and tired of the war advised Baum that Burgsinn, six kilometres further north was the best place to cross the Sinn. In Burgsinn, Baum added three more prisoners to the 200 plus he had already captured. These three prisoners were a German general and part of his staff. The general identified himself in German and, since time was a critical factor, Baum did not take time to interrogate him, believing any information the general may reveal would have little or no effect on the immediate mission of the task force. Near the town of Grafendorf, the task force encountered approximately 700 Russian prisoners working on a road gang. When the Americans appeared, the Russians jumped their German guards and disarmed them. More Russians were freed in Grafendorf proper. Baum turned the 200 plus German prisoners over to the Russians who assured him they would conduct guerilla

warfare in that area until the Americans arrived in force. The task force then continued toward the town of Hammelburg. Baum encountered his first German tanks near the village of Ober, a mile and half from Hammelburg. The Germans and Americans exchanged fire and the Germans withdrew leaving both sides undamaged. Baum was apprehensive because he knew there must be more German tanks in the area and that a tank battle would be forthcoming.

'Baum elected to bypass Hammelburg and, near the village of Pfaffenhausen, his apprehension of a tank fight proved correct as the task force was engaged by a significant number of German tanks. While the medium tanks and two assault guns slugged it out with the German Panzers, Baum sent his light tanks, one assault gun, most of the half-tracks and a platoon of infantry on to the POW camp to start liberating the prisoners. After $2\frac{1}{2}$ hours of fighting, Baum broke through the German lines at the expense of five half-tracks and three jeeps. The Germans lost three tanks and three or four ammunition carriers. Additional fighting took place around the POW camp as the German guards fired on the task force with bazookas, rifles and machine guns.

'The POW camp was two miles south of Hammelburg and was divided into two compounds, one compound housing Yugoslavian prisoners. The Americans mistook the grey Yugoslav uniforms for Germans and started firing into that part of the POW camp. After the tank guns had set fire to a number of barracks in the camp, a Yugoslav officer asked the German camp commander to send several

Below: Map 12 The Hammelburg mission.

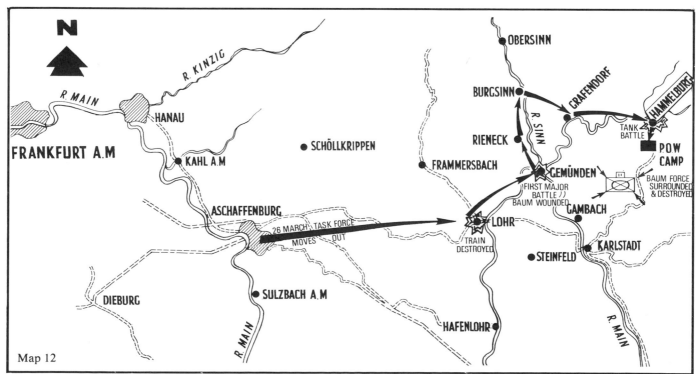

Map 12

Americans out to stop the firing. The camp commander, a German general named Von Goeckel, asked the senior American POW, Colonel Paul B. Goode, to undertake the task. Colonel Goode agreed and took three other American officers with him, one of whom was Lieutenant-Colonel John K. Waters, Patton's son-in-law. A German interpreter accompanied the Americans and they walked out of the camp through the main gate carrying the American flag and a white sheet tied to a pole. Before the party reached the task force, Colonel Waters was shot by a German soldier hiding in a barnyard nearby. Waters was taken to a hospital in the village where he was treated by a Serbian doctor. Task Force Baum had liberated the POW camp. The freed prisoners became almost hysterical with joy at the sight of the Americans, and it took Baum several hours to restore order to the camp. This time lost in trying to organise the prisoners to load up and move out back to the Aschaffenburg area may very well have been the crucial element in Baum's mission which cost him "the old ball game" because the Germans had used this time to good advantage in preparing to destroy Baum's force. The tank battalion in Hammelburg still had some operational guns, and figuring that the Americans would return the same way they came, prepared to ambush Baum on his return to Hammelburg. Additionally, a German reconnaissance plane had spotted the task force about 2 o'clock that afternoon near Weickersgruben and had radioed the position and true strength to the German 7th Army

headquarters in the area. The German 7th Army commander, General Von Obstfelder, had been working since early in the morning of the 26th to muster enough forces to destroy the raiders. He didn't know the exact size of the force he was opposing, however, until he received the report from the reconnaissance plane. Baum had liberated 5,000 prisoners, 1,291 of whom were Americans. He loaded approximately 250 of them on his tanks and half tracks and advised the others to follow on foot or strike out on their own directly west for Aschaffenburg. Task Force Baum then departed for its return trip to the Aschaffenburg area.

'The Americans had hardly gotten outside the gate of the POW camp when the first tank was knocked out by anti-tank fire from a bazooka. Most of the liberated prisoners saw all hopes of escape fade and quietly walked back into the POW camp to await liberation at a later date. Baum then turned his force toward the town of Hessdorf, 5 miles south-west of Hammelburg instead of trying to fight his way through the ambush. Upon reaching Hessdorf around midnight, Baum ran into two roadblocks and had to change direction again, this time shifting north to Hollrich. By this time, other German forces, rallied by General Obstfelder, was closing in on Baum. At Hollrich, Baum lost three more tanks, a tank commander, and a large number of infantrymen. Baum then moved his forces up a trail to the top of a hill a mile east of Hollrick and regrouped. The task force had now been reduced to three medium tanks, six light

Below: Infantrymen of 65th Infantry Division, Third Army, pass burning buildings in a little German town after it has been cleared of all enemy resistance./*US Army*

tanks, 12 halftracks, about 100 men and 60 liberated officers in fighting condition. The force was low on gasoline, so he ordered gas siphoned from eight of the half tracks and burned them. He gave his men a pep talk, placed the wounded in a building nearby and marked it with a red cross. Baum then formed the column to move out when the Germans attacked. Baum could see he was surrounded. An unknown number of assault guns were moving up from the south, six heavy tanks and two infantry companies were approaching from the southwest, six Tiger tanks were firing from positions from the northeast and a column of tanks was approaching from the direction of Weickersgruben.

'The German attack was rapid, violent and well co-ordinated, with artillery shelling Baum's forces while the tanks and infantry attacked. The task force fought until all of the tanks and assault guns were destroyed. Baum's men fought like tigers, but were hopelessly outnumbered and out-gunned. Their means to resist having been destroyed, Baum broke the remainder of his men into small groups and told them to try to make it back on their own. Baum, Stiller and an unidentified lieutenant tried to evade the Germans, but were captured about 1930 hours that evening. Baum was wounded for the third time when a German sergeant shot him with a pistol while capturing him. The Germans did not know that Baum had been the commander of the task force and he was taken back to Hammelburg to the camp he had momentarily liberated where he was passed off as a former POW

in the camp. The Germans thought Major Stiller had been the commander. The Hammelburg mission had ended. Task Force Baum had been destroyed and most of the survivors were captured.

'As mentioned earlier, this raid was to become another controversy in Patton's career. The focal point of this controversy was the presence of Patton's son-in-law, Lieutenant-Colonel John K. Waters, in the Hammelburg camp. Critics of Patton quickly seized upon the incident for another editorial assault on him by claiming that Patton had ordered the raid for the sole purpose of rescuing Colonel Waters. Others, in defence of Patton, claimed that the raid was a sound tactical move and had nothing to do with Waters' presence in the camp. The real purpose of the raid probably lies somewhere between these two extremes. The first point to consider is whether or not Patton even knew his son-in-law was in the Hammelburg Camp. Waters had been captured in Tunisia in February 1943, and sent to Italy. He was moved to Poland and was reported to be in a POW camp near Szubin in early 1945. The Russians overran that part of Poland, but the Germans had already moved the prisoners before the Russians arrived. The fact that Waters had been at Szubin was revealed by the Russian commander in a message to the American military mission in Moscow and word was sent through various channels until it eventually reached Patton. However, Waters' new location was unknown. Allied intelligence later reported that the camp at Hammelburg

Below: As machine gunners (on left of picture) set up their LMG to provide cover, infantrymen of the 26th Infantry Division, Third Army, dash across the Schleuse River near Waldau, Germany, 9 April 1945, to attack German units dug in the surrounding pine forest./*US Army*

Below: The crew of a Sherman of 6th Armd Div, watch the smoke rising from the burning railway station in nearby Mühlhausen, Germany, 5 April 1945./*6 Armd Div Assoc/George F. Hofmann*

was a principal camp for Allied officers and that many of those at Szubin had been transferred to Hammelburg. With only this scant information, it is difficult to see how General Patton could have known positively that Colonel Waters was at Hammelburg. Based on his diary entries, it is apparent that Patton hoped or even believed that Waters was in Hammelburg, but that is a long way from knowing he was there. On 23 March Patton wrote to his wife, Beatrice: "We are headed right for John's place and may get there before he is moved". This letter to Mrs Patton, rather than being a positive statement as to Waters' location, was probably to reassure Mrs Patton as to Waters' safety for, as mentioned previously, the information was simply not available to Patton for him to be certain that Waters was at Hammelburg. There are obviously dissenting opinions and one such opinion was stated by General (then Lieutenant-Colonel) Creighton W. Abrams whose Combat Command B provided the forces for the Hammelburg mission. In a letter to the Chief of Military History, dated 13 September 1967, Abrams stated that when Major Alexander Stiller, Patton's aide, spoke with him (Abrams) and General Hoge, Stiller said he wanted to go along "only because General Patton's son-in-law, Colonel Waters, was in the prison camp". This statement probably reflects Patton's hope that Waters was in the camp rather than an absolute knowledge that he was there. Whether Patton knew or hoped Waters was at Hammelburg could be a moot point if the resulting actions were the same. This leads to the heart of the controversy, namely the reason for the Hammelburg raid. If Patton believed that Waters was there, did Waters' presence in fact motivate the raid or was he incidental to the real purpose?

'A study of Patton's character reveals one important trait which would have made it unlikely that he would risk the lives of almost 300 of his soldiers for no other reason than to rescue his son-in-law. That trait was his love for his men. It touched him deeply to see his men wounded or killed and, on more than one occasion, he had wept over one of his men. Patton's nephew, Frey Ayer Jr, once asked his uncle why he swaggered around and ranted and waved his pistols so much; Patton's answer sums up his feelings for his men. Patton said: "In any war, a commander, no matter what his rank, has to send to sure death, nearly every day, by his own orders, a certain number of men. All are his personal responsibility, to them as his troops and to their families. Any man with a heart would, then, like to sit down and bawl like a baby, but he can't. So he sticks out his jaw and swaggers and swears". His concern for his men was further evidenced by the fact that,

169

to a great extent, he measured an officer's fitness to command by the number of casualties his unit sustained. Patton was constantly checking the casualty figures in each command in evaluating his subordinate commanders. His concern for the welfare of his men, therefore, would at the very least, prove it to be out of character for Patton to order the Hammelburg raid for the express purpose of rescuing Colonel Waters. Assuming for the moment that Waters was not the primary reason for the raid, it may be reasonable to assume that Waters was at least a secondary reason. Patton could have been influenced to some degree by Waters' presence if only subconsciously. What is more probable is that Patton ordered the raid for other reasons, with Waters' rescue as a bonus. If so, what were the other reasons? According to Patton, as mentioned earlier in this article, the mission was launched to rescue the American POWs in the camp and to create a diversionary action to deceive the Germans as to the true direction of the Third Army's next attack. These two objectives certainly were feasible and the soundness of them could be found in both precedent and the rules of warfare. General Douglas MacArthur, through a similar daring move, had liberated 5,000 POWs and civilian internees at the prison camps at Santo Thomas and Bilibid in Manila. This action by MacArthur probably had some influence on Patton's decision to stage the Hammelburg raid, for as Patton stated "he

would make MacArthur look like a piker". Not that he would undertake so dangerous a mission just to outdo MacArthur, but it at least indicated that this type of manoeuvre was possible, albeit the circumstances and location were different. The idea of using the raid as a diversion to deceive the Germans was certainly a sound tactic, both as general policy in warfare and in this particular instance. Third Army was disposed in such a manner to make German intelligence uncertain as to Patton's intention and direction once he launched his offensive from the west bank of the Main River. A foray to the east stood a good chance of making the Germans believe that was the direction of the main effort of the Third Army. In fact, they were deceived. The only questionable aspect of the Hammelburg mission should be the size of the force sent and not the motives behind the mission. The fact that Generals Eddy and Hoge were against the mission entirely probably had a great deal of influence in sending a small force rather than the combat command Patton had initially intended to send. There is some disparity in available source material as to the influence General Omar Bradley had on this mission. In addition to the reference of Bradley's opinion made earlier, Patton also stated in a letter to Mrs Patton on 5 April 1945: "My first thought was to send a combat command, but I was talked out of it by Omar and others. . . ." In contradiction to Patton's statements,

Below: Doughboys of the 44th Armd Inf Bn, 6th Armd Div, dash across open space to escape sniper fire in Oberdoria, Germany, 4 April 1945. /*US Army*

General Bradley in his autobiography states: "I did not learn of the expedition until it had been on the road two days ... Certainly had George consulted me on the mission I would have forbidden him to stage it". One can only speculate as to the true story, however, this writer believes General Patton's version is close to the truth, based on the character of these two men and an entry in Patton's diary on 18 January 1944, long before the Hammelburg incident occurred. The character of Patton and Bradley differed in a number of ways, but most pertinent here is Patton's boldness and Bradley's timidity, and Bradley's political nature versus Patton's total lack of political considerations throughout his life. Bradley would be much more apt to "sway with the tide" and keep his record clean by denying knowledge of an operation that had failed, whereas Patton was always willing to "stand up and be counted" and accept full responsibility for his mistakes, as he certainly did in the Hammelburg incident. The diary entry of 18 January referred to above illustrates this point. Patton had just been informed that Bradley had been made commander of all ground troops in England when he entered the following in his diary: "Bradley is a man of great mediocrity. At Gafsa when it looked as though the Germans might turn our right flank ... he suggested that we withdraw corps headquarters to Feriana. I refused to move. In Sicily, when the 45th Division approached Ofala, he halted them for fear of a possible German landing east of Termini. I had to order him to move and told him I would be responsible for his rear and that his timidity had cost us one day. He tried to stop the landing operation east of Cap d'Orlando because he thought it was dangerous. I told him I would take the blame if it failed and that he could have the credit if it was a success ...". The fact that Patton was willing to take the blame for failure and give Bradley credit for success could very well have been repeated prior to the Hammelburg raid. However, as previously stated, this is only speculation and the absolute truth could probably not be proven one way or the other. Be that as it may, there is little doubt that the partial failure of Task Force Baum was caused by insufficient strength. Note the term "partial failure", for in some ways the mission was a resounding success, proving at least in part that the raid was a sound tactical manoeuvre.

'Most of the critics of the Hammelburg raid give the impression that the entire task force was annihilated and accomplished nothing in the process. Statements have been made that 300 men were sacrificed to satisfy Patton's whim. The record does not bear this out. Interviews with captured German officers and official German records bear testimony to the fact that Task Force Baum accomplished the mission of creating a diversionary action. General Von Obstfelder believed that Task Force Baum would be followed by the 4th Armored Division and possibly the entire Third Army because he still did not know they were swinging north. Other German units, elements of an estimated three divisions, were diverted to the Hammelburg area to stop Task Force Baum and to block the suspected follow-on attack. Some of those units would have been used against Third Army in the north had they not been diverted. The effect of the diversion of those units on the subsequent advance of the Third Army was evidenced by the fact that the 4th Armored Division didn't fire a shot for the first 90-100 miles in the attack. In addition to creating a diversion, the Task Force inflicted considerable damage on the Germans while enroute to Hammelburg. Baum's forces had destroyed 12 German trucks, three tanks, three or four ammunition carriers, at least six locomotives and 12 trains, a number of anti-aircraft guns, disrupted troop movement schedules, notified the Air Force of a lucrative target (the marshalling area at Gemunden), and captured over 200 prisoners. In addition, it can be assumed that the 700 Russian prisoners released around Grafendorf must have caused considerable problems for the Germans if for no other reason than requiring additional forces to be diverted to recapture them. The same was true of the liberated American POWs who chose to strike out on their own in an attempt to make it back to the American lines. There was also the psychological effect on both the Germans and Americans. The Germans suffered a blow to their morale, both military and civilian, in the realisation that their defences were insufficient to prevent an American raid deep into their territory. The entire area was thrown into confusion and caused a great deal of panic. The American POWs were given a morale boost by the knowledge that they were not forgotten and a brighter outlook toward permanent liberation, since they learned from the task force how close the main American forces were. The American casualty picture from the raid was not as dismal as that painted by the critics. Of the 293 officers and men comprising the task force, only nine were killed, 32 wounded and 16 missing. The remainder were captured and returned at a later date. As for Colonel Waters, both he and Captain Baum were liberated along with the other wounded American prisoners, by a task force from Combat Command B of the 14th Armored Division commanded by Lt-Colonel James Lann of the 47th Tank Battalion. The rest of the prisoners had been moved from the Hammelburg camp shortly after the raid by Task Force Baum.'

The Last Roundup

Germany on its Last Legs

When April 1945 began 3rd Army armoured spearheads were bursting out from positions 60 miles east of the Rhine, and by the end of the month the enemy were on their last legs, unable to offer any properly organised resistance. Their tanks were almost all destroyed or captured, their replacement system broken down and their communications shattered. Complete collapse was not far off, as Third Army continued its drive deep into the Fatherland. About the middle of the month orders were received to shift Third Army's direction of advance to the southeast, into Bavaria, in order to attack the German-Austrian 'National Redoubt' area. This change

Below: Map 13 The Last Roundup: the Rhine to VE-Day, 22 March-8 May 1945.

of direction was another enormous undertaking which can be likened to their 90 degree turn during the Battle of the Bulge, but once again it was achieved without a hitch. On 21 April the campaign to cross the Danube, enter Czechoslovakia and Austria began, with 'Lucky' attacking southeast. Enemy resistance was encountered at Neumarkt, Regensburg and on the Altmuhl, Danube and Isar rivers (see Sketch Map 13). On 26 April they captured a field order from the German 1st Army, which disclosed that the enemy intended to attack Third Army's open left flank with the 11th Panzer Division. The attack did not materialise, however, and the complete panzer division later surrendered en

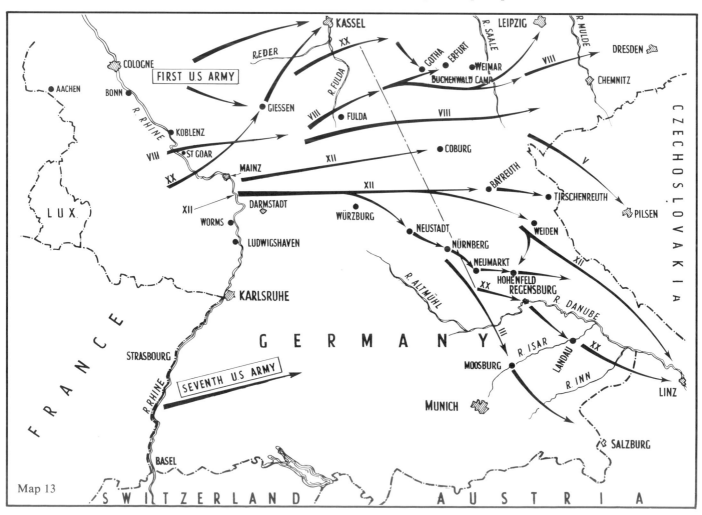

Map 13

Above: On the last lap. Tanks and halftracks of 4th Armd Div, kick up clouds of dust as they roll along across open country towards Erfurt, Germany, 12 April 1945. /*US Army*

Left: US armour rolls through Bayreuth, 14 April 1945./*IWM*

Below left: Destruction in the railway yards at Bayreuth. /*Col Crosby P. Miller*

Above: Patton plans the 'coup de grace'. Gen Patton and Maj-Gen James A. Van Fleet, CG III Corps, kneel down to examine a map layout of the Danube River, 26 April 1945. /*US Army*

Right: A Sherman of 11th Armd Div, follows a jeep into the burning town of Kronach, near Bayreuth./*US Army*

masse. By the end of the month armoured units of XII Corps were 15 miles inside Austria and enemy resistance had all but completely collapsed. The first eight days of May saw the end of the German war machine. Third Army had split the Reich in half, its armoured spearheads were at the Czech border, across the Danube, Isar and Inn rivers and deep into Austria. Once higher headquarters lifted their restraining orders Third Army was able to plunge ahead into Czechoslovakia and to capture Pilsen. They were also able to blast into the 'National Redoubt' area so swiftly that even if the Germans had wanted to make a last stand there they just weren't given the opportunity!

Spoils of War

During this final sweep through Germany the biggest treasure trove of the war was accidentally discovered by XII Corps in a small village called Merkers, northeast of Fulda, as the XII Corps history relates:

'Into Merkers, an undistinguished village about 15 miles southwest of Eisenach in mid Germany slogged the weary infantrymen of Maj-Gen Herbert L. Earnest's 90th Division. Their job was the usual one of follow through after Lt-Gen George S. Patton's advance tank forces; unsnarling knots of resistance, sorting out prisoners and slave labourers. Of the latter there were many for Merkers' big salt mines. That night after curfew, two of the 90th military police stopped two women in the village street. The women explained they were going for the midwife. The MPs went along just to be certain. They passed an entrance to a salt mine. Said one of the *Hausfrauen*: "That's where the bullion is hidden". MP ears perked up: "How's that again?" the woman repeated the gossip she had heard – Germany's gold had been salted away in that mine. The MPs took a look. The mine was held by eight German civilians. Two were polite, worldly men from Berlin: one moon-faced Werner Vieck, a Reichsbank official, the other pale, gaunt Dr Paul Ortwin Rave, curator of the German state museums, assistant director of Berlin's National Gallery. They talked quite frankly about their secret, now that it was no longer secret. The mine, they said, held: about 100 tons of gold bars (worth approximately 100 million dollars); Banker Vieck said it was Germany's entire gold reserve. Three billion paper Reichmarks; probably the greatest store of currency in Germany, perhaps the only reserve. Great stacks of foreign currency, two million American dollars, 110,000 British pounds, four million Norwegian crowns, a million French francs, lesser amounts of Spanish, Portuguese and Turkish money. Hundreds of crates and boxes – a huge cache of priceless works of art: Rembrandts, Raphaels, Renoirs, Durers, Van Dycks; tapestries and engravings; a Titian Venus, original Goethe manuscripts. All this and more was stored in chambers 2,100 feet deep. The Americans went down, opened a few bundles of currency, looked into wooden cases that covered paintings and

Below: GIs of the 11th Armd Div, fire at enemy across the border in the blazing town of Kepple, Austria./*US Army*

statues. On many cases they noted significant stencilling: Paris, Brussels, Vienna. But Curator Rave insisted that these were not stolen treasures – this store of art belonged to the Reich, and had been removed from Berlin "because the Russians were pushing too close". Banker Vieck regretted that he could not show the cache of gold, somebody had lost the key to the chamber. The Americans obligingly blew out a wall, and there was the gold, each 25lb bar wrapped in a sack, each sack tagged "Reichsbank". There were sacks of gold coin, some of them too heavy for a man to lift. There seemed to be even more gold stacked in the dimlit, salt-crusted chamber than Vieck had said. Gold was something for reparation experts to worry about. Gen Earnest's intelligence experts were more interested in the three billion German marks. That currency might turn out to be a prize of golden military value. Banker Vieck remarked that the German Army desperately needed it to meet its payrolls. It was irreplaceable: Germany's money-engraving plants had been bombed out.'

The Corps history goes on to amplify the fascinating story, which was copied from a wartime magazine, with the following footnote:
'XII Corps men who actually got down to look at the treasure might quibble over certain details. The "salt-encrusted chamber" was

176

Left: The fabulous Merkers treasure mine. The bags to the right of the small railway track contain gold coin and bars – about 200 tons of the precious metal was hidden in this disused salt mine and 'liberated' by Third Army, 7 April 1945./*Herbert S. Benjamin Associates Inc*

Below left: A helmet, full of golden coins from the Merkers treasure mine, takes two to lift. /*Herbert S. Benjamin Associates Inc*

Right: Third Army finance officers, aided by a Reichsbank official (in civilian clothes), check over the money bags found in the Merkers salt mine. /*IWM*

Below: Men of Third Army inspect some of the crated works of art, found in the mine. Besides hundreds of famous sculptures there were over 2,000 valuable paintings. /*US Signal Corps*

Above: Nazi prisoners walk along the centre island of the autobahn near Giessen, as vehicles of 6th Armd Div roll past them on both sides. /US Army

Right: Two of the 120 British, Scottish, Canadian and New Zealand POWs waving at their liberators from 15th Tank Bn, 6th Armd Div, in the town of Lengenfeld, Germany. (Note the 75mm howitzer on the M5 chassis. This was known as the M8 Howitzer Motor Carriage and was introduced in order to provide the Armoured Force with a howitzer equipped vehicle for close support. 46 rounds were carried. It was found in the HQ companies of medium tank battalions, until gradually replaced by 105mm howitzers mounted on the Sherman chassis.)/6 *Armd Div Assoc/George F. Hofmann*

extremely well lighted by a row of electric lights along the ceiling. The gold bars appeared to be loaded three to a sack, instead of one, and the total was reported to be not 100 tons but 200. No mention is made of the suitcases containing jewellery and even – the horrified whisper ran – gold teeth from the concentration camps. Rumour at least had it that the original tip off was given to our troops not by the Krauts but by some British POWs in a camp near Merkers, who had been used as labourers to get the treasure into place. Col Lieber, who was Gen Eddy's representative, sent to the mine as soon as Gen Earnest reported the apparent importance of the discovery, remembers that a woman was said to have given the tip off, but British POWs led him and his party to the entrance of the treasure room which he ordered blown out when the door could not be opened.'

Death Marches and Death Camps

Other dramatic discoveries made in the closing days of the war were such stark evidence of Nazi brutality as to make the average GI almost doubt his own eyes. First were the emaciated survivors of the infamous death marches, when the SS moved prisoners away from the advancing Allies. The XII Corps history tells the dreadful story thus:

'On 16 April, 2,800 political prisoners were started on a march from Flossenberg by the SS; on 18 and 20 April more were put on the road, so that by 20 April, an estimated 15,000 German-held political prisoners and forced labourers were conducted on an SS "March of Death". They were driven for three days and three nights; as the weak fell by the wayside, they were either murdered or left to die. No food was provided during the period and, in their weakened condition after years of concentration camp inhumanities, many had insufficient energy to withstand the torturous journey. Survivors report the cruellest treatment throughout the march; shootings by SS guards were reported to be continuous. The slaughter continued right up to the arrival of our armour; then the SS guards departed leaving the human wreckage to stagger away; the strongest, taking to the highways; the weak crawling into the woods and barns or other shelter. About 3,000 died on the march; about 3,000 were able to get out of the immediate area where turned loose, the balance of 9,000 holed up in the general area of Cham, Roding, Posing and Neuenberg. Near the town of Neuenberg the SS guards had one final orgy of butchery. Col Frank Weaver, Asst G-5, and Capt Merle Potter, found such aftermath of this activity that the

Above: Captured German officers watch from the side of the autobahn as vehicles of 6th Armd Div, approach Giessen, 30 miles north of Frankfurt, which was entered 28 March 1945./*US Army*

Far right: When 5th Inf Div entered Volary, Czechoslovakia, they discovered that the SS had buried in a shallow mass grave 30 Jewish women prisoners who had been starved to death on the infamous 300 mile death march across Czechoslovakia. They made the Germans exhume and view the bodies, before giving them a decent burial./*US Signal Corps*

Right: Happy Allied POWs freed by the 6th Armd Div near Ziegenhain, Germany. /*6 Armd Div Assoc/George F. Hofmann*

Below: Murdered Polish prisoners lie where they were shot through the head in the Ohrdruf Concentration Camp, another infamous deed perpetrated by the SS, just before Third Army arrived on 8 April 1945./*US Army*

latter returned to the village and supervised a mass burial for 204 victims of the "march". Col Hayden Sears, formerly CO of the 17th Armored Corps and more recently of the 4th Armored Division, is credited with the organisation of a custom by this time widely popular throughout XII Corps. In accordance with it, the people of Neuenberg were required to supply coffins for the poor wretches slaughtered within their township, dig the graves and attend the burial services. At the conclusion of the ceremony, in the name of the Corps CG, a message was read in German over the public address system of a sound track to the assembled men, women and children of the village "Only God Himself" the message ended "has the terrible might and infinite wisdom to visit upon you and your leaders the total punishment you deserve ... May the memory of this day and of these tragic dead rest heavily upon the conscience of every German so long as each of you shall live". The worst discovery of this nature was reserved almost for the last. On 5 May 1945, a reconnaissance party from Troop D, 41st Cavalry Squadron, 11th Armored Division, advancing down the beautiful Danube valley, uncovered near Linz two concentration camps, Mauthausen and Gusen. The former was such a spectacle of horror as subsequently to compete in the opinion of the world with Dachau and Buchenwald for the title of worst example of its kind. It was certainly the most hideous thing that many members of XII Corps had ever seen. "Here were 16,000 political prisoners, representing every country in Europe, all reduced to living skeletons and ridden with disease", the I&E pamphlet history of the 11th Armored Division reports. "The bodies of more than 500 were stacked

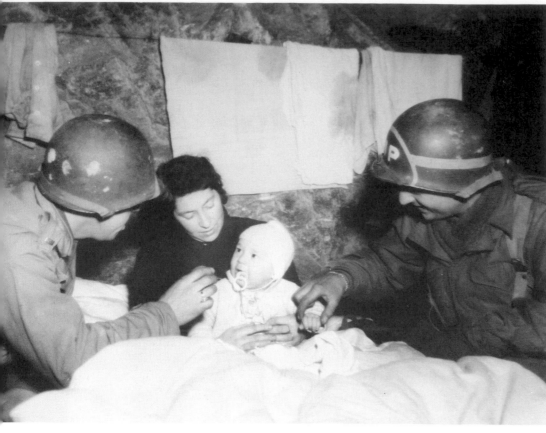

Left: 300 refugees took shelter in a cave near Rohrbach, Germany, for six days during the shelling of the town which preceded its capture by Third Army troops, 14 December 1944./*US Army*

Right: Close up of a group of German prisoners. Note the mess kits (*Kochgeschirr*) which some are carrying. This consisted of a deep pot with a cover which could be utilised as a plate, strapped together with a leather or web strap. One man holds his canteen (*Feldflasche*). /*IWM*

Below right: Thousands of prisoners were now stumbling through vast stockades, such as this one, for counting. /*US Army*

Below: Major E. L. Booch, provost marshal of the 11th Armd Div, Third Army, talks to two Nazi boy soldiers, captured near Kulmbach, Germany, 15 April 1945. /*US Army*

in an area between two barracks. The few long term prisoners still alive said that at least 45,000 bodies had been burned in the huge crematorium in four years. Other thousands were killed in the gas chambers, injected with poison or beaten to death". Details of such camps have since received so much public notice in connection with postwar trials of guards and superintendents of the hell-holes, that this volume need not repeat the stories of the torture chambers, killing pens, the walking dead, the emaciated bodies stacked like cordwood. Suffice it that a visit to Mauthausen was an unforgettable experience – unfortunately. As one XII Corps Headquarters officer wrote home: "It is really the smell that makes a visit to a Death Camp stark reality. The smell and the stink of the dead and the dying. The smell and stink of the starving. Yes, it is the smell, the stink, the odour of a Death Camp that makes it burn in the nostrils and memory. I will always smell Mauthausen, just as I can smell the bodies we found from the Floosenburg death march . . .".'

The End of the War

'The stars were out on the night of 9 May. The GI looked over at his buddy. "You watch for red flares for a while, I have some business to attend to" he said quietly. He moved over into a patch of bushes, raised his M-1 into the air and shot off a whole clip at nothing – nothing at all'.

182

That is how the history of the 76th Infantry Division describes the feelings of one GI on VE-Day, and they were probably very typical of the vast majority of Allied soldiers. They were strangely lacking in the exultant thrill of victory which all had expected to feel. However, General Patton produced a rousing General Order for VE-Day which included the following passages:

'... During the 281 days of incessant and victorious combat, your penetrations have advanced farther in less time than any other army in history, you have fought your way across 24 major rivers and innumerable lesser streams. You have liberated or conquered more than 82,000 square miles of territory, including 1,500 cities and towns, and some 12,000 inhabited places. Prior to the termination of active hostilities, you had captured in battle 956,000 enemy soldiers and killed or wounded at least 500,000 others. France, Belgium, Luxembourg, Germany, Austria and Czechoslovakia bear witness to your exploits. All men and women of the six corps and 39 divisions that have at different times been members of the Army have done their duty. Each deserves credit. The enduring valour of the combat troops has been paralleled and made possible by the often unpublicised activities of the supply, administrative and medical services of this Army and of the Communications Zone troops supporting it. Nor should we forget our comrades of the other armies and of the Air Force, particularly of the XIX Tactical Air Command, by whose side or under whose wings we have had the honour to fight. In proudly contemplating our achievements let us never forget our heroic dead whose graves mark the course of our victorious advances, nor our wounded whose sacrifices aided so much our success ...

Left: Gen Jacob D. Devers, CG 6th and 12th Army Groups, presents the 4th Armd Div with the Presidential Unit Citation for their outstanding combat work in France and Germany. Major-General William M. Hoge, CG 4th Armd Div, stands behind Gen Devers, whilst Sgt James T. Foley, 47, Catherine Street, Hartford, Conn, holds the division flag. Landshut, Germany 14 June 1944./*US Army*

Below: Maj-Gen Robert Grow, Patton's other outstanding armoured commander, receives the French Legion of Honor, from Gen Koeltz, French Army, 28 April 1945. Gen Grow commanded 6th Armd Div throughout almost the whole period of Third Army's active operations./*US Army*

During the course of this war I have received promotion and decorations far above and beyond my individual merit. You won them: I as your representative wear them. The one honour which is mine and mine alone is that of having commanded such an incomparable group of Americans, the record of whose fortitude, audacity, and valour will endure as long as history lasts . . .".*

The Occupation, Problems for Patton

The fighting over, Third Army along with the rest of the victorious Allied troops had now to face the problems and frustrations of sorting out the total chaos all around them. Thousands of German soldiers were filling the POW cages, equal numbers of displaced persons from all over Europe had to be looked after, the civil government were non-existent, the economy in ruins and the population almost starving. Much had to be done to restore order out of the chaos and at the same time Germany had to be de-nazified and de-militarised. Non-fraternization was the rule of these early days, although it shortly proved impossible to maintain. This tangled web was not the sort of environment which Patton, always the soldier and man of action, enjoyed. He did his best in his usual forthright manner, seeing as his first duty the reorganisation of his area of Germany, so that the people at least would have the bare necessities of life in order to survive the coming winter. Once again he fell foul of the press of his own country and a group of them deliberately goaded him into losing his temper at a press conference and saying things which were then blown up out of all proportion and used against him. He was accused of keeping known Nazis in

XII Corps History by Lt-Col George Dyer.

positions of power and public opinion, and in particular, the very strong Jewish lobby in America was turned against him, so that once again his career took a slide for the worse. As I have said earlier, as a completely un-biased outsider, I cannot understand why America should choose to treat one of their greatest war heroes so badly. It was inevitable that he would lose command of his beloved Third Army and be once again given a 'paper command' – this time the 15th Army, which, as Martin Blumenson explains: 'controlled no troop units except those necessary for its own housekeeping . . . its sole mission being the preparation of historical and analytical studies on the tactics, techniques, organisations and administration of the war in Europe'.* 'The more I see of people the more I regret that I survived the war' wrote Patton in his diary in one of his darker moments.

Patton Hands Over

At noon on 7 October 1945 the transfer of command ceremony took place in which General Patton handed over to General Lucian K. Truscott. It was a simple ceremony and Patton made a short speech:

The Patton Papers by Martin Blumenson.

'General Truscott, Officers and Men: All good things must come to an end. The best thing that has ever come to me thus far is the honour and privilege of having commanded the Third Army. The great successes we have achieved together have been due primarily to the fighting heart of America, but without the co-ordinating and supply activities of the General and Special Staffs, even American valour would have been impotent. You officers and men here represent the fighting, the administrative and the supply elements of this Army. Please accept my heartfelt congratulations on your valour and devotion to duty, and my fervent gratitude for your unwavering loyalty. When I said that all good things come to an end, I was referring to myself and not to you because you will find in General Truscott every characteristic which will inspire in you the same loyalty and devotion which you have so generously afforded me. A man of General Truscott's achievements needs no introduction. His deeds speak for themselves. I know that you will not fail him. Goodbye and God bless you.'

The band then played Auld Lang Syne at the end of which the Colour Bearer approached with the colours of the Third Army. Patton took the colours and handed them on to General Truscott, saying that he could think of no more worthy recipient. General Truscott then handed them back to the Colour Sergeant. There followed a formal lunch with speeches, and here is how Colonel George Fisher remembers the event:

'The skies were dripping . . . when Patton officially turned over the command, so the formal ceremony was staged in the spacious Bad Tolz gymnasium. The General attended religious services that morning as usual, after which he went directly to the gym. Nothing in his dress or bearing reflected the torture of his soul as he stepped forward to hand over the symbol of his command. "All good things must come to an end" was the burden of his brief remarks. The luncheon that the headquarters mess officer spread out that noon really deserved a better appetite than most of us could muster. All the old corps and division commanders who could be found were there. Their testimonies varied in length but no wise in sincerity. Some thoughts strayed to George Washington and his farewell address at Fraunces' Tavern. Chaplain O'Neill may have remembered the Last Supper. Along about mid-afternoon Patton had had enough. He arose, squared his shoulders, and moved resolutely off to his waiting car.'*

*The Patton Papers by Martin Blumenson.

187

'This is a Hell of a Way for a Soldier to Die'

On 9 December 1945 General Patton was travelling in his car along the Frankfurt-Mannheim road with his Chief of Staff Major-General 'Hap' Gay. The car was a 1939 Cadillac, driven by Pfc Horace L. Woodring. Shortly before midday they were in collision with a big truck belonging to a quartermaster corps unit. The front of the car was smashed, but Gay, Woodring and the driver of the truck were unhurt. Patton, however, had been thrown forward and then hurled back. He was bleeding from cuts on his head and appeared to be paralysed. He was driven to the 130th Station Hospital at Heidelberg, which was commanded by an old friend General Geoffrey Keyes. There he was taken to surgery where it was discovered that he had broken his neck and was paralysed from the neck downwards. Mrs Patton arrived during the afternoon of 11 December and by the 13th General Patton had shown such improvement that his doctors began to consider the possibility of flying him back to the States. But it was not to be. On the 19th a crisis suddenly developed, he had great difficulty in breathing and the pressure on his spinal cord increased. For two days he struggled for survival, but at 5.50pm on 21 December he died of acute heart failure having confided to his brother-in-law that 'this is a hell of a way for a soldier to die'.

'They buried him in the drizzle of a fog-shrouded December morning in the huge American Military Cemetery at Hamm in Luxembourg, where he joined 6,000 other dead heroes of the Third Army. For two days before the funeral, while he was lying in state in the Villa Reiner, one of the stately homes of Heidelberg, the GIs claimed him as one of their own. They came in seemingly endless procession to pay their last respects to the great soldier who, unlike themselves, would not be going home soon, or ever. Even in his grave he remained close to them. Nearest to him on top of the gently sloping hillside was the grave of a private first class, John Hrzywarn of Detroit. Patton was sent on his long journey with the Psalm David had sung in the wilderness of Judah. . . . "O God, thou art my God; early will I seek thee; my soul thirsteth for thee, my flesh longeth for thee in a dry and thirsty land, so as I have seen thee in the sanctuary". It was Patton's own favourite Psalm, devout as well as defiant. "My soul followeth hard after thee; but those that seek my soul, to destroy it, shall go into the lower parts of the earth.

Right: Patton's funeral service was held in Christ Church, Heidelberg, on 23 December 1945. /*Associated Press*

Above: Master Sergeant William G. Meeks, Patton's orderly in North Africa, Sicily, Italy, France and Germany, is photographed at GSP, Jr's funeral service in Heidelberg, Germany, 23 December 1945. */US Army*

Right: Patton's burial. The coffin is carried along a troop lined path in the Military Cemetery at Hamm, just outside Luxembourg, 24 December 1945. The negro bearer is Master Sergeant William G. Meeks, who was Gen Patton's orderly for eight years./*Associated Press*

They shall fall by the sword; they shall be a portion for foxes. But the king shall rejoice in God; everyone that sweareth by him shall glory; but the mouth of them that speak lies shall be stopped". In the final moment of the ceremony, Master Sergeant William George Meeks, the elderly negro from Junction City, Kansas, who had served the General faithfully as his orderly for years, presented to Beatrice the flag that had draped the casket. There were tears in Meeks' eyes – his face was screwed up with strain. He bowed slowly and handed the flag to Mrs Patton. Then he saluted stiffly to her. For an instant their eyes met and held. Sergeant Meeks turned away. A 12-man firing squad raised its rifles and a three-round volley of salutes echoed into the Luxembourg hills.

'Next morning the *New York Times* wrote the most moving of the editorials with which the world press bade him farewell: "History has reached out and embraced General George Patton. His place is secure. He will be ranked in the forefront of America's great military leaders. ... Long before the war ended, Patton was a legend. Spectacular, swaggering, pistol-packing, deeply religious and violently profane, easily moved to anger because he was first of all a fighting man, easily moved to tears because underneath all his mannered irascibility he had a kind heart, he was a strange combination of fire and ice. Hot in battle and ruthless too, he was icy in his inflexibility of purpose. He was no more hell-for-leather tank commander but a profound and thoughtful military student. He has been compared with Jeb Stuart, Nathan Bedford Forrest and Phil Sheridan, but he fought his battles in a bigger field than any of them. He was not a man of peace. Perhaps he would have preferred to die at the height of his fame, when his men, whom he loved were following him with devotion. His nation will accord his memory a full measure of that devotion".'*

*Patton: Ordeal and Triumph by Ladislas Farago.

Left: The Italian marble cross which marks his grave at Hamm./*Patton Museum*

Below left: A monument dedicated to Patton was unveiled at Ettelbruck, Luxembourg, by Prince Felix of Bourbon-Parma, the Prince of Luxembourg on 16 May 1954. The photograph shows Gen Leander Doan, CG of the 2nd US Armd Div, making a speech during the ceremony. /*Associated Press*

Below: Gen Patton's statue near the monument at Ettlebruck./*Patton Museum*

Above: Four Star General. Portrait of General George S. Patton, Jr, taken at the end of the war in Europe./*IWM*

It would be wrong for me to finish this book on a note of sadness and I'm sure that Third Army's great commander would not have wished me to do so. More fittingly perhaps, let me close with what is my favourite Patton quotation from his famous 'off the cuff' speeches to his troops in England before D-Day:

'I'm not supposed to be commanding this Army. I'm not supposed even to be in England. Let the first bastards to find out be the goddam Germans. I want them to look up and howl, *"ACH, IT'S THE GODDAM THIRD ARMY AND THAT SON-OF-A-BITCH PATTON AGAIN!"*.'